NEW TESTAMENT

BIG PICTURE
of the
BIBLE

LORNA DANIELS NICHOLS

WINEPRESS WP PUBLISHING

Unless otherwise noted, all Scriptures are taken from the Holy Bible, *New Living Translation,* Copyright © 1996, 2004 by Tyndale Charitable Trust. Used by permission of Tyndale House Publishers, Wheaton, Illinois 60189. All rights reserved.

Scripture references marked AMP are taken from *The Amplified Bible,* Old Testament, © 1965 and 1987 by The Zondervan Corporation, and from The Amplified New Testament, © 1954, 1958, 1987 by The Lockman Foundation. Used by permission.

Scripture references marked CEV are taken from *The Contemporary English Version:* Thomas Nelson, 1997, © 1995 by the American Bible Society. Used by permission. All rights reserved.

Scripture references marked KJV are taken from the *King James Version of the Bible.*

Scripture references marked KJ21 are taken from The Holy Bible, *21st Century King James Version* (KJ21®), Copyright © 1994, Deuel Enterprises, Inc., Gary, SD 57237, and used by permission.

Scripture references marked MSG are taken from *The Message Bible* © 1993 by Eugene N. Peterson, NavPress, PO Box 35001, Colorado Springs, CO 80935, 4th printing in USA 1994. Published in association with the literary agency—Alive Comm. PO Box 49068, Colorado Springs, CO 80949. Used by permission.

Scripture references marked NASB are taken from the *New American Standard Bible,* © 1960, 1963, 1968, 1971, 1972, 1973, 1975, 1977 by The Lockman Foundation. Used by permission.

Scripture references marked NCV are taken from the *New Century Version.* Copyright © 1987, 1988, 1991 by Thomas Nelson, Inc. Used by permission. All rights reserved.

Scripture references marked NIV are taken from the Holy Bible, *New International Version®, NIV®.* Copyright © 1973, 1978, 1984 by the International Bible Society. Used by permission of Zondervan. All rights reserved.

Scripture references marked NKJ are taken from the *New King James Version,* © 1979, 1980, 1982 by Thomas Nelson, Inc., Publishers. Used by permission.

Scripture references marked TNIV are taken from the Holy Bible, *Today's New International® Version TNIV©.* Copyright 2001, 2005 by International Bible Society®. Used by permission of International Bible Society®. All rights reserved worldwide.

Scripture references marked ESV are taken from The Holy Bible: *English Standard Version,* Copyright © 2001, Wheaton: Good News Publishers. Used by permission. All rights reserved.

ISBN 13: 978-1-57921-928-4
ISBN 10: 1-57921-928-4
Library of Congress Catalog Card Number: 2007935555

Printed in China.

AIE-08085

DEDICATION

This book is dedicated to my father, George Earl Daniels, Jr. Thank you so very much for your dedication and commitment to our family. Your love, hard work, and values capture the essence of what fatherhood is all about. You instilled in each of your seven children a sound work ethic, financial stewardship, and great moral and family values. We are all better people because of the leadership and practical wisdom you modeled for us.

I am blessed that you are my father. I am overjoyed that you are a Christ-follower and profess Him as your Lord and Savior.

TABLE *of* CONTENTS

Preface..xi

Acknowledgments xiii

Introduction.. 1

Using This Study 3

Historical Background... 5

- Old Testament Summary.. 5

- Between the Old and New Testaments 8

- New Testament Background... 10

Chapter 1: Jesus' Birth and Early Ministry 13

- Summary 14

- Section 1: God's Plan Unfolds 19

- Section 2: Jesus' Birth and Youth 22

- Section 3: Baptism and Temptation 25

- Section 4: Early Ministry—Part 1 27

- Section 5: Early Ministry—Part 2 30

- Review 34

Chapter 2: Jesus' Ministry in Galilee 39

- Summary 40

- Section 1: Galilean Ministry Begins 45

- Section 2: Jesus' Message 48

- Section 3: Miracles and Confrontations 51

- Section 4: Jesus' Parables 55

- Section 5: Rejection and Opposition 60

- Review 65

Chapter 3: Final Phase of Jesus' Ministry.. 71

- Summary 72

- Section 1: Mentoring the Disciples 77

- Section 2: Conflict with Religious Leaders 79

- Section 3: Preparing the Disciples 83

- Section 4: One Man Should Die 85
- Section 5: On the Way to Jerusalem 88
- Review 91

Chapter 4: Jesus' Death and Resurrection 97
- Summary 98
- Section 1: Entering Jerusalem 103
- Section 2: Debates and Warnings 106
- Section 3: Jesus' Farewell 110
- Section 4: Jesus' Arrest and Trial 114
- Section 5: The Crucifixion and Resurrection 119
- Review 125

Chapter 5: Establishing The Church 131
- Summary 132
- Section 1: The Outpouring of the Holy Spirit 136
- Section 2: Good News in Jerusalem 140
- Section 3: Good News in Samaria and Judea 143
- Section 4: Good News to the Gentiles 146
- Section 5: The Apostles Face Persecution 149
- Review 152

Chapter 6: Spreading the Good News 157
- Summary 158
- Section 1: Paul's First Missionary Journey 165
- Section 2: Paul's Second Missionary Journey 169
- Section 3: Paul's Third Missionary Journey 173
- Section 4: Paul's Arrest 177
- Section 5: Building the Faith 180
- Review 187

Review Answers 193
Appendix 1: How We Got the New Testament 199
Appendix 2: Selecting a Bible 200
Appendix 3: Comparison of Bible Translations 201
Appendix 4: Organization of the New Testament 202

Appendix 5: New Testament Summary of Major Events.. 204

Appendix 6: New Testament Rulers... 205

Appendix 7: Messianic Prophecies Fulfilled by Jesus of Nazareth 206

Appendix 8: God's Plan of Redemption and Salvation... 210

Appendix 9: Accepting God's Free Gift of Redemption and Salvation 211

Glossary 213

Bibliography... 221

ILLUSTRATIONS

MAPS OF KEY LOCATIONS

Chapter 1   17

Chapter 2   43

Chapter 3   75

Chapter 4   101

Chapter 5   134

Chapter 6   162 & 163

PICTURES

The Flight into Egypt   18

The Bread of Life   44

The Transfiguration   76

The Resurrection   102

Philip Baptizes the Ethiopian Eunuch   135

Paul in Athens   164

IX

PREFACE

What do you do when you are facing tough times and personal hardships? Where do you turn when the answers to life's many challenges just aren't available? Do you seek professional advice, read self-help books, or simply continue struggling on your own? Did you know that one of the oldest, most reliable and trusted best-sellers of all time has all the answers you need? It's the Bible!

For years, I experienced constant torment caused by chronic headache pain. Every day, every waking minute, I had headache pain. It didn't stop. After years of pain and with no apparent solution in sight, I finally cried out to God for help.

Up to that time, I had thought I could do almost anything I wanted—without God's help. My accomplishments thus far were testament to that (or so I thought!). I finished college in three years and immediately went into a management position with a large corporation. Promotions soon followed. And then I met Mr. Right. We were married and I soon realized that Mr. Right was definitely Mr. Wrong! We divorced and I immersed myself back into my career. My responsibilities increased and so did my stress level.

Then the headaches started—Excruciating headaches! I'd wake every morning with a headache and go to bed every night with a headache. Nothing helped. I visited doctor after doctor—allergists, neurologists, psychiatrists, acupuncturists, even a pain management clinic. No one had an answer to my problem. As my life spiraled out of control, I began experiencing severe bouts of depression.

With no place to turn, I cried out to God. Through His grace, I remembered something my mother told me in my youth. She said that God would speak to me through the Bible. Scripture is God's formula for success. I began meditating on Scripture every morning before starting my work day. Over time, as I read God's Word, the pain started to diminish.

As I cultivated my relationship with God, He began doing incredible things in my life. He led me to a Christian headache specialist who diagnosed my problem and prescribed medicine that relieved my headache pain. My employer offered me an early retirement package which I readily accepted. And soon after that, I met and married a wonderful man, my soul mate and life partner, chosen by God.

My healing came from the greatest self-help book of all times—the Bible! God's message of hope was what I needed to overcome the inner struggle that plagued me. Over the years, the Bible has become my source for inspiration and mental well-being. Why don't more people read the Bible on a regular basis? Could it be that many find it too difficult to understand—or simply can't see how it relates to them today? In response to this obstacle and God's call, I wrote *Big Picture of the Bible—Old Testament* and *Big Picture of the Bible—New Testament*. Both books are designed to help you read, more fully understand, and embrace God's Word.

As you begin your study of *Big Picture of the Bible—New Testament,* please use it as a tool to assist in your Bible reading—not as a substitute. My prayer for you is that God will plant in you a strong desire to read His Word more often and more consistently. Everything you need to live a successful life is in God's Word. God wants to speak to you. Allow Him to lead you into a deeper, more personal encounter with Him through the pages of the Bible.

The Lord instructed Joshua, *"Study this Book of Instruction continually. Meditate on it day and night so you will be sure to obey everything written in it. Only then will you prosper and succeed in all you do"* (Joshua 1:8). Jesus later explained, *"Ask and it will be given to you; seek and you will find; knock and the door will be opened to you. For everyone who asks receives; he who seeks finds; and to him who knocks, the door will be opened"* (Matthew 7:7–8 NIV).

Lorna Daniels Nichols

ACKNOWLEDGMENTS

First and foremost, my sincere thanks to God for Your inspiration and guidance. I especially thank You for sending all the right people at the right time, and with the right talents to assist me with this book. My gratitude and affection for each of them is without measure. My personal thanks to:

My husband, best friend and wonderful partner, John W. Nichols III, for your love, patience, support, and encouragement throughout the long hours of study and writing for this project.

My sister, Rhonda L. Daniels, for your artwork. Your talent brings to life the personalities of the New Testament. Your persistence and enthusiasm are contagious.

My sister, Rita L. Daniels, for editing and proofing the manuscript numerous times. Your in-depth scrutiny and editing skills were a true blessing. You were always there when I needed you and ready to provide sound input and feedback.

Mary Ruth Crawford for the final touches you added to the manuscript. Once again, your command of English grammar and writing skills were exactly what I needed for the *Big Picture of the Bible* project.

Gino Santa Maria for designing the maps and icons, identifying key locations and concepts. God has given you an incredible gift and we are blessed that you continue to use it to glorify His name.

My many friends and relatives who have read, edited, and given me their invaluable input on this project—Claudia Inman Brown, Dianne Dawson Daniels, Bonita McClellan Sams, Bob Bucheck, and Madeline Norris Legler.

A special thanks to Grace Church—Saint Louis and Pastor Ron Tucker for the opportunity to teach and further develop material for *Big Picture of the Bible*.

May God bless and keep each of you in His care always!

INTRODUCTION

What Is the Bible?

The Bible is a compilation of writings written by men inspired by God. Although men wrote the Bible, its words are not those of mere men, but those of God. The authors of the Bible were divinely chosen by God to write His words and deliver His message. Apostle Peter makes this point clear in Scripture when he writes, *"Above all, you must realize that no prophecy in Scripture ever came from the prophet's own understanding, or from human initiative. No, those prophets were moved by the Holy Spirit, and they spoke from God"* (2 Peter 1:20–21).

Writings included in our Bible were authored by at least forty men over a period of about 1600 years. These writings were collected, organized, and published as the sixty-six books of our Bible. These books, when combined, tell the story of God's love and desire for a close personal relationship with each of us.

The Bible is sectioned into two main divisions: the Old Testament and the New Testament. The word "testament" could easily have been translated "covenant." Both terms are used to describe the various promises and agreements God entered into with mankind.

What Is the Old Testament?

There are thirty-nine Old Testament books, written from about 1445 B.C. to 430 B.C. Most of the Old Testament was written in Hebrew, a Semitic language similar to Arabic. A small portion was written in Aramaic, a language spoken in Palestine (Israel) during Jesus' days. The Old Testament provides a record of God's relationship with mankind, covering history from the beginning of the world to about 400 years before the birth of Jesus Christ. It includes the covenants God entered into with men during this period. The primary focus of the Old Testament is on how God taught the world about the One True God through His relationship and interactions with the nation of Israel. Throughout the pages of the Old Testament is God's promise of a Messiah, the Anointed One, who would provide a way for all mankind to enjoy a close personal relationship with the One True God.

What Is the New Testament?

There are twenty-seven New Testament books, written in Greek between 45 A.D. and 100 A.D. The New Testament includes writings, covering the historical period from just prior to Jesus' birth to about seventy years after His death and resurrection. It provides the Good News of the new covenant God entered into with humanity after Jesus completed His mission on earth. The New Testament's primary focus is on how God fulfilled His promise of a Messiah through Jesus Christ, providing a way for all mankind—Jews and non-Jews alike—to commune with Him in an intimate and personal way.

 Note: See Appendix 1 for information about how we got the New Testament and Appendix 4 for the organization of the New Testament.

Why Read the Bible?

The Bible is the Word of God. It is God's message to mankind. It tells us what God (the Creator) wants us (His creation) to know about fellowshipping with Him and living a life that is full of successes and not failures. When we read the Bible, we gain a better understanding of who God is and why we need Him in our lives. God loves us and wants each of us to enjoy a good life, full of promise and direction. This can only happen if we allow God to guide us instead of living life apart from Him, doing things our own way.

The Bible provides all the power, wisdom, and knowledge needed to help us develop a close personal relationship with God, who is ready, willing, and able to help us navigate through life's challenges. God speaks to us as we read the Bible, guiding and equipping us for success. Apostle Paul said, *"All Scripture is God-breathed and is useful for teaching, rebuking, correcting and training in righteousness, so that the man of God may be thoroughly equipped for every good work"* (2 Timothy 3:16–17 NIV).

 Note: See Appendix 2 for information on selecting a Bible and Appendix 3 for a comparison of various Bible translations.

Who Is God?

God is the Creator of the universe and everything in it. God is not limited by time or space and has no beginning or end. God is all-knowing, all-powerful, and He is in all places at all times.

God is a being with a personality. He has emotions just as we do. God feels, thinks, acts, sympathizes, hopes, desires, and enters into relationships. God is merciful, righteous, and just. However, one of the most important characteristics of God's nature is that of love. Scripture tells us that God is love (1 John 4:8, 16).

Who Is Jesus?

Jesus is God made human (John 1:1–3, 14; Colossians 2:9). Jesus came to earth and is the exact representation of God (Hebrews 1:3). The Bible explains that God revealed Himself to us through Jesus Christ. God is love and so is Jesus. God is merciful, righteous, and just; and so is Jesus. By sending Jesus, God was saying to mankind, "Here I am. This is who I am. Come fellowship with Me and let Me guide you through life's journey." It is possible to develop a close personal relationship with God and commune with Him now and throughout eternity when we accept Jesus Christ as our Lord and Savior.

Who Is the Holy Spirit?

The Holy Spirit is God. He is the Spirit of God. After Jesus delivered God's message and completed God's mission on earth, He sent the Holy Spirit to live inside of everyone who believes in God's Word. The Holy Spirit helps us recognize sin and points us toward the righteousness of God (John 14:16–17; 16:7–8). By sending the Holy Spirit to live inside of us, Jesus is saying, "I am with you always, living inside of you through the Holy Spirit. I am here to help you develop a close personal relationship with God. I will encourage you, strengthen you, and guide you to the Truth of God." The Holy Spirit helps us grow in righteousness so that we become more like Jesus, displaying God's character and reflecting God's glory.

What Is the Trinity?

Our one God is three distinct beings: God the Father; Jesus the Son; and the Holy Spirit. These three beings are collectively referred to as the Trinity. All three are fully God, and yet these three beings are one God, and not three Gods.

The Trinity, although not a biblical term, is commonly used to describe our (one) God in (three) beings. It is a profound mystery and difficult to understand because humans are not created in this way. We must remember that this existence is unique to God.

USING THIS STUDY

Most first-time Bible readers mistakenly assume they can read the Bible sequentially to understand the complete story and overall message of God's Word. Most fail to realize that the books of the Bible are organized by category instead of chronological sequence. *Big Picture of the Bible* provides a summary of Bible stories and events in historical sequence so that readers can see the continuity and overall message of the Bible. Its bulleted format and Scriptural headings make this study an easy-to-read supplement for Bible reading and Bible study.

Big Picture of the Bible has been designed to be used either as an individual or group study. It is not a replacement for reading the Bible, but should supplement it. When using this study, it is recommended that you follow a lesson plan similar to this:

✓ Find a good Bible translation you can read and understand. *Big Picture of the Bible* is not a translation, but a tool to help you with your study.

✓ Each chapter begins with an opening prayer and summary. The chapters are divided into five sections so you can easily read a section each day and read through a chapter each week. However, you can read at your own pace. Read each chapter according to whatever schedule you've chosen for yourself.

✓ Read the recommended Bible reading listed at the end of each section to experience God's Word speaking to you.

✓ You might decide to follow along in your Bible and read all scriptures or scriptures other than those selected as recommended reading. If so, you will find the corresponding Bible scriptures for *Big Picture of the Bible* summaries included in the heading lines.

✓ Go to the Review section located at the end of each chapter and answer the questions before proceeding to the next chapter. This will help you verify your understanding and reinforce the material covered in each chapter.

✓ After completing this study, make the Bible a part of your daily activity.

Icons Used in this Study

As you read through *Big Picture of the Bible*, you will see the following icons. They are there to guide you in thought, prayer, or to provide supplemental information to enhance your knowledge of the section you're reading.

Prayer for beginning and ending each chapter. The prayers at the end of the chapter are prefaced with scripture, on which you may wish to meditate before praying the author's prayer.

Indicates an instance in which Jesus Christ fulfills God's Plan of Redemption and Salvation or an Old Testament prophecy about the Messiah.

Supplemental information provided by the author to enhance the reader's knowledge of the section.

Recommended Bible Reading. References include passages from both the Old and New Testaments and complement one another.

 Review Questions. A set of questions is provided at the end of each chapter, along with space to answer them. Answers are found in the back of the book.

 Personal Reflections. Questions designed for prayerful thought as you discover how God is speaking to you through this study.

Bible Versions Used in This Study

AMP—Amplified Bible

CEV—Contemporary English Version

ESV—English Standard Version

KJV—King James Version

KJ21—21st Century King James

MSG—The Message

NASB—New American Standard Bible

NCV—New Century Version

NIV—New International Version

NKJ—New King James Version

NLT—New Living Translation (2nd Edition)

TNIV—Today's New International Version

 Note: See Appendices 2 and 3 for more information about Bible Versions and Translations.

HISTORICAL BACKGROUND
OLD TESTAMENT SUMMARY

The Old Testament is an account of God's relationship and interactions with humanity from the beginning of time to about 400 years before Jesus' birth. It chronicles the events God so lovingly orchestrated to provide a way for mankind to live in fellowship with Him here on earth and throughout eternity. The Old Testament is divided into two major historical periods. The first period covers an unspecified number of years and is documented in Genesis 1–11. This period focuses on God's interactions with specific individuals who lived in the beginning of mankind's existence. The second period covers about 2,000 years. It begins in Genesis 12 and continues through the rest of the Old Testament. During this period, the Old Testament tells of God's interactions with a specific group of people—the nation of Israel.

FIRST HISTORICAL PERIOD

THE BEGINNING OF MANKIND (CREATION TO 2091 B.C.)

The first historical period of the Old Testament begins in Genesis. It opens with God creating the world and then quickly moves to the first man and woman, Adam and Eve, rebelling against God. Their rebellion, commonly referred to as the Fall, marked the beginning of sin and unrighteousness in the world. Our righteous and holy God could not co-exist with sin and unrighteousness, so a barrier was created spiritually separating all mankind from God. Immediately after the Fall, God initiated a plan to remove this barrier and restore His relationship with humanity. God's plan is called "Redemption and Salvation through Jesus Christ" and we see it unfolding throughout the remaining pages of the Old Testament.

 Note: See Appendix 8 for a more detailed explanation of God's Plan of Redemption and Salvation, and Appendix 9 for information on Accepting God's Free Gift of Redemption and Salvation.

God's Plan of Redemption and Salvation is initiated through Seth, a son of Adam and Eve. Seth became the father of a godly line of descendants. After Seth's story, the Old Testament provides an account of the great Flood, which covered the earth during Noah's day. Noah, a descendant of Seth, was the only righteous person living on earth at the time. God saved Noah and his family from the flood. The Old Testament then records the division of people and languages at the Tower of Babel. After the Tower of Babel, the descendants of Shem, one of Noah's sons, are listed and the first historical period comes to a close.

SECOND HISTORICAL PERIOD

GOD'S RELATIONSHIP WITH THE PATRIARCHS (2091–1805 B.C.)

God entered into a covenant with a man named Abraham, a descendant of Seth, Noah, and Shem. Abraham was a righteous man who served the One True God. In the covenant with Abraham, God promised to bless all the nations of the earth through Abraham's offspring and to make Abraham's descendants a nation of kings. Jesus Christ is the manifestation of these promises. God also promised to give Abraham and his descendants the land of Canaan (Israel) and to always be Abraham's God and the God of His descendants. God told Abraham that his part in keeping this covenant was to obey and have himself and all his male offspring circumcised as a constant reminder of the agreement.

Abraham did not live to see the fulfillment of all God's promises. However, it is through Abraham that God's Plan of Redemption and Salvation begins to unfold. God's covenant with Abraham was passed on to his son, Isaac, and then to Isaac's son, Jacob, who had twelve sons. After God changed Jacob's name to Israel, his twelve sons and their families were called the twelve tribes of Israel. They would later become the nation of Israel.

The Old Testament book of Genesis continues with the story of Jacob's 11th son, Joseph, who became a great and powerful man in Egypt. Joseph saved his family (Jacob's entire household of about seventy people) from famine by arranging their migration to Egypt. Genesis closes with God's Plan of Redemption and Salvation unfolding in Egypt through Jacob's descendants.

ESTABLISHING THE NATION, LAW, AND WORSHIP (1526–1406 B.C.)

When Exodus, the second book of the Old Testament, opens, 400 years have passed since Jacob and his household migrated to Egypt. Jacob's descendants had greatly increased to about two and a half million people and were called Hebrews or Israelites. The Egyptians enslaved the Israelites and greatly oppressed them. The Lord divinely empowered a man named Moses to deliver the Israelites from slavery and lead them out of Egypt to Canaan, the land God promised Abraham.

God delivered the Israelites from the Egyptians by performing a series of miracles. God's miracles included sending ten plagues that devastated Egypt; sparing Israel's firstborn sons from death in an event known as the Passover; and parting the Red Sea so the Israelites could walk across and escape the Egyptians. The Passover miracle foreshadowed God's Plan of Redemption and Salvation. The Israelites were instructed to sacrifice a lamb and smear its blood over the doorpost of their homes. When God's angel of death saw the blood, he passed over the Israelites homes. Israel's firstborn sons were saved because of the lamb's blood. In the New Testament, Jesus became the sacrificial Passover Lamb, whose blood was shed to save humanity.

The books of Exodus, Leviticus, Numbers, and Deuteronomy provide a record of God's relationship and interactions with the Israelites as they traveled to Canaan, the Promised Land. Along the way, the Lord cultivated His relationship with the Israelites, giving them the Ten Commandments, providing plans for building the Tabernacle (a mobile tent used as a place of worship), organizing the priesthood, and teaching them how to live righteous lives. The Ten Commandments were placed inside the Ark of the Covenant, a chest symbolizing God's presence with the people of Israel.

In addition to the Ten Commandments, God gave Moses over 600 other laws and then entered into a covenant with Israel. In this covenant, Israel was God's treasured possession and in right standing with Him through obedience to His laws. Moses sealed this Old Testament covenant with animal's blood. Each time a person disobeyed God's laws, animal's blood was required for atonement of sin and right standing with God. In the New Testament, God entered into a new covenant with all mankind. The New Testament covenant was sealed with the blood of Jesus and fellowship with God is restored through faith in Jesus Christ.

When the Israelites finally reached the southern border of Canaan, they sent spies to explore the land. After hearing the spies' report that giants lived in Canaan, the Israelites became discouraged. The Israelites did not believe they could conquer the giants living in the land God promised their forefathers. As a result of their lack of faith, God became angry and would not let them enter Canaan. The Lord made the Israelites wander in the desert for forty years until those who lacked faith died and a new generation emerged. Joshua and Caleb, two spies who had faith in God, were the only Israelites from the older generation whom God allowed to enter the Promised Land. Before the new generation crossed into Canaan, Moses died and Joshua succeeded him as leader of Israel.

LIVING IN THE PROMISED LAND (1406–1050 B.C.)

The Old Testament continues the story of the Israelites in the book of Joshua, which covers about thirty years of history. A major portion of Joshua is about the military battles Israel fought to take possession of Canaan from the various peoples living in the land. Joshua and the Israelites had great success in battle. After vast territories had been conquered, God told Joshua to divide and allocate the land to the tribes. God instructed the tribes to continue fighting until all the Canaanites had been driven out of the land. The book ends with Joshua's death.

Israel's story continues in the book of Judges, which covers about 330 years of history. The Israelites never totally drove the Canaanites out of the land. As a result, the Canaanites influenced the Israelites and led the nation into idolatry. Judges describes a very dark period of moral decay and idolatry in Israel.

After Judges, the Old Testament records the story of Ruth, who lived during the period of the Judges. Although most of Israel had turned away from God, some people continued to serve the Lord. Ruth's Jewish mother-in-law, Naomi, was one of them. Ruth was a Moabite (non-Jew) who learned about the God of Israel from Naomi. Her tremendous love and respect for Naomi led her to the Lord. God rewarded Ruth's faith, blessing her to become an ancestor of King David and Jesus Christ.

Toward the end of the period of the Judges, Samuel—a priest, prophet, and last judge of Israel—led the nation back to God. When the people asked Samuel for a king, God instructed Samuel to anoint Saul as Israel's first king.

ESTABLISHING THE KINGDOM (1050–930 B.C.)

In the Old Testament, the story of Israel's kings is recorded in 1st and 2nd Samuel, 1st and 2nd Kings, and 1st and 2nd Chronicles. Saul, the first king of Israel, refused to obey the Lord. As a result, God's Spirit left Saul. After Saul's death, David became king of Israel. He established Jerusalem as the nation's capital and moved the Ark of the Covenant there as its permanent location. David loved the Lord and was a man after God's own heart. He made mistakes, but was quick to ask the Lord for forgiveness. God entered into a covenant with David promising him a kingdom that would last forever. This covenant was fulfilled through Jesus Christ, a descendant of King David, whose kingdom is forever.

After David's death, his son, Solomon, succeeded him as king. Solomon built the first Temple for the Lord in Jerusalem. The Temple was an elaborate sanctuary for worship built in the same pattern as the Tabernacle. Solomon later married hundreds of women from other nations and allowed them to bring their pagan practices with them to Israel. Solomon's wives eventually led him and the nation into idolatry.

THE DIVIDED KINGDOM (930–586 B.C.)

After King Solomon's death, his son, Rehoboam, succeeded him as king. Soon afterward, the people asked Rehoboam for relief from the heavy taxes imposed by his father. When he refused, ten tribes revolted and two separate nations were formed. The ten revolting tribes joined together and were called the Northern Kingdom of Israel. The tribes of Judah and Benjamin kept Solomon's son, Rehoboam, as their king and were known as the Southern Kingdom of Judah.

All the kings in the Northern Kingdom of Israel were ungodly and practiced idolatry. A few of the kings in the Southern Kingdom of Judah served God, but many were ungodly and led the people into idolatry. God sent prophets again and again to urge both nations to turn away from idolatry and come back to Him. The prophets were often inspired by God to reveal future events about the coming of the Messiah, God's Anointed One. The prophecies about the Messiah unveiled God's plan to restore His relationship with humanity through Jesus Christ. The prophets' ministries and inspired messages are told in the seventeen prophetic books of the Old Testament.

CAPTIVITY, EXILE, AND RETURN (586–430 B.C.)

After several hundred years of evil kings and idolatry, God's patience finally ran out with both kingdoms. The Assyrians conquered the Northern Kingdom of Israel in 722 B.C.; and King Nebuchadnezzar and the Babylonians destroyed the Southern Kingdom of Judah in 586 B.C. After Nebuchadnezzar demolished the Temple and the city of Jerusalem, he captured most of the people and took them to Babylon. There were twenty kings and nine dynasties in the Northern Kingdom over a period of about 200 years. The Southern Kingdom of Judah had twenty kings over a period of about 300 years but only one dynasty, as all were descendants of King David.

The Old Testament books of Ezra, Nehemiah, and Esther continue the story of the Jews, the name given to the Israelites. The Persians captured Babylon in 539 B.C. and took over the Babylonian Empire, which included control of the Jewish exiles. King Cyrus of Persia issued a decree in 538 B.C., allowing the Jewish exiles to return to Jerusalem and rebuild the Temple. The first group of exiles returned under the leadership of Zerubbabel. The Temple was rebuilt in 515 B.C. and Jerusalem's city wall was restored in 445 B.C. God's promise to King David, regarding an everlasting royal dynasty, was passed on to Zerubbabel, a descendant of King David, whose name appears in Matthew and Luke's gospels as an ancestor of Jesus Christ.

Not all Jewish exiles returned to Judah when Cyrus' decree was issued. A young woman named Esther and her cousin Mordecai, who raised her, were among those who did not go back. They chose to stay in Persia. Through a series of God-orchestrated events, Esther became queen of Persia. God used Queen Esther to save the Jews from annihilation. The Jewish holiday known as Purim commemorates this event.

The Old Testament comes to an end with God's promise of a Messiah. In the book of Malachi, God prophetically announces, *"Look! I am sending my messenger, and he will prepare the way before me. Then the Lord you are seeking will suddenly come to his Temple"* (Malachi 3:1). Malachi was the last of the Old Testament prophets.

BETWEEN THE OLD AND NEW TESTAMENTS

PERSIAN PERIOD: (539–331 B.C.)

The Old Testament ends in about 430 B.C. with the writings of the prophet Malachi. Over 400 years passed between Malachi, the last book of the Old Testament, and Matthew, the first gospel in the New Testament. These years are often called the "Four Hundred Years of Silence." There were no prophets or inspired messages to reveal more of God's Plan of Redemption and Salvation. Although these years are called "the silent years," God was orchestrating events in and around the Jews' homeland, called Palestine. In the Old Testament, Palestine was called Canaan and later became known as Israel. During the silent years, God set the stage for the birth of the Messiah.

At the close of the Old Testament, the Persians controlled Palestine, the land God promised Abraham. The Jews enjoyed relative peace under Persian rule. Palestine remained a province of Persia until 331 B.C.

GREEK PERIOD: ALEXANDER THE GREAT (331–323 B.C.)

In about 336 B.C., Alexander the Great of Greece and his army began conquering territories previously controlled by the Egyptians, Assyrians, Babylonians, and Persians. The Persian Empire fell to Alexander the Great in 331 B.C. and the Jews' homeland became a province of Greece. When Alexander marched through Jerusalem, he showed favor to the Jews, sparing the city from destruction. He also provided special incentives, which allowed a number of Jews to migrate to Alexandria, Egypt.

During the period of Greek rule, Alexander the Great spread Greek culture and language to every city in his empire. Before long, Greek culture permeated the lifestyle of most cities under Alexander's rule. Greek became the common language for transacting business and eventually became the universal language spoken throughout the empire. This common language helped set the stage for God's Plan of Redemption and Salvation. After Jesus' death and resurrection, the Greek language greatly facilitated the spreading of the Good News. As the apostles traveled from Jerusalem to the rest of the world, they were able to communicate the Good News in Greek across cultural boundaries. If this common language had not been introduced at the right time, the apostles' missionary work would have been seriously hampered.

Alexander the Great died at the young age of thirty-three. Since he had no heirs, his empire was divided among his four generals. The story of the Jews centers around two of Alexander's generals. After the empire was divided, Egypt was given to a general named Ptolemy, and Syria went to Seleucus, another one of Alexander's generals. Since the Jews' homeland was situated between Egypt and Syria, both generals wanted it as part of their territory. The Jews' homeland eventually went to Ptolemy of Egypt; however, an ongoing rivalry persisted over control of Palestine.

GREEK PERIOD: THE PTOLEMIES RULE (321–198 B.C.)

The Ptolemies (Ptolemy's family dynasty who ruled Egypt) controlled the Jews' homeland from 321 B.C. to 198 B.C. During this period, conditions were peaceful for the Jews. As a result of Alexander's earlier incentives, a large number of Jews were living in Alexandria, Egypt. The Hebrew Old Testament was translated into Greek to accommodate the needs of the increased number of non-Hebrew speaking Jews. This translation is called the Septuagint and is the version of Scripture used during Jesus' time.

Although the Jews prospered under the Ptolemies, the two dynasties (the Ptolemies and Seleucids, Seleucus' family dynasty who ruled Syria) feuded continuously over territorial boundaries. The Seleucids finally defeated the Ptolemies in 198 B.C. and took over as rulers of Palestine.

GREEK PERIOD: THE SELEUCIDS RULE (198–143 B.C.)

When the Seleucids took control of Palestine, they promoted Greek culture and religion in the Jews' homeland. During the reign of Seleucid ruler, Antiochus IV Epiphanes, the spread of Greek culture became more of a demand than a request. Antiochus Epiphanes became obsessed with stamping out Judaism, the religion of the Jewish people, and forcing the Jews to embrace Greek culture. He is most noted for converting the Temple in Jerusalem into a pagan shrine and sacrificing a pig on its altar. According to the law of Moses, pigs were ceremonially unclean and to sacrifice one on the altar was the ultimate insult to Jews.

Outraged by Antiochus Epiphanes' attempt to destroy Jewish culture and religion, a priest named Mattathias led a rebellion against the Seleucids. When Mattathias died, his son, Judas, took over the uprising. Judas' nickname was Maccabeus, which means "the hammer." For this reason, the rebellion against the Seleucids was called the "Maccabean Revolt." After winning numerous battles, Judas captured Jerusalem from the Seleucid army in 165 B.C. The Temple was then cleansed and rededicated. Hanukkah is the Jewish holiday commemorating this event. The holiday is also called "Feast of Dedication" or "Feast of Lights." The Seleucids finally relinquished control of Palestine in 143 B.C. and the Jews' homeland became an independent state.

INDEPENDENT PERIOD: MACCABEAN OR HASMONEAN RULE (143–63 B.C.)

After Judas gained control of Jerusalem, he established a line of priests from within his own family. He then set up a government run by the priests, who were in charge of both religious and civic oversight. Judas' family name was Hashmon and the era of his family's priestly rule is called the "Hasmonean Period."

The Hasmoneans governed the independent Jewish state. Although the Jews' homeland was free of foreign rule, the period was marked with tremendous unrest and civil war. When a power struggle for the priesthood escalated among members of the Hasmonean family, the Romans came in 63 B.C. to bring peace to the area. Under the leadership of General Pompey, the Romans resolved the in-fighting by making the Jews' homeland a part of the Roman Empire.

ROMAN PERIOD: (63 B.C.–636 A.D.)

Roman rule of the Jews' homeland began in 63 B.C. Ironically, the Romans brought a measure of peace to the area through forced domination, called *Pax Romanus* or "Peace of Rome." They appointed a local king over the area, but real power belonged to Rome.

The Romans were great builders. They constructed roadways from Rome to all parts of the empire, hence the saying, *"All roads lead to Rome."* With Roman peace and roadways leading out of Jerusalem to all parts of the world, God set in motion His Plan of Redemption and Salvation. During this time of peace, Jesus Christ was born. The Roman roadways would later facilitate God's plan as the apostles traveled outside of Jerusalem spreading the Good News of Jesus Christ.

NEW TESTAMENT BACKGROUND

Old Testament prophecies foretold of the Messiah's coming. God promised to send a Messiah, who would fulfill His Plan of Redemption and Salvation to restore His relationship with humanity. The New Testament is about how God implemented His Plan with the birth of Jesus Christ and finished it through Jesus' death and resurrection. God became a man in the person of Jesus Christ and was born to a virgin girl named Mary through the power of the Holy Spirit.

 Note: Jesus' birth marks the beginning of a new period on our calendar. Events, which occurred before Jesus' birth, are labeled B.C., for before Christ. Those occurring after Jesus' birth are time stamped A.D., for *Anno Domini*, which means "in the year of our Lord."

Political Environment:

When the New Testament opens, Palestine was a province of Rome. While the Greeks advanced their own culture in provinces under their control, the Romans granted their provinces religious, political, and civic freedoms. As a result, the Romans were extremely tolerant of the Jews' religious practices, but maintained strict control. Jews hated Roman subjugation and anxiously awaited the prophesied Messiah. They believed the Messiah would liberate them and establish a Jewish kingdom, free of foreign rule.

When the Romans took over Palestine, they set up a state of occupation patrolled by Roman soldiers, and appointed a local king as they did in other provinces. At the time of Jesus' birth, the Roman emperor was Caesar Augustus and Herod the Great was the local king whose power came from Rome. Caesar Augustus established a governor's position in 6 A.D. The governor lived in Palestine and represented Roman authority in the Jews' homeland. At the time of Jesus' arrest, the Roman governor was Pontius Pilate. (See Appendix 6 for a list of New Testament rulers.)

The Roman government heavily taxed the Jews and employed local people to collect taxes for Rome. Jewish tax collectors often overtaxed their own people. Jews despised tax collectors, calling them traitors and sinners. Jesus chose a tax collector named Matthew as one of his disciples.

King Herod the Great, a Jewish convert from Idumea, was politically motivated and had won favor with Rome. After his appointment, Herod greatly expanded and beautified the Temple in Jerusalem, which pleased the Jews. Herod was extremely evil and ruled with brutal force. He was responsible for the deaths of his first wife, three of his sons, as well as the deaths of baby boys two years old and younger in Bethlehem during the time of Jesus' birth.

Religious Environment:

In Jesus' day, Jews were extremely nationalistic and thought of everyone in the world as either a Jew or a Gentile (non-Jew). The Jews believed in the One True God and separated themselves from people who practiced pagan and all other religions or philosophies. Major emphasis was placed on obedience to the Old Testament law of Moses for right standing with God. As a result, Jews offered animal sacrifices for the atonement of sin and practiced other purification rituals as outlined in Leviticus.

According to Jewish law, priests had to be descendants of Aaron, Moses' brother. However, the high priest of Jesus' day was a position appointed by the Roman government. The priests served in the Temple, offering animal sacrifices for the people and performing other religious duties. People observed religious festivals and often traveled to the Temple in Jerusalem for annual holidays. In the New Testament, Jesus traveled to Jerusalem on several occasions to celebrate religious festivals. Jesus was in Jerusalem for Passover at the time of His arrest and crucifixion. Passover was the major Jewish holiday, which celebrated the Jews' deliverance from Egyptian slavery.

The Temple was in Jerusalem and had been greatly enhanced in size and grandeur by King Herod. Jews were required to pay a Temple tax to help support its operation and maintenance. Although Jews traveled to Jerusalem for religious holidays, synagogues existed in Jewish neighborhoods in and outside of Palestine. The synagogue, translated "house of assembly or congregation," was the local gathering place for studying the Scriptures and worshiping God. People met in the synagogue for weekly Sabbath day services. The Sabbath day began on Friday at sundown and ended at sundown on Saturday. It was observed as a day of rest in accordance with God's Sabbath commandment. When Jesus performed healing miracles on the Sabbath, he was often chastised by religious leaders for working on the day of rest.

For Jews, religion and education were intermingled. The Torah, the first five books of the Bible, was the primary source of religious and all other educational studies. Rabbis and Jewish mothers taught the Old Testament Scriptures to children at an early age. Exceptionally gifted rabbis often traveled from town to town, teaching Scripture and had disciples, who were students and devoted followers.

An understanding of the religious atmosphere in Jesus' day requires some background information on the various groups that existed. The groups which made up the religious and political environment of the New Testament were as follows:

1. **Pharisees** were a very strict religious party, committed to the law of Moses and other Old Testament Scriptures. They were well-respected among the Jews for their religious zeal. The Pharisees assumed responsibility for interpreting Scripture to make it applicable to new situations. As a result, the Pharisees added numerous man-made rules and oral traditions to God's law. While the Pharisees were extremely focused on obedience to the law, they often ignored God's love and grace. They believed in angels and a bodily resurrection.

2. **Sadducees** were a wealthy, political minded religious party, which included high ranking priests and aristocrats. They were less popular than the Pharisees among the common people. While they recognized the first five books of Moses, they refused to accept other Old Testament Scriptures. They did not accept the Pharisees' man-made rules and did not believe in angels or life after death. Since Rome allowed them to keep certain leadership responsibilities, they often collaborated with Rome to maintain their authority.

3. **Herodians** were a political group who supported King Herod. They were ambitious for political power and influence. Although nothing much is known about their religious beliefs, they partnered with the Pharisees to oppose Jesus in Mark 3:6; 12:13; and Matthew 22:16.

4. **Zealots** were a political group who openly resisted Roman occupation of the Jews' homeland. They were the terrorists of Jesus' day and were responsible for several uprisings against Rome. Zealots believed that only God should rule Palestine and felt this belief justified their murderous acts. One of Jesus' disciples was called Simon the Zealot.

5. **Essenes** were a strict religious order that existed in Jesus' day, but were not mentioned in the New Testament. They separated themselves from other Jews and lived in closed religious communities as they waited for the Messiah.

6. **Scribes** were a special class of men responsible for interpreting, teaching, and making copies of the Scriptures. They were well-educated and influential leaders in their communities.

7. **The Sanhedrin Council** was a Jewish high court authorized by Rome to maintain religious and limited civil order in Palestine. It was comprised of seventy men who were Jewish priests, religious leaders, and/or religious teachers. The council included a large number of Pharisees and Sadducees. The high priest presided over the council. The Sanhedrin council held hearings and ruled on cases within the confines of Roman law. The council did not have authority from Rome to issue a death sentence. Consequently, its members had to petition Pilate, the Roman governor, to hear their case against Jesus and for him to order Jesus' crucifixion.

People and Land:

The Jews' homeland was a major passage route for land and sea travel. The Mediterranean Sea bordered its western coast. Travelers headed from Syria to Egypt or vice versa had to pass through Palestine. For this reason, Palestine was important for world commerce and an attractive location to foreign rulers. Greek was the universal language of the common people. However, most Jews in Palestine spoke both Greek and Aramaic. Palestine was divided into three territories west of the Jordan River—Judea, Samaria, and Galilee. There were two territories east of the Jordan—Decapolis and Perea.

1. **Judea** was located west of the Jordan River in southern Palestine. In the Old Testament, Judea was the territory in which the Southern Kingdom of Judah was located. A few cities in Judea mentioned in the New Testament were: Jerusalem, the location of the Temple; Bethlehem, King David and Jesus' birthplace; and Bethany, the home of Lazarus, whom Jesus raised from the dead. Although some Gentiles lived in Judea, it was predominantly Jewish. Jews living in Judea were often better educated and more affluent than in other areas.

2. **Samaria** was located west of the Jordan in central Palestine. In the Old Testament, Samaria was the capital city of the Northern Kingdom of Israel. After the fall of Israel, poor Jews who escaped the exile and Gentile migrants lived in Samaria. Their offspring formed an interracial group of people, called the Samaritans. Their religion was a blend of Judaism and pagan beliefs. Jews despised Samaritans and looked down on them because they were not racially, culturally, or religiously pure.

3. **Galilee** was west of the Jordan River in northern Palestine. When the kingdom was divided in the Old Testament, the land of Galilee was part of the Northern Kingdom of Israel. In Jesus' day, Jews and Gentiles lived in Galilee. The area was more rural and less affluent than Judea. Jesus and most of His disciples were from Galilee. A few cities located in Galilee include: Nazareth, Jesus' hometown; Capernaum, the home base for Jesus' ministry; Cana where Jesus turned water into wine; and Bethsaida, Peter and Andrew's hometown.

4. **Decapolis**, translated "ten cities," was located east of the Jordan River in northern Palestine next to Galilee and was not a province of Rome. Ten cities had been incorporated to form a single metropolitan area.

5. **Perea** was located east of the Jordan River, next to Samaria and Judea, and south of Decapolis. The New Testament does not mention Perea by name. However, it is the territory referred to as "beyond the Jordan," where John was baptizing.

6. **The Diaspora** is a name used for dispersed Jews living outside of Palestine. Although these Jews did not live in Palestine, they maintained their religious faith, and built local synagogues for religious study and worship.

When Jesus was about thirty years old, He began his public ministry, teaching and performing healing miracles. After a three-and-half-year ministry, Jesus voluntarily gave up His life as a sacrifice to redeem and save humanity. Jesus suffered and died on a cross as the world's Passover Lamb. After three days in the grave, Jesus rose from the dead and appeared to His disciples on several occasions. Jesus' resurrection appearances proved He was indeed the promised Messiah. Through His death and resurrection, Jesus fulfilled God's Plan of Redemption and Salvation. The apostles and other believers first communicated the Good News of salvation through Jesus Christ in Jerusalem and then spread it to the rest of the world.

CHAPTER 1

JESUS' BIRTH AND EARLY MINISTRY

OPENING PRAYER

Heavenly Father,

You are All-Powerful, All-Knowing, and Eternal. All wisdom and knowledge belong to You and are Yours to give. Open the eyes of my heart and illuminate Your Word. Guide me through this New Testament study and enlighten me with spiritual wisdom and understanding. Help me to more fully comprehend the significance of Jesus' birth and earthly ministry.

Amen

CHAPTER SUMMARY

JESUS' BIRTH AND EARLY MINISTRY

(Matthew, Mark, Luke, and John)

When the New Testament opens, about 400 years have passed since the prophet Malachi wrote the last book of the Old Testament. Many things changed during that time. Most notably, the Jews' homeland is now a province of the Roman Empire. The Roman army occupied the Jews' homeland in about 63 B.C. and forced the Jews to submit to Roman authority. Although the Romans made Herod the Great the local king of the Jews, it was clear real power belonged to Caesar Augustus, emperor of Rome. The Jews despised their Roman oppressors and longed to be free from foreign rule. The hope for Israel's future was firmly rooted in Old Testament prophecies. The Jews believed a leader—referred to in Scripture as the Messiah—would soon come and free them from Roman subjugation. *Messiah* is a Hebrew word which is translated "Christ" in Greek, and "Anointed One" in English. Prophecies about the Messiah are referred to as Messianic prophecies.

Old Testament Scripture is filled with prophecies about the coming of a Messiah. Centuries earlier, God revealed to Abraham that all families on earth would be blessed through his offspring (Genesis 12:3; 22:18). The Lord told Moses, *"I will raise up a prophet like you . . ."* (Deuteronomy 18:18). God told King David, *"I will raise up your offspring to succeed you . . . and I will establish the throne of his kingdom forever"* (2 Samuel 7:12–13 NIV).

Isaiah revealed that God would send a Messiah, who would bring peace and rule from David's throne eternally (Isaiah 9:6–7). Micah told us the Lord Himself would guide us (Micah 2:13) and the Messiah would be born in Bethlehem (Micah 5:2). According to Jeremiah, God would place a righteous Branch on King David's throne, a King who would rule with wisdom (Jeremiah 23:5–6). Ezekiel spoke about a Shepherd, a descendant of King David, whom God would send to lead His people (Ezekiel 34:23–24). Malachi prophesied that God would send a messenger to prepare the way for His Anointed One (Malachi 3:1).

<u>Years from Messianic Prophecy to Jesus' Birth</u>

- 2,000 years from Abraham to Jesus Christ

- 1,400 years from Moses to Jesus Christ

- 1,000 years from David to Jesus Christ

- 700 years from Isaiah to Jesus Christ

- 700 years from Micah to Jesus Christ

- 600 years from Jeremiah to Jesus Christ

- 570 years from Ezekiel to Jesus Christ

- 430 years from Malachi to Jesus Christ

God promised to send a Messiah, a righteous King, who would rescue a world spiritually separated from Him. The Jews of Jesus' day believed it was time for these prophecies to be fulfilled. They waited—with great expectancy and anticipation—for the Messiah to come. The Jews envisioned a day when one of King David's descendants would free them from Roman oppression and take his rightful place as King of the Jews.

Although Jesus of Nazareth faithfully fulfilled God's role for the Messiah, people did not recognize Him when He appeared. The Jews were looking for an earthly king to free them from Roman domination, but God sent a heavenly Savior to free all people from sin's captive power.

Jesus' story is told in the Bible's four gospels. The word gospel means "Good News." The first four books of our New Testament are those of gospel writers: Matthew, Mark, Luke, and John. Although all four wrote about Jesus, each told His story from different perspectives, giving us four distinct pictures of Jesus Christ.

Matthew wrote for a Jewish audience, presenting Jesus as the "King of Israel," heir to King David's throne. Mark's gospel targeted a Roman audience and presents Jesus as the "Servant," humbly fulfilling God's Plan of Redemption and Salvation. Luke describes Jesus as the "Son of Man," identifying with humanity to make God's gift of salvation possible for all people. John emphatically declares Jesus as the "Son of God," emphasizing His divinity.

John's gospel opens declaring Jesus was with God from the beginning. John tells us Jesus was God made human. Matthew and Luke's gospels explain how God became human in the person of Jesus Christ. A young virgin girl named Mary conceived through the power of the Holy Spirit and gave birth to Jesus, the long-awaited Messiah. Before Jesus' birth, Mary's cousin, whose name was Elizabeth, gave birth to a son named John. Elizabeth's son grew up to become the great prophet John the Baptist. John's purpose in life was to prepare everyone for Jesus' ministry. John preached in an area near the Jordan River, admonishing people to turn away from sin and begin living for God. John baptized those who turned to God as a symbolic representation of their sins being washed away.

Mary's fiancé, Joseph, married her and raised Jesus as his own son in a town called Nazareth. According to Luke's gospel, Jesus was an obedient child, who pleased His heavenly Father in every way. When Jesus was about thirty years old, He sought out His cousin, John, to be baptized and then began His public ministry. Apostle John is the only gospel writer to describe Jesus' early ministry, which includes accounts of Jesus' first public miracle in Cana of Galilee; His first clearing of the Temple in Jerusalem; Nicodemus' visit with Jesus; Jesus' ministry near the Jordan River; and Jesus' conversation with the Samaritan woman. Jesus' early ministry began shortly after His baptism and covered a period of about one year.

The Four Gospel Writers

Gospel Writer	What We Know About the Writer and His Message
Matthew, One of Jesus' Twelve Disciples and an Apostle	Matthew, also called Levi, was a tax collector, who became a follower of Jesus Christ. Jesus later chose Matthew as one of His twelve disciples, named apostles, who would spread the message of God's Kingdom. As a disciple, Matthew wrote what he saw Jesus do and what he heard Him say. Matthew's gospel was written to help the Jews see that Jesus of Nazareth was—in fact—the Messiah, the long-awaited King of Israel. Matthew knew Jews were familiar with Scripture and would embrace fulfilled prophecy if they could only see it. With this in mind, Matthew set out to show how Jesus of Nazareth fulfilled prophecies about the Messiah. As a result, there are more references to Old Testament Scripture in the book of Matthew than any other gospel.

Mark, Companion of Apostle Peter	Mark, also called John Mark, was a student and friend of Apostle Peter. The book of Acts tells us that a group of Jesus' followers met at the house of Mark's mother to pray for Peter when he was imprisoned. (See Acts 12:12.) While Mark was not one of the twelve disciples, he wrote what he heard Peter say about Jesus. Mark's gospel seems to be written with a Roman audience in mind. Mark knew Romans were people of action and were impressed by those who got things done. Mark's gospel pictures Jesus as a Servant—on a mission to serve humanity—and tells more about what Jesus did than what Jesus said. Mark appealed to a Roman audience, using a style that was concise and to the point. As a result, Mark's gospel is the shortest of the four gospels.
Luke, Physician and Companion of Apostle Paul	Luke was a close friend and traveling companion of Apostle Paul. Luke meticulously researched the details of Jesus' life and was the only gospel writer who was not Jewish. He was a well-educated physician, author, and historian. Luke clearly addressed his gospel and his subsequent letter, Acts, to a man named Theophilus, who was quite possibly a high-ranking Roman official. However, Luke's gospel seems to be written with a Greek audience in mind. His gospel is very detailed, full of historical references and geographical landmarks, which were characteristic of that period's Greek thought and writing style. Luke painted a picture of Jesus as the Son of Man, the One who made salvation possible not only for Jews, but for all people.
John, One of Jesus' Twelve Disciples and an Apostle	John was a fisherman, who became a follower of Jesus Christ. Jesus later chose John as one of His twelve disciples, named apostles. Scripture depicts John as one of Jesus' closest disciples in a trio which also included Peter and his brother, James. John's gospel provides the most information about what Jesus said to His disciples in the upper room before His arrest and crucifixion. John clearly spelled out the purpose of his gospel saying, *"Jesus did many other miraculous signs in the presence of his disciples, which are not recorded in this book. But these are written that you may believe that Jesus is the Christ, the Son of God, and that by believing you may have life in his name"* (John 20:30–31 NIV). John's gospel emphasizes Jesus' divinity and was written to all people for all times.

	Approximate Timeline	**Location**	**Biblical Scriptures**	**Author**
God's Plan Unfolds	In the Beginning–6/5 B.C.	Jerusalem, Nazareth, Judea	Matthew 1:1–25 Luke 1–80; 3:23–38 John 1:1–18	Matthew Luke John
Jesus' Birth and Youth	6/5 B.C.–6/7 A.D.	Nazareth, Bethlehem, Jerusalem, Egypt	Matthew 2:1–23 Luke 2:1–52	Matthew Luke
Baptism and Temptation	26 A.D.	Judea	Matthew 3:1–4:11 Mark 1:1–13 Luke 3:1–4:13 John 1:19–28	Matthew Mark Luke John
Early Ministry —Part 1	26/27 A.D.	Cana, Judea, Galilee	Luke 3:23 John 1:29–2:13	Luke John
Early Ministry —Part 2	26/27 A.D.	Jerusalem, Judea, Samaria	Luke 3:19–20 John 2:14–4:42	Luke John

MAP OF KEY LOCATIONS

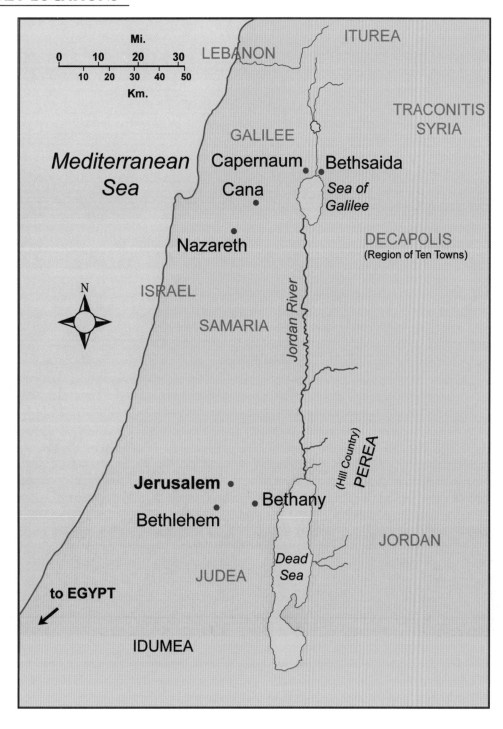

THE FLIGHT INTO EGYPT

"Now when they had departed, behold, an angel of the Lord appeared to Joseph in a dream, saying, 'Arise, take the young Child and His mother, flee to Egypt, and stay there until I bring you word; for Herod will seek the young Child to destroy Him.'" (Matthew 2:13 NKJ)

SECTION 1: GOD'S PLAN UNFOLDS

Jesus' Genealogy: (Matthew 1:1–17; Luke 3:23–38; John 1:1–18)

- Matthew opens his gospel with a record of Jesus' ancestry and declares Jesus to be the prophesied Messiah.

- Luke's gospel introduces Jesus as *". . . the son, so it was thought, of Joseph"* (Luke 3:23 NIV). Luke traces Jesus' ancestry starting with Joseph back to King David and continues all the way back to Adam, the first man.

- Apostle John begins his gospel declaring Jesus as the Word who was with God from the beginning. John addresses Jesus' divinity saying, *"In the beginning was the One who is called the Word. The Word was with God and was truly God. From the very beginning the Word was with God. And with this Word, God created everything. . . . The Word became a human being and lived here with us. We saw his true glory, the glory of the only Son of the Father"* (John 1:1–3, 14a CEV).

Note: Why is Jesus' genealogy important? Centuries earlier, God revealed through the prophets that the Messiah would be a descendant of King David. (See Isaiah 9:6–7; Jeremiah 23:5–6; and Ezekiel 34:23–24.) With this in mind, both Matthew and Luke recognized the importance of tracing Jesus' ancestry back to King David. In order for Jesus to be the Messiah of prophecy, He had to be in David's lineage. By recording Jesus' genealogy, Matthew and Luke provide the historical evidence needed to support the claim that Jesus of Nazareth was indeed the long-awaited Messiah. Matthew's genealogy appears in Matthew 1:1–17 and Luke's genealogy is recorded in Luke 3:23–38. The two genealogies are different. The commonly held view is that Matthew records Joseph's lineage (Jesus' legal earthly father), while Luke provides Mary's lineage (Jesus' actual bloodline). King David appears in both lineages as an ancestor of Joseph and Mary. Matthew's genealogy shows Jesus' legal claim as King of Israel, tracing Jesus' ancestry from Father Abraham to Joseph, the husband of Mary. Luke traces Jesus' ancestry all the way back to Adam and then states, *"Adam was the son of God"* (Luke 3:38). In doing so, Luke firmly establishes Jesus' relationship to God and all mankind.

The Angel's Birth Announcements: (Luke 1:5–80; Matthew 1:18–25)

- During the reign of King Herod the Great, a priest named Zechariah was on duty in the Temple at Jerusalem. Priests took turns serving in the Temple and it happened to be Zechariah's turn.

- Zechariah and his wife, Elizabeth, were righteous and served the God of Israel. Both were descendants of Aaron, Israel's first high priest and brother of the prophet Moses. They were getting up in age and were still childless.

- While Zechariah was busy serving in the Temple, an angel suddenly appeared near the altar. The angel told Zechariah his wife was going to have a son and the baby was to be named John.

- The angel explained to Zechariah that his son would be great before the Lord in spirit and power like the prophet Elijah. Zechariah's son would preach a message of repentance and would prepare Israel for the coming Messiah.

- Since he and his wife were well along in years, Zechariah asked the angel, *"How can I be sure of this?"* (Luke 1:18a NIV).

- The angel hastily replied, *"I am Gabriel. I stand in the presence of God, and I have been sent to speak to you and to tell you this good news"* (Luke 1:19 NIV).

- Gabriel then told Zechariah he would be unable to speak until the birth of his son because he did not believe the Lord's message.

- Elizabeth soon became pregnant. She rejoiced and thanked God for blessing her to conceive in her old age. Zechariah could not say anything for he had been rendered mute.

- When Elizabeth was six months pregnant, God sent the angel Gabriel to Nazareth to deliver a message to a young virgin girl named Mary.

- Mary was engaged to a man named Joseph. Mary and Joseph were both descendants of King David and lived in the town of Nazareth in Galilee.

- When Gabriel appeared to Mary, he announced she would soon have a Son who would be called the Son of the Most High God. Mary's Son would sit on King David's throne and His kingdom would last forever.

- Puzzled by Gabriel's announcement, Mary asked, *"But how can this happen? I am a virgin"* (Luke 1:34). Gabriel explained that the Child would be conceived by the power of the Holy Spirit. Mary's Child would be the long-awaited Messiah.

- Gabriel then informed Mary that Elizabeth, one of her relatives, had become pregnant in her old age. Although people thought Elizabeth was barren, she had conceived, for nothing is impossible with God.

- Mary humbly replied, *"I am the Lord's servant. May everything you have said about me come true"* (Luke 1:38). Gabriel then left.

 About 700 years before Jesus' birth, the prophet Isaiah revealed that the Messiah would be born to a virgin. Isaiah wrote, *". . . the Lord himself will give you the sign. Look! The virgin will conceive a child! She will give birth to a son and will call him Immanuel (which means 'God is with us')"* (Isaiah 7:14). In this prophecy, Isaiah said the Child would be called *Immanuel*, a Greek word, meaning "God with us." Jesus is "God with us." Jesus lives in us when we accept Him as our Lord and Savior (Romans 8:9–11; Galatians 2:20).

- After the angel left, Mary made arrangements to visit Elizabeth. She was soon on her way to the hill country of Judea where her relatives lived.

- When Mary arrived, she greeted Elizabeth. At the sound of Mary's voice, Elizabeth's baby jumped for joy and was filled with the Holy Spirit in her womb.

- Overjoyed and humbled, Elizabeth declared Mary had truly been blessed above all women and commended her very young relative for her faith in the Lord.

- Mary responded with a song of praise, thanking God for blessing her and being merciful to Israel as He promised Abraham. She stayed with Zechariah and Elizabeth about three months and then returned to Nazareth.

- When time came for Elizabeth to have her baby, she gave birth to a boy. The baby's parents named him John as they had been instructed by the angel.

- Suddenly, Zechariah was able to speak again. Inspired by the Holy Spirit, Zechariah began to prophecy saying God has sent a Savior from King David's lineage, fulfilling His covenant with Abraham.

- Zechariah then blessed John, his son, in a prophecy saying, *"And you, my little son, will be called the prophet of the Most High, because you will prepare the way for the Lord. You will tell his people how to find salvation through forgiveness of their sins"* (Luke 1:76–77).

In a prophecy written 430 years earlier, the prophet Malachi revealed the Messiah would suddenly appear in the Temple. As a sign of the Messiah's coming, a messenger—a prophet—would first appear to prepare the way for the Messiah. Malachi wrote, *"Look! I am sending my messenger, and he will prepare the way before me. Then the Lord you are seeking will suddenly come to his Temple. The messenger of the covenant, whom you look for so eagerly, is surely coming," says the* LORD *of Heaven's Armies"* (Malachi 3:1).

Zechariah and Elizabeth's baby was the messenger of prophecy who would precede the coming of the Messiah. When Gabriel appeared to Zechariah, the angel explained that God had a special mission for his son. God chose Zechariah and Elizabeth's baby to be His messenger who would prepare the way for the Messiah's ministry.

- In time, Mary became visibly pregnant. When Joseph, Mary's fiancé, discovered she was pregnant, he decided to quietly call off the marriage. He did not want her to experience the pain and embarrassment of public ridicule.

- While contemplating the situation, Joseph fell asleep. An angel of the Lord then appeared to him in a dream. The angel told Joseph he should not be afraid to marry Mary for the Child she was carrying had been conceived by the Holy Spirit.

- The angel also said Mary would have a Son and her Son should be named *Jesus*, meaning "The Lord is salvation" or "The Lord saves." Mary's Child would be a Savior for all people, reconciling mankind with God.

- After hearing the angel's message, Joseph married Mary. However, he did not have relations with her until after the Child was born.

God revealed numerous details about the Messiah to the prophet Isaiah. In one of his Messianic prophecies, Isaiah wrote, *"For to us a child is born, to us a son is given, and the government will be on his shoulders. And he will be called Wonderful Counselor, Mighty God, Everlasting Father, Prince of Peace . . . He will reign on David's throne and over his kingdom, establishing and upholding it with justice and righteousness from that time on and forever"* (Isaiah 9:6–7).

Jesus is "Wonderful Counselor," "Mighty God," "Everlasting Father," "Prince of Peace," and so much more. This prophecy was fulfilled through Jesus Christ, who came on a rescue mission to save the world. Jesus is the One who upholds justice and righteousness in a kingdom that will last forever.

RECOMMENDED BIBLE READING

John 1:1–18 **In the Beginning**
Genesis 1:1–2:4 **The Account of Creation**
Genesis 12:1–3 **Mankind Will Be Blessed**

SECTION 2: JESUS' BIRTH AND YOUTH

The Savior's Birth: (Luke 2:1–40; Matthew 2:1–23)

- During the final months of Mary's pregnancy, Caesar Augustus, emperor of Rome, ordered a census. Everyone was required to register in the town of their family's origin.

- Since Joseph was a descendant of King David, he and Mary had to register in David's hometown of Bethlehem. They made the long journey from Nazareth to Bethlehem, a distance of about seventy miles.

- While Mary and Joseph were in Bethlehem, it came time for the Baby to be born. Mary gave birth to a Boy. She placed her Baby in a lowly manger (a food trough for animals) because there was no room in Bethlehem's inn.

- Meanwhile, shepherds were in fields caring for their flocks. They watched as God's glory filled the night sky with radiant light.

- An angel suddenly appeared to the shepherds. The angel said, *"Do not be afraid, for behold, I bring you good tidings of great joy which will be to all people. For there is born to you this day in the city of David a Savior, who is Christ the Lord. And this will be the sign to you: You will find a Babe wrapped in swaddling cloths, lying in a manger"* (Luke 2:10–12 NKJ).

- A vast number of angels joined in the heavenly announcement. They praised God for the Child, who would bring peace and God's favor to all mankind. After witnessing the glorious announcement, the shepherds ran to see the Baby whom the angel declared to be the Savior.

Note: What was Jesus' date of birth? The exact date of Jesus' birth is unknown. According to *Halley's Handbook*, Jesus' birth is placed at 6 or 5 B.C., instead of 1 B.C., because of a mathematical error that occurred when the Roman calendar was converted to our present-day calendar. After the conversion, the calendar showed Herod the Great's death as having occurred in 4 B.C. Paul Benware, author of *Survey of the New Testament*, explains that Scripture tells us Herod was alive when Jesus was born and died while Jesus was a Child living in Egypt with His parents. (See Matthew 2:19–20.) Taking this into account, most historians place Jesus' birth at 6 or 5 B.C. on our present-day calendar.

- When Mary's Baby was eight days old, Mary and Joseph took Him to the Temple in Jerusalem to be circumcised. They named the Baby Jesus.

- Mary and Joseph returned to the Temple shortly afterward to complete the rites and offerings required by Jewish law after the birth of a child.

Note: Jewish parents had to perform several religious ceremonies after a child's birth to keep God's covenant and laws: 1.) A male child was circumcised and given a name eight days after his birth. (See Leviticus 12:3.) God initiated this rite as a sign of His covenant with Abraham. (See Leviticus 17:9–14.) Circumcision has been performed from generation to generation among the Jews, identifying them as part of God's covenant with Abraham; 2.) When Jewish mothers gave birth, they were considered ceremonially unclean and prohibited from worshiping in the Temple. They were not unclean due to sin, but because of the health issues associated with childbirth. Forty days after the birth of a son and eighty days after the birth of a daughter, the mother had to bring animals as required by Jewish law to the priest as an offering to God. The priest would then sacrifice the animals on the altar, which purified the mother. (See Leviticus 12:1–8); 3.) When a mother gave birth to her first son, the child had to be presented to God one month after his birth. All firstborn male children belonged to God and were to perform work in His service. (See Exodus 13:2, 11–16; Numbers 18:15–16.)

- While at the Temple, the Holy Spirit revealed to two people that Mary's Child was the Messiah. The first to receive this revelation was an elderly man named Simeon, who walked upright before the Lord.

- When Simeon saw the Baby Jesus, he praised God and said, *"Sovereign Lord. . . . I have seen your salvation, which you have prepared for all people. He is a light to reveal God to the nations, and he is the glory of your people Israel!"* (Luke 2:29–32).

- The Holy Spirit also revealed Baby Jesus' identity to a widowed prophetess named Anna. She praised God and began telling everyone Mary's Child was the long-awaited Messiah.

- Shortly after Jesus' birth, wise men arrived in Jerusalem looking for the newborn King of the Jews. The wise men said the newborn King's star appeared to them in the east and they followed it to Jerusalem.

- After hearing the wise men's story, King Herod was greatly disturbed. He feared a Child had been born who would someday take his kingdom away from him.

- Herod quickly assembled some prominent Jewish religious leaders and asked, *"Where is the Messiah supposed to be born?"* The religious leaders answered, *"In Bethlehem in Judea"* (Matthew 2:4–5).

- After consulting the religious leaders about the prophesied location of the Messiah's birth, Herod met privately with the wise men.

- Herod instructed the wise men to go to Bethlehem and search for the Child. He added, *"When you find him, come back and tell me so that I can go and worship him, too!"* (Matthew 2:8b).

Note: Herod did not really want to worship the Child. He lied to the wise men so that they would return with information about the Child's whereabouts. Herod wanted to kill the Child because from his point of view, the newborn King represented a threat to his reign as king.

God revealed the Messiah's birthplace to the prophet Micah 700 years before Jesus' birth. According to Micah's prophecy, the Messiah would be born in Bethlehem, *"But as for you, Bethlehem Ephrathah, too little to be among the clans of Judah, from you One will go forth for Me to be ruler in Israel His goings forth are from long ago, from the days of eternity"* (Micah 5:2 NASB).

Although Jesus grew up in Nazareth of Galilee, He was born in Bethlehem Ephrathah in Judea. Jesus' parents were in Bethlehem at the time of His birth because Caesar Augustus had ordered a census. Only God could have orchestrated such perfect timing to fulfill Micah's prophecy.

- As the wise men traveled to Bethlehem, the star appeared again. It guided them directly to the Child. They worshiped the Child and gave Him gifts of gold, frankincense, and myrrh.

Note: Gold was an expensive gift offered to Jesus as King. Frankincense was an incense ingredient used for religious worship. Myrrh was a spice used in burial preparation.

- Having been warned by God in a dream about Herod's plan to harm the Child, the wise men traveled a different route back home.

- An angel then appeared to Joseph in a dream and told him to flee to Egypt because Herod was going to try to kill the Child. Joseph immediately got up and took his family to Egypt where the Child would be safe.

- When Herod realized the wise men were not returning to Jerusalem with information about the Child's whereabouts, he was furious. He ordered his soldiers to kill all the boys in Bethlehem who were two years old or younger.

- A few years later, Herod died. An angel appeared to Joseph and told him to return to Israel. Joseph left Egypt and traveled back to Nazareth in Galilee with his family.

 According to the gospel of Matthew, Joseph and Mary's escape to Egypt and return to Israel fulfilled a prophecy about the Messiah. Over 700 years earlier, the prophet Hosea wrote, *"When Israel was a child, I loved him, and I called my son out of Egypt"* (Hosea 11:1). (See Matthew 2:15.)

Jesus' Youth: (Luke 2:41–52)

- When Jesus was twelve years old, He and His family traveled to Jerusalem for the annual Passover celebration as they did each year.

- After the celebration, Jesus' family packed up and started the long journey back to Nazareth. While en route, Mary and Joseph discovered Jesus was not with them.

- Mary and Joseph returned to Jerusalem and searched for Jesus. They were surprised to find Him in the Temple discussing the Scriptures with religious teachers. The priests and teachers of religious law were amazed at Jesus' knowledge of the Scriptures.

- As Mary approached Jesus, she said to Him, *"Son, why have you done this to us? Your father and I have been very worried, and we have been searching for you!"* (Luke 2:48 CEV).

- Jesus responded to His mother saying, *"Why did you have to look for me? Didn't you know that I would be in my Father's house?"* (Luke 2:49 CEV).

 Note: This is the first time Jesus acknowledged His divinity in Scripture, referring to God as His Father.

- Jesus returned to Nazareth with His parents. He grew in spiritual wisdom and insight. He was an obedient Child, well-pleasing to God—His Heavenly Father.

RECOMMENDED BIBLE READING

Luke 2:1–20 **Jesus' Birth**

Matthew 2:1–12 **The Wise Men's Visit**

Micah 5:1–4 **Little Town of Bethlehem**

SECTION 3: BAPTISM AND TEMPTATION

John the Baptist (Matthew 3:1–12; Mark 1:1–8; Luke 3:1–17; John 1:19–28)

- Tiberius Caesar was emperor of Rome when John, Zechariah and Elizabeth's son, began his ministry. Pilate was the Roman governor of Judea; Herod Antipas, son of Herod the Great, was ruler of Galilee; Herod Philip, another son of Herod the Great, was ruler of Iturea and Traconitis; and Annas and Caiaphas were the high priests.

- John lived in the wilderness and preached on both sides of the Jordan River. He exhorted people to repent, turn away from sin, and walk upright before the Lord. John boldly delivered God's message, baptizing those who turned away from sin and to God. For this reason, he became known as John the Baptist.

 Note: Water baptism was a washing ritual used in Old Testament times to cleanse a person from sin, disease, and anything considered unclean according to Jewish law. John used water baptism as a symbol of one's sins being washed away.

John the Baptist was the forerunner of Jesus Christ. God ordained him from birth as the prophet who would prepare people for the Messiah's coming. Isaiah wrote about John saying, *"Listen! It's the voice of someone shouting, 'Clear the way through the wilderness for the LORD! Make a straight highway through the wasteland for our God!'"* (Isaiah 40:3).

John started preaching in about 26 A.D., shortly before Jesus began His public ministry. John delivered a message of repentance for the remission of sins. He confronted people, challenging them to repent. John baptized those who acknowledged their sins and asked God for forgiveness.

- People traveled from all over Judea to hear John's message. Since the Jews were anxiously awaiting the coming of the Messiah, many wondered if John was their long-awaited Savior.

- One day, religious leaders in Jerusalem sent priests to the wilderness where John was preaching to ask about his ministry. They asked if he was the Messiah or Elijah or the Prophet foretold in Scripture.

 Note: Over 1,400 years before Jesus' birth, God spoke to the prophet Moses saying, *"I (God) will raise up for them a prophet like you from among their brothers; I will put my words in his mouth, and he will tell them everything I command him"* (Deuteronomy 18:18 NIV). The Jews were very much aware of this prophecy and wanted to know if John the Baptist was the prophet mentioned in Scripture.

- Responding to the religious leaders' question, John said he was not the Messiah, but was the one God had chosen to prepare the way for the Messiah. John explained that another was coming who would be greater than he. John said he baptized with water, but the Messiah would baptize with the Holy Spirit.

John Baptizes Jesus (Matthew 3:13–17; Mark 1:9–11; Luke 3:21–22)

- As John was baptizing in the Jordan River, Jesus came to him one day. Jesus wanted John to baptize Him.

- John was reluctant, saying he was not worthy of such an honor. John felt their roles should be reversed and Jesus should be baptizing him.

- Jesus said to John, *"For now this is how it should be, because we must do all that God wants us to do"* (Matthew 3:15 CEV). After Jesus explained that it was God's will for John to baptize Him, John baptized Jesus.

- As Jesus came up out of the water, the Holy Spirit descended on Him from heaven in the form of a dove. A voice from heaven then said, *"You are my own dear Son, and I am pleased with you"* (Luke 3:22b CEV).

 Note: Jesus was about thirty years old when He was baptized. Jesus' baptism marked the beginning of His public ministry, which lasted about three-and-a-half years. All three members of the Trinity are mentioned in Luke 3:21–22. God, the Father, spoke from heaven; the Holy Spirit descended in the form of a dove; and Jesus, in human form, was baptized. It is important to note that Jesus was not baptized because He was in need of repentance. Jesus was baptized on behalf of all mankind because the world was in need of repentance.

Satan Tempts Jesus (Matthew 4:1–11; Mark 1:12–13; Luke 4:1–13)

- After Jesus was baptized, the Holy Spirit led Him into the wilderness. Jesus had been alone in the desert for forty days without food when Satan (the Devil) appeared. Satan, who is always full of guile, tried to entice Jesus into disobeying God, His Father.

- Satan knew Jesus had not eaten in weeks so he said to Him, *"If you are the Son of God, tell these stones to become bread"* (Matthew 4:3 NIV). Quoting Scripture, Jesus responded, *"It is written: 'Man does not live on bread alone, but on every word that comes from the mouth of God'"* (Matthew 4:4 NIV). (See Deuteronomy 8:3 for cross-reference.)

- The Devil transported Jesus to the top of the Temple in Jerusalem and ordered Him to jump. Satan insisted it would prove Jesus was the Son of God. Refusing the wiles of the Devil, Jesus quoted Scripture again, *"It is also written: 'Do not put the Lord your God to the test'"* (Matthew 4:7 NIV). (See Deuteronomy 6:16 for cross-reference.)

- The Devil then swept Jesus away to the summit of a very high mountain and pointed to all the nations of the world. Satan promised to give Jesus the entire world and all its glory if He would bow down and worship him.

- Jesus fired back at the Devil saying *"Away from me, Satan!"* Jesus then quoted Scripture for a third time saying, *"For it is written: 'Worship the Lord your God, and serve him only'"* (Matthew 4:10 NIV). (See Deuteronomy 6:13 for cross-reference.)

- The Devil had nothing more to say and left. Angels came and ministered to Jesus' needs.

 Note: Jesus resisted Satan's attacks with the Word of God. By quoting Scripture, Jesus showed us how powerful God's Word is against Satan.

RECOMMENDED BIBLE READING

Mark 1:1–13	**Jesus' Baptism and Temptation**
Isaiah 40:1–11	**Prophecy of the Messiah's Coming**
Malachi 3:1	**Prophecy about John the Baptist and Jesus**

SECTION 4: EARLY MINISTRY—PART 1

Jesus, the Messiah: (John 1:29–51)

- After overcoming Satan's temptations in the wilderness, Jesus returned to the area where John was baptizing. One day, John saw Jesus walking toward him and shouted out, *"Behold! The Lamb of God who takes away the sin of the world!"* (John 1:29 NKJ).

- God had previously revealed to John how he would recognize the Messiah. John said, *"I didn't know he (Jesus) was the one, but when God sent me to baptize with water, he told me, 'The one on whom you see the Spirit descend and rest is the one who will baptize with the Holy Spirit.' I saw this happen to Jesus, so I testify that he is the Chosen One of God"* (John 1:33–34).

Note: John the Baptist explained how he knew Jesus was the Messiah. God had revealed to John that at the time of the Messiah's baptism, the Holy Spirit would descend upon His Anointed One. When Jesus was baptized, John saw the Holy Spirit descending on Jesus in the form of a dove. Having witnessed God's revelation come true before his very eyes, John knew at that moment Jesus was indeed the Messiah. Although John was related to Jesus, he did not fully realize Jesus was the Messiah until His baptism. (See Luke 1:36.)

- Two of John's disciples heard him declare Jesus to be the Messiah. They decided to follow Jesus. One of these men was Andrew, Simon Peter's brother. Andrew immediately found Simon and shared the news about Jesus with him.

- After hearing the news, Simon went back with Andrew to meet Jesus. When Jesus saw Simon, He looked him in the eye and said, *"Your name is Simon, son of John—but you will be called Cephas (which means 'Peter')"* (John 1:42b).

Note: What is in a name? *Cephas* is Aramaic and is translated *Peter* in Greek. The names "Cephas" and "Peter" mean "rock" in both languages. By changing Simon's name to Peter, Jesus revealed that Peter would grow spiritually into a rock-solid ambassador in God's Kingdom. During Jesus' days on earth, Peter was anything but rock-solid. He was impulsive and often spoke without thinking. However, Peter experienced tremendous spiritual growth after Jesus' death and became rock-solid in his faith during the days of the early church.

- After His encounter with Andrew and Peter in Judea, Jesus traveled back home to Galilee.

- Jesus sought out a man named Philip, who was from Bethsaida, Andrew and Peter's hometown. When Jesus found Philip, He asked him to become one of His disciples.

- After meeting Jesus, Philip left to find his friend, Nathanael. When Philip found Nathanael, He said to him, *"We have found the very person Moses and the prophets wrote about! His name is Jesus, the son of Joseph from Nazareth"* (John 1:45).

- Nathanael was surprised to learn the Messiah was from Nazareth. He asked Philip, *"Can anything good come from Nazareth?"* (John 1:46).

- After hearing Philip's news, Nathanael decided to go meet Jesus for himself. As the two approached, Jesus called out to Nathanael saying, *"Now here is a genuine son of Israel—a man of complete integrity"* (John 1:47).

- Surprised by Jesus' remark, Nathanael asked Him, *"How do you know about me?"* (John 1:48).

- Jesus told Nathanael He had seen him sitting underneath a fig tree long before Philip found him. Amazed, Nathanael shouted out, *"Rabbi! You are the Son of God, the King of Israel!"* (John 1:49 MSG).

- Jesus then said to Nathanael, *"Do you believe this just because I told you I had seen you under the fig tree? You will see greater things than this"* (John 1:50).

 Note: *Rabbi* is a Hebrew word translated "master" or "lord," or more literally, "great one." It is the title given to Jewish religious teachers and still used today. Jesus was often called "Rabbi" by His followers to show their respect for Him as a Great Teacher.

Jesus' First Miracle in Public: (John 2:1–12; Luke 3:23)

 Note: According to Luke, Jesus was about thirty years old when He began His ministry. (See Luke 3:23.) John is the only gospel writer to describe Jesus' early ministry which began shortly after His baptism and covered a period of about one year.

- Shortly after Nathanael and Philip became disciples, Jesus, His mother, and His disciples attended a wedding celebration in Cana of Galilee.

- During the celebration, the groom's supply of wine ran out. When Mary became aware of the situation, she found Jesus and told Him there was no more wine. Jesus said to His mother, *"Dear woman, why do you involve me? My time has not yet come"* (John 2:4 NIV).

- Mary went over to the servants and told them to do whatever Jesus said. Shortly afterward, Jesus instructed the servants to fill six very large jars with water.

- The servants did exactly what Jesus told them. After they finished filling the jars with water, Jesus told them to give the master of ceremonies a drink.

- When the servants dipped from one of the jars, they discovered the water had miraculously turned into wine.

- The master of ceremonies took a sip of the wine and was elated by its taste. He did not know the wine had been made from water. It tasted like a high quality fine wine.

- Calling the groom over, the master of ceremony said to him, *"Everyone brings out the choice wine first and then the cheaper wine after the guests have had too much to drink; but you have saved the best till now"* (John 2:10 NIV).

- Turning the water into wine was the first miracle Jesus performed publicly in full view of His disciples. Seeing Jesus perform this miracle strengthened the disciples' faith in Him.

Jesus Attends the Passover Celebration: (John 2:13)

- Jesus later traveled to Jerusalem for the annual Passover celebration.

 Passover is a Jewish holiday that is still celebrated annually in the March/April timeframe. It is a reminder of how God delivered the Israelites from slavery in Egypt. God instructed the Israelites to slaughter a lamb and smear its blood on the doorframes of their houses. At midnight, God's destroyer (angel of death) killed all the Egyptians' firstborn sons and firstborn animals. The angel of death passed over the houses with blood smeared on the doorframes, so the Israelites' firstborn were spared. This was the "Passover" miracle. (See Exodus 12:1–30.)

Passover foreshadowed the significance of "blood" for the remission of sins, *". . . without the shedding of blood there is no forgiveness"* (Hebrews 9:22b NIV).

- Jews and Gentiles came from all over Israel and other countries to worship in the Temple.

Note: The Temple in Jerusalem during Jesus' time was not the same structure King Solomon built in 959 B.C. When the Babylonians conquered Jerusalem in 586 B.C., they completely destroyed King Solomon's Temple. The Jews who survived the invasion were forcibly carried away to Babylon where they lived in exile. The exiled Jews were allowed to return to Jerusalem in 538 B.C. Zerubbabel, heir to King David's throne and ancestor of Jesus Christ, led the first group of exiles from Babylon to Jerusalem. Those who returned rebuilt the Temple on its original site on top of Mount Moriah. The second Temple was finished in 515 B.C. under Zerubbabel's leadership. It was much smaller and less impressive than Solomon's Temple. In 20 B.C., Herod the Great started a massive Temple renovation project. He enlarged the Temple and greatly enhanced its appearance with expensive stones, gold overlays, and beautiful gated walls. After Herod's death, the renovation effort continued and was still going on at the time of Jesus' ministry. During a Jewish uprising, the Romans completely destroyed Herod's Temple in 70 A.D.

- As Jesus entered the Temple courtyard, He saw crowds of people buying animals from local merchants to be used as sacrificial offerings for Passover.

Note: What was the purpose of sacrificial offerings? After God miraculously freed the Jews from Egyptian slavery, He led them into the wilderness to Mount Sinai. While there, God gave the Jews—through the prophet Moses—specific procedures for five types of sacrificial offerings: Burnt Offerings, Grain Offerings, Fellowship (Peace) Offerings, Sin Offerings, and Guilt Offerings. (See Leviticus 1–7.) The people were to give a portion of their livestock or grain as an offering to atone for sin and make peace with God. The people brought animals to the priests, who slaughtered and burned them on an altar as an offering to God.

Recommended Bible Reading

John 2:1–12 **Jesus' First Public Miracle**

Isaiah 11:1–5 **The Branch from David's Lineage**

SECTION 5: EARLY MINISTRY—PART 2

Jesus Chases the Merchants Out of the Temple: (John 2:14–25)

- As Jesus arrived in the Temple courtyard, merchants were standing behind tables and booths selling animals and exchanging foreign money for the local currency.

- When Jesus saw the Temple courtyard being used as a marketplace, He made a whip out of some rope. In a fit of righteous indignation, Jesus chased the merchants and those exchanging currency out of the Temple.

- As Jesus turned over the merchants' tables and booths, He said to them, *"Get these things out of here. Stop turning my Father's house into a marketplace!"* (John 2:16).

- When some religious leaders saw what was happening, they confronted Jesus, asking who had given Him permission to chase the merchants out of the Temple.

- Jesus replied, *"Destroy this temple, and in three days I will raise it up"* (John 2:19). Outraged, the religious leaders pointed to the Temple and said it had taken forty-six years to build the structure. If the Temple were destroyed, it would take much longer than a mere three days to rebuild it.

- The religious leaders did not realize Jesus was referring to His own body as a Temple. Apostle John added a commentary note in his gospel saying, *"Later, after he (Jesus) was raised from the dead, his disciples remembered he had said this. They then put two and two together and believed both what was written in Scripture and what Jesus had said"* (John 2:22 MSG).

 Note: What did Jesus mean when He said, *"Destroy this temple, and in three days I will raise it up?"* Jesus was not saying He would rebuild Herod's Temple in three days. Jesus was referring to His body as a Temple and was announcing His resurrection, which would happen three days after His death.

- Jesus performed several miracles while in Jerusalem. Many people witnessed His miracles and believed He was indeed the Messiah.

Jesus' Discussion with Nicodemus: (John 3:1–21)

- One night, a Pharisee named Nicodemus visited Jesus. Nicodemus told Jesus His miracles were proof positive He had been sent by God.

- Jesus said to Nicodemus, *"I tell you the truth, unless you are born again you cannot see the Kingdom of God"* (John 3:3).

- Puzzled by Jesus' statement, Nicodemus wondered how a man could be born again. After all, no one could enter the womb a second time.

- Jesus explained, *"Humans can reproduce only human life, but the Holy Spirit gives birth to spiritual life"* (John 3:6). Everyone who believes in Him would be born again of the Holy Spirit and would live with God forever.

- Jesus then said, *"And as Moses lifted up the bronze snake on a pole in the wilderness, so the Son of Man must be lifted up, so that everyone who believes in him will have eternal life"* (John 3:14–15).

 Note: Jesus compared the purpose of His mission on earth to an event that occurred in the Old Testament. While in the desert, the Israelites often complained about God's provisions as they journeyed to Canaan under Moses' leadership. On one occasion, God disciplined the Israelites by sending venomous snakes that killed people with their bites. Moses prayed for the people and God instructed him to make a bronze snake. God told Moses to put the bronze snake on top of a pole and lift it up high. Anyone who had been bitten by a snake lived when they looked up at the bronze snake and believed they would be healed. (See Numbers 21:4–9.) This incident foreshadowed Jesus' death and resurrection. Jesus was telling Nicodemus He would be lifted up on a cross. Those who look up at the cross and believe in Him will receive eternal life.

> During His discussion with Nicodemus, Jesus summed up God's Plan of Redemption and Salvation in a few words. Jesus said, *"For God so loved the world that he gave his one and only Son, that whoever believes in him shall not perish but have eternal life. For God did not send his Son into the world to condemn the world, but to save the world through him"* (John 3:16–17 NIV).
>
> Jesus' message to Nicodemus about His mission was very succinct and exceptionally clear. God (the Creator) loved us (His creation) so much He sent Jesus (His Son) to live on earth for a while. Those who accept Jesus as God's Plan of Redemption and Salvation will be blessed with eternal life.

John the Baptist's Testimony: (Luke 3:19–20; John 3:22–36)

- Jesus and His disciples left Jerusalem, but stayed in Judea near the area where John was baptizing.

- One day, a disciple of John the Baptist came to John saying Jesus was baptizing and attracting more people than John.

- John responded, saying he was not the Messiah. John explained that God sent him to prepare the way for the Messiah. Because of this, his ministry would diminish as the Messiah's ministry increased.

- John the Baptist later publicly denounced Herod Antipas' marriage to Herodias because she was the wife of Herod's brother. After John openly criticized Herod for this and other crimes, Herod put John in prison.

Jesus' Discussion with the Samaritan Woman: (John 4:1–42)

- After hearing about John the Baptist's imprisonment, Jesus left Judea and traveled back to Galilee by way of Samaria.

- When Jesus came to Samaria, He stopped to rest at a well built by Jacob, patriarch of the Jews.

- While Jesus was at the well, a Samaritan woman came with a jar to draw water. When Jesus saw her, He asked for a drink of water.

- Utterly shocked, the woman asked Jesus why He, a Jew, was speaking to her, a Samaritan, for Jews despised Samaritans and did not associate with them.

Note: Samaritans were a mixed race. Jews looked down on Samaritans because they were not pure descendants of Abraham. They were the offspring of intermarriages between Gentiles and poor Jews left behind in Israel during the exile. Samaritans mixed Judaism with various forms of pagan worship. As a result, Jews despised Samaritans because they were not racially, culturally, or religiously pure. By talking to the Samaritan woman, Jesus taught a valuable lesson about God. Men and women are equal in His sight. God is impartial and does not subscribe to favoritism.

- Responding to the woman's question, Jesus said, *"If you knew the gift of God and who it is that asks you for a drink, you would have asked him and he would have given you living water"* (John 4:10 NIV).

- Jesus told the woman that a person who drinks a glass of water would eventually become thirsty again and need more water. However, people would never be thirsty (spiritually) again after they received His living water.

- Jesus said He would give her a continuous flow of living water that would forever quench the thirst.

Jesus is the One who gives Living Water. In the Old Testament God is described as One who quenched the thirst. (See Psalm 42:1–2.) Jeremiah called the Lord a Fountain of Living Water. (See Jeremiah 17:13.) Zechariah provided one of the clearest prophecies in Scripture depicting the Messiah as a fountain that cleanses away sin, *"On that day a fountain will be opened for the dynasty of David and for the people of Jerusalem, a fountain to cleanse them from all their sins and impurity"* (Zechariah 13:1).

When Jesus told the Samaritan woman He could give her living water, He was declaring Himself to be the Messiah. Only the Messiah could offer living water that quenches spiritual thirst, cleanses sin, and leads to eternal life with God.

- When the woman asked Jesus for His living water, He instructed her to bring her husband to Him. The woman said she was not married.

- Jesus responded, *"You are right when you say you have no husband. The fact is, you have had five husbands, and the man you now have is not your husband. What you have just said is quite true"* (John 4:17b–18 NIV).

- Amazed, the woman wondered how Jesus could possibly know so much about her. She decided Jesus must be a prophet.

- Jesus explained, *"Yet a time is coming and has now come when the true worshipers will worship the Father in spirit and truth . . ."* (John 4:23 NIV).

- As Jesus explained about true worship, the woman said, *"I know that Messiah '(called Christ)' is coming. When he comes, he will explain everything to us"* (John 4:25 NIV).

- Jesus then said, *"I am he . . . You don't have to wait any longer or look any further"* (John 4:26 MSG).

- When Jesus said this, the woman left her jar at the well and ran into the village. She told everyone she met about Jesus.

- After hearing the woman's story, a large number of Samaritans went to see Jesus. He ministered to them and many believed He was indeed the Savior of the world.

RECOMMENDED BIBLE READING

John 4:1–42	**The Samaritan Woman Meets Jesus**
Isaiah 44:1–5	**Water to Quench the Thirst**
Jeremiah 17:12–13	**The Fountain of Living Water**

MEDITATION & PRAYER

Apostle Paul exhorts us to have the same attitude as that of Jesus Christ:

"Is there any encouragement from belonging to Christ? Any comfort from his love? Any fellowship together in the Spirit? Are your hearts tender and compassionate? Then make me truly happy by agreeing wholeheartedly with each other, loving one another, and working together with one mind and purpose. Don't be selfish; don't try to impress others. Be humble, thinking of others as better than yourselves. Don't look out only for your own interests, but take an interest in others, too. You must have the same attitude that Christ Jesus had. Though he was God, he did not think of equality with God as something to cling to. Instead, he gave up his divine privileges; he took the humble position of a slave and was born as a human being."

(Philippians 2:1–7)

Dear Heavenly Father,

Fill me with Your tender love and compassion. Remove from me the spirit of selfishness and pride, and create in me a spirit of fellowship and goodwill. Teach me to be more like Your Son, Jesus Christ, who in humble submission, gave up His divine privileges. Jesus came to earth and showed us how to live a life that pleases You. Jesus is the perfect image of Your love, righteousness, and unity. Help me to have the same attitude as Christ. Make me an instrument of Your glory so that others will see Christ in me.

Amen

REVIEW QUESTIONS

1. What was the political atmosphere in Israel at the time of Jesus' birth? Who were the Jews waiting for and why?

_____

_____

_____

_____

2. Who were the four gospel writers? What did you learn about each of them? How did each portray Jesus Christ in his gospel?

_____

_____

_____

_____

3. Why was Jesus' genealogy important?

_____

_____

_____

4. How did God announce the Messiah's birth to Mary and Joseph? To the shepherds? To the wise men?

_____

_____

_____

_____

5. Why did Jesus' birth occur in Bethlehem instead of Nazareth, Mary and Joseph's hometown? Why was this important?

_____

_____

_____

_____

6. Who was John the Baptist? What was God's purpose for his life? Why did John baptize people?

_____

_____

_____

_____

7. How did God reveal to John that Jesus was the Messiah?

_____

_____

_____

_____

8. Why was the Samaritan woman shocked when Jesus spoke to her? What lessons did Jesus teach during His encounter with the Samaritan woman?

_____

_____

_____

_____

PERSONAL REFLECTIONS

9. Gabriel appeared to Zechariah announcing the birth of John the Baptist. He then appeared to Mary announcing Jesus' birth. How did each respond to Gabriel's announcement? If an angel appeared to you, would your response be more like Zechariah's or Mary's? Why?

_____

_____

_____

_____

_____

10. Satan tempted Jesus at a time when He was most vulnerable. Jesus resisted Satan's attacks by quoting Scripture. In what areas are you most vulnerable to Satan's attacks? As you read your Bible, begin making a list of scriptures you can use to ward off Satan's attacks in these areas?

_____

_____

_____

_____

11. Isaiah wrote about Jesus, saying He would be called "Wonderful Counselor, Mighty God, Everlasting Father, and Prince of Peace." What do these names mean to you?

_____

_____

_____

_____

12. Jesus said to Nicodemus, *"You must be born again."* What does being "born again" mean to you?

_____

_____

_____

_____

_____

13. Which of the Messianic prophecies mentioned in this chapter were most meaningful to you? (See Appendix 7.) How do these prophecies affect your personal belief about Jesus as the Messiah?

_____

_____

_____

_____

_____

14. According to John 3:16, *"For God loved the world so much that he gave his one and only Son, so that everyone who believes in him will not perish but have eternal life."* Write a prayer thanking God for His great gift of love.

_____

_____

_____

_____

CLOSING PRAYER

Isaiah prophesies about God's gift to the world:

"For a child has been born—for us!
    the gift of a son—for us!
He'll take over
    the running of the world.
His names will be: Amazing Counselor,
    Strong God,
Eternal Father,
    Prince of Wholeness.
His ruling authority will grow,
    and there'll be no limits to the wholeness he brings.
He'll rule from the historic David throne
    over that promised kingdom.
He'll put that kingdom on a firm footing
    and keep it going
With fair dealing and right living,
    beginning now and lasting always.
The zeal of God-of-the-Angel-Armies
    will do all this."

(Isaiah 9:6–10 MSG)

Lord God,

I thank You for the most precious gift the world has ever known. Nothing compares to the love and compassion You demonstrated when You gave the world Your Son, Jesus Christ. He is truly an Amazing Counselor, Strong God, Eternal Father and Prince of Wholeness. His ruling authority abounds. His healing power is limitless and His kingdom is timeless. I am truly grateful and will praise Your name all the days of my life.

Amen

Chapter 2

Jesus' Ministry in Galilee

Opening Prayer

Dear Lord God,

Prepare my heart and mind to receive a better understanding of the Good News of Jesus Christ. Speak to me through the Holy Spirit as I read about Jesus' mission and ministry in Galilee. Help me to see how Jesus' words and actions demonstrated Your righteous and loving character. Teach me, through Jesus, Your ways so that I might bring honor and glory to Your name.

Amen

CHAPTER SUMMARY

JESUS' MINISTRY IN GALILEE

(Matthew, Mark, Luke, and John)

After John the Baptist was imprisoned, Jesus left Judea and began ministering in Galilee. Jesus was greatly concerned about the hundreds of man-made rules the religious leaders added to the laws God gave Moses. These additional rules imposed a tremendous burden on the people. Particularly challenging were the rules about what constituted work on the Sabbath. Jesus interpreted the law of Moses with compassion. He said, *"Don't suppose that I came to do away with the Law and the Prophets. I did not come to do away with them, but to give them their full meaning"* (Matthew 5:17 CEV).

Jesus taught and performed miracles throughout Galilee and the surrounding area. He preached in synagogues, on mountainsides, near lakeshores, and any place where people gathered. This phase of Jesus' ministry lasted about two years and is described in all four gospels. On one occasion, Jesus spoke to a large crowd about God's Kingdom in a message called, "The Sermon on the Mount." In this message, Jesus told the people to:

- Serve God wholeheartedly without hypocrisy.

- Let others see God's character in you and give God the glory.

- Put God first and make Him a priority in your life.

- Keep a godly perspective while going about your daily routine.

- Love your neighbors and pray for your enemies.

- Do not retaliate or judge others.

- Choose God's way, for it leads to eternal life.

Jesus became well-known for His healing miracles. Large crowds followed Him in hopes of witnessing a miracle. The gospel writers documented many of Jesus' miracles, which included:

- Restoring sight to the blind, speech to the mute, and hearing to the deaf.

- Healing lepers and others sick with dreaded diseases.

- Bringing dead people back to life.

- Calming storms and walking on water.

- Feeding 5,000 people with five loaves of bread and two fish.

- Feeding 4,000 people with seven loaves of bread and a few fish.

Jesus' followers initially grew in numbers and then dwindled as religious leaders opposed His ministry. Many found Jesus' message radically different from what was taught in Jewish synagogues. Others felt his teachings were too difficult to accept. While many of Jesus' followers abandoned Him, His true disciples—many of whom were women—continued to believe in Him.

Jesus chose twelve disciples and declared them apostles. An apostle is a person sent on a mission. Jesus commissioned the twelve disciples to preach, teach, and perform miracles. Jesus' twelve disciples, called apostles, are listed in Matthew 10:2–4; Mark 3:16–19; and Luke 6:14–16.

The Twelve Disciples Whom Jesus Made Apostles

Apostle	What We Know About Him
Peter, Simon	Peter was a fisherman. Jesus changed his name from Simon to Peter, meaning "rock." Peter was one of Jesus' central three disciples and was somewhat impulsive. Peter denied knowing Jesus during His trial, but was a bold witness for Christ on Pentecost and later emerged as leader of the church in Jerusalem. Peter wrote two New Testament letters.
James, Son of Zebedee, Son of Thunder	James was John's brother and one of Jesus' central three disciples. He was a fisherman in business with John and their father, Zebedee. He was ambitious and short-tempered, but fully committed to Jesus. James was the first of the twelve disciples to be martyred.
John, Son of Zebedee, Son of Thunder	John was a fisherman with his brother, James, and their father. He was one of Jesus' central three disciples. John was ambitious and judgmental, but later became very loving and gentle. Before Jesus died on the cross, He gave John responsibility for His mother's care. John was later exiled to the island of Patmos. He wrote the Gospel of John, three letters, and Revelation.
Andrew	Andrew was Peter's brother and a fisherman. When Andrew discovered Jesus was the Messiah, he immediately found Peter and brought him to Jesus. Andrew was eager to share the Good News with others.
Philip	Philip was from Bethsaida, which was Peter and Andrew's hometown. He was one of the first disciples Jesus asked to follow Him. Philip told Nathanael about Jesus.
Bartholomew, Nathanael	Bartholomew is called Nathanael in John's gospel. Nathanael asked if anything good could come from Nazareth. After his encounter with Jesus, Nathanael became a believer, declaring Jesus as the Son of God. Jesus called Nathanael a "true son of Israel" and "an honest man."
Matthew, Levi, Son of Alphaeus	Matthew was a tax collector. After becoming one of Jesus' disciples, Matthew hosted a dinner party and introduced his fellow tax collectors to Jesus. He wrote the Gospel of Matthew.
Thomas, The Twin	Thomas was a twin. He didn't believe the other disciples' claim that Jesus had risen from the dead, making him the original 'doubting' Thomas. After Jesus showed Thomas His wounds, he declared Jesus as Lord and God.
James, Son of Alphaeus	Scripture identifies this disciple as the son of Alphaeus. It is interesting to note that Mark's gospel refers to Matthew as Levi, the son of Alphaeus (See Mark 2:14). This James could have been Matthew's brother; however, scripture never identifies them as brothers. During the crucifixion, Mark refers to him as James, the Less or James, the Younger. (See Mark 15:40). This James is often confused with Jesus' half-brother, James, and John's older brother, James, who was also a disciple.
Simon, The Zealot	Zealots were militant extremists strongly opposed to Roman rule. Zealots believed only God should rule Palestine and felt this belief justified their murderous acts. Simon gave up this lifestyle to follow Jesus.
Judas, Son of James, Thaddaeus	Judas is called Thaddaeus in Matthew and Mark's gospels. Matthew also refers to this disciple as Lebbaeus (See Matthew 10:2). Luke called this disciple Judas, son of James. John's gospel referred to this disciple as Judas, not Iscariot.
Judas, Iscariot	Judas was in charge of the disciples' money bag and was the disciple who betrayed Jesus.

	Approximate Timeline	Location	Biblical Scriptures	Author
Galilean Ministry Begins	27–29 A.D.	Nazareth, Capernaum, Galilee	Matthew 4:1–25; 8:1–4, 14–17; 9:1–17	Matthew
			Mark 1:14–2:22	Mark
			Luke 4:14–5:39	Luke
			John 4:43–5:47	John
Jesus' Message	27–29 A.D.	Galilee	Matthew 5:1–7:29; 12:1–21	Matthew
			Mark 2:23–3:19	Mark
			Luke 6:1–49; 11:1–13, 33–36; 12:22–34	Luke
Miracles and Confrontations	27–29 A.D.	Capernaum, Nain, Galilee	Matthew 8:5–13; 8:23–34;11:1–30; 12:22–50	Matthew
			Mark 3:20–35; 4:35–5:43	Mark
			Luke 7:1–50; 8:1–3; 19–56; 11:14–32	Luke
Jesus' Parables	27–29A.D.	Galilee and Judea	Matthew 13:1–52; 20:1–16	Matthew
			Mark 4:1–23	Mark
			Luke 8:4–18; 13:18–21; 10:25–37 12:13–33; 14:15–24; 15:1–16:31; 18:1–14	Luke
Rejection and Opposition	27–29 A.D.	Nazareth, Galilee, Tyre, Sidon, Decapolis	Matthew 10:1–42; 13:53–58; 14:1–16:12	Matthew
			Mark 6:1–8:26	Mark
			Luke 9:1–17	Luke
			John 6:1–71	John

MAP OF KEY LOCATIONS

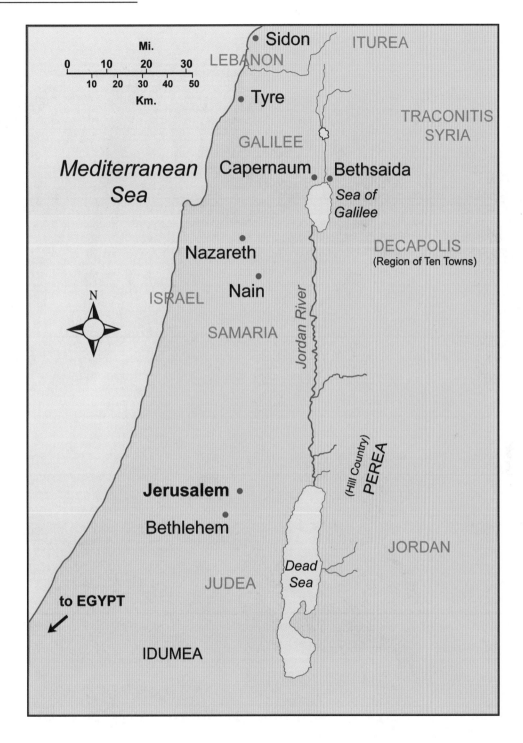

THE BREAD OF LIFE

"Then Jesus declared, 'I am the bread of life. He who comes to me will never go hungry, and he who believes in me will never be thirsty . . . I am the living bread that came down from heaven. If anyone eats of this bread, he will live forever.'" (John 6:35, 51a NIV)

SECTION 1: GALILEAN MINISTRY BEGINS

Jesus Begins His Galilean Ministry: (Matthew 4:1–17; Mark 1:14–15; Luke 4:14–30; John 4:43–54)

- Jesus returned to Galilee preaching a message of repentance. He traveled to synagogues throughout Galilee preaching and performing miracles. He soon became well-known as a Healer.

- One day, a government official from Capernaum begged Jesus to heal his son. The official's son was at home, and very close to death.

- Jesus assured the official his son would live. As the official returned home, his servants met him on the road. They told him his son was alive and well.

- The official asked his servants when had his son's health improved. He discovered his son was healed at the exact same time Jesus said his son would live.

- After healing the official's son, Jesus traveled to His hometown of Nazareth. He went into the synagogue and read from Scripture saying, *"The Spirit of the LORD is upon me, for he has anointed me to bring Good News to the poor"* (Luke 4:18a).

- Jesus announced the Scripture He read had come true that very day.

- Although the people of Nazareth were impressed with Jesus' eloquence and knowledge, they did not believe He was the Messiah. They all knew Him as Mary and Joseph's Son.

- Overhearing the people's comments, Jesus said a prophet is never recognized in his own hometown. Clarifying His point, Jesus reminded them that God sent the prophets Elijah and Elisha to help foreigners, rather than those living in their own homeland of Israel.

- When the people heard this, they became angry and attacked Jesus. He slipped away and left Nazareth.

Jesus' Disciples Follow Him: (Matthew 4:18–22; Mark 1:16–20)

- As Jesus walked along the shore of the Sea of Galilee, he saw Simon Peter and his brother, Andrew, fishing with nets. The brothers were commercial fishermen.

- Calling out to the brothers, Jesus told them to drop their nets and follow Him. Jesus said He would show them how to fish for (attract) people. Peter and Andrew left their nets and joined Jesus as disciples.

- As Jesus walked further up shore, He saw two more brothers, James and John. They were in a boat with their father, Zebedee. They, too, were commercial fishermen and partners with Peter and Andrew.

- Jesus invited James and John to become His disciples. They left their father in the boat and followed Jesus.

Jesus' Miracles: (Matthew 4:23–25; 8:1–4, 14–17; 9:1–8; Mark 1:21–2:12; Luke 4:31–5:26)

- Jesus later went to Capernaum and taught in the local synagogue. The people were impressed with the power and authority of Jesus' message.

- While Jesus was teaching one Sabbath day, a demon-possessed man called out to Him. The demon recognized Jesus as the One sent from God. Jesus commanded the demon to come out of the man. At Jesus' command, the demon obeyed, leaving the man unharmed.

- After teaching in the synagogue, Jesus went to Simon Peter's house. Peter's mother-in-law was very sick in bed with a high fever. Jesus prayed, rebuking the fever, and Peter's mother-in-law was immediately healed.

- As news of Jesus' miracles spread, people began bringing their sick family members and friends to Jesus. He miraculously healed all who were sick.

- One day, Jesus was preaching near the Sea of Galilee when He noticed an empty boat. Jesus stepped into the boat and began preaching to the people who were standing on the seashore.

- When Jesus finished His message, He told Peter to row the boat into deeper waters and lower his net. Peter explained that they had been fishing all night and hadn't caught anything.

- Peter agreed to try again only because Jesus said to do so. Following Jesus' instructions, Peter and his partners caught a vast number of fish.

- Peter was so amazed he fell to his knees in front of Jesus. Peter confessed he was a sinner and not worthy to be in Jesus' presence. Jesus said to Peter, *"There is nothing to fear. From now on you'll be fishing for men and women"* (Luke 5:10b MSG).

- After this miracle, the four fishermen—Peter, Andrew, James, and John—had such great faith in Jesus they left their business to follow Him full time.

- As Jesus' popularity increased, the Pharisees and other religious leaders started showing up to hear His messages.

- One day while Jesus was teaching to a capacity crowd inside of a house, some men walked in carrying a paralyzed man on a mat. They wanted Jesus to heal their friend.

- The men tried to reach Jesus, but were unable to squeeze through the crowd. Determined to get their friend to Jesus, the men climbed on top of the roof and lowered their paralyzed friend down in front of Jesus.

- Moved by the men's faith, Jesus reached out to the paralyzed man and told him his sins were forgiven.

- When the Pharisees heard Jesus say the man's sins had been forgiven, they were outraged. Interrupting Jesus, they blurted out only God could forgive sins.

- Looking directly at the Pharisees, Jesus said He would prove His authority to forgive sins. Jesus then commanded the paralyzed man to stand and pick up his mat.

- The paralyzed man immediately stood up, grabbed his mat, and walked home praising God.

 Miracles were a major part of Jesus' ministry. Miracles demonstrated His power and authority over the laws of nature, sickness, disease, and even death. Old Testament prophecy revealed that the Messiah's miracles would be a sign He had been sent by God. The prophet Isaiah wrote about the Messiah's miracles saying, *"Then will the eyes of the blind be opened and the ears of the deaf unstopped. Then will the lame leap like a deer, and the mute tongue shout for joy"* (Isaiah 35:5–6a NIV).

Jesus Eats with Tax Collectors and Sinners: (Matthew 9:9–17; Mark 2:13–22; Luke 5:27–39)

- Jesus later met a man named Matthew, also called Levi, who was a tax collector. Jesus invited Matthew to become one of His disciples.

 Note: Jews despised tax collectors because they collected taxes on behalf of the Roman government. Tax collectors often overtaxed their own people (the Jews) and kept the overage for themselves.

- After leaving his business to follow Jesus, Matthew hosted a dinner party. Jesus was the guest of honor. Matthew invited his tax collector friends and others whom the religious leaders called sinners.

- During the party, Matthew introduced his friends to Jesus. The Pharisees and other religious leaders complained, saying Jesus was eating and drinking with sinners.

- Jesus responded to the religious leaders' accusations saying, *"Healthy people don't need a doctor—sick people do. . . . For I have come to call not those who think they are righteous, but those who know they are sinners"* (Matthew 9:12–13).

Jesus Accused of Blasphemy: (John 5:1–47)

- Jesus later traveled to Jerusalem to celebrate one of the Jewish holy days. While at the pool of Bethesda, Jesus met a man who had been sick for thirty-eight years.

- Looking directly at the man, Jesus commanded him to stand up, pick up his mat, and begin walking. As soon as Jesus spoke the words, the man was healed. This healing miracle occurred on a Sabbath day.

- As the man walked away with his mat in hand, some religious leaders chastised him for carrying his mat on a Sabbath. According to the religious leaders, carrying a mat was work and therefore forbidden on the Sabbath.

- The religious leaders then confronted Jesus about healing the man on a Sabbath. Jesus responded saying, *"My Father is always working, and so am I"* (John 5:17).

- Infuriated by Jesus' remark, the religious leaders said Jesus had made Himself equal with God. Jesus responded saying John the Baptist had testified about Him; His miracles and teachings proved God sent Him; Scripture foretold of His coming; and Moses wrote about Him.

- Jesus then called them hypocrites, for they would rather praise each other than honor God by believing in Him.

 Note: The Pharisees and other religious leaders were outraged because Jesus would not follow their man-made rules and traditions. Jesus socialized with sinners; healed on the Sabbath; and made claims which implied He was equal to God—all of which were contrary to their religious beliefs.

RECOMMENDED BIBLE READING

Luke 4:14–30 **Jesus' Galilean Ministry Begins**

Isaiah 61:1–3 **Prophecy about the Messiah's Mission**

SECTION 2: JESUS' MESSAGE

Jesus Disobeys Sabbath Rules: (Matthew 12:1–21; Mark 2:23–3:12; Luke 6:1–11)

- As Jesus and His disciples were walking through a field one Sabbath day, they stopped and gathered some wheat. When some Pharisees saw this, they reprimanded Jesus for gathering the wheat, saying it was work, and therefore forbidden on the Sabbath. Jesus responded to their complaints saying, *"The Sabbath was made to meet the needs of people, and not people to meet the requirements of the Sabbath. So the Son of Man is Lord, even over the Sabbath!"* (Mark 2:27–28).

Note: The Sabbath law stated, *"Remember the Sabbath day, to keep it holy. Six days you shall labor and do all your work, but the seventh day is the Sabbath of the Lord your God. In it you shall do no work . . ."* (Exodus 20:8–10 NIV). The Pharisees objected because, in their sight, Jesus was breaking God's law of the Sabbath. Jesus pointed out the purpose of the Sabbath was to prevent people from overworking and losing sight of God.

- On another Sabbath day, a man with a deformed hand was among those in the synagogue listening to Jesus' message. Some Pharisees were also in the synagogue and were eager to see if Jesus would heal the man. They were looking for a reason to bring charges against Jesus.

- Jesus turned to the Pharisees and asked which is allowed on the Sabbath, good deeds or evil deeds. Should life be saved or destroyed? After saying this, Jesus healed the man. The religious leaders were outraged because, in their sight, healing the man on the Sabbath was a violation of God's Sabbath law.

- As Jesus left the synagogue, a large crowd followed Him. Many people had been healed that day, so those who were sick pressed their way through the crowd for Jesus to make them well. Jesus healed many who had been demon-possessed. Each time the evil spirits saw Jesus, they recognized Him as the Son of God.

Jesus Commissions 12 Apostles: (Mark 3:13–19; Luke 6:12–16)

- Walking up the side of a mountain, Jesus found an isolated area and stayed there all night in prayer.

- When Jesus finished praying, He chose twelve disciples from among His followers and called them apostles. Jesus commissioned the twelve disciples, whom He named apostles, to teach and perform miracles.

Jesus' Sermon on the Mountain: (Matthew 5:1–7:29; Luke 6:17–49; 11:1–13, 33–36; 12:22–34)

- One day, a large crowd gathered near a mountain to hear Jesus. After walking up the mountainside, Jesus sat down and taught the people.

Note: Jesus' message to the crowd is called "The Sermon on the Mount." (See Matthew 5:1–7:29.) In this sermon, Jesus taught about the blessed rewards of living for God. These blessed rewards are often called "The Beatitudes." (See Matthew 5:1–12.) Jesus also taught about the importance of living for God, the One Who gives eternal life, and provided a model prayer, known as "The Lord's Prayer." (See Matthew 6:9–13.)

- Jesus taught the people saying:

  ➢ God will eternally bless those who strive to walk upright before Him. Be happy! God has great rewards stored up in heaven for those who live for Him.

  ➢ You are the salt of the earth. Your life should enhance the world in the same way salt adds flavor to food. You are the light of the world. Your righteous actions should shine as light shines for all to see.

➢ Jesus did not come to get rid of the law, but to fulfill it—make it effective. If you obey God's laws and teach them to others, you will receive a great reward in God's Kingdom. Obey God. Do not be like the Pharisees and other religious leaders, who pretend to love God but do not obey Him.

➢ Moses taught people not to break their vows (promises). However, righteous people should not have to make vows at all. You should be so trustworthy that your word alone is enough.

➢ If a person harms you—according to the law of Moses—you have the legal right to injure that person in the same way in which you were injured. Hence the phrase, "an eye for an eye and a tooth for a tooth." However, your desire should not be to get even, but rather to show love and mercy. You should be kind even to those who have harmed you.

Note: The law of Moses, which stated "an eye for an eye and a tooth for a tooth," was originally established for judges. (See Exodus 21:23–25.) The law's purpose was to prevent excessively cruel punishments and ensure just retribution for crimes. According to the law, the punishment should fit the crime. After the law was established, people misinterpreted its purpose and began using it as a guide for personal vengeance. Jesus taught against misusing the law for retaliation.

➢ According to the law of Moses, you should love your friends and hate your enemies. However, Jesus taught that you should love everyone, even those who hate or persecute you. How does loving your friends make you any different from the Devil? The Devil loves his friends too! Godly people should show love to both friend and foe.

➢ There is no reward in telling people about your good deeds. God knows everything you do and the spirit in which it is done. God looks at the heart and will reward accordingly.

➢ Likewise, there is no reward in praying in public to impress others. This is hypocritical. Pray in earnest, in private, and succinctly. There is no need to ramble on and on, repeating the same words.

➢ Our prayers should be similar to this: *"Our Father in heaven, Hallowed be Your name. Your kingdom come. Your will be done On earth as it is in heaven. Give us this day our daily bread. And forgive us our debts, As we forgive our debtors. And do not lead us into temptation, But deliver us from the evil one. For Yours is the kingdom and the power and the glory forever. Amen"* (Matthew 6:9–13 NKJ).

➢ If you forgive those who injure or sin against you, God will forgive your sins. However, if you refuse to forgive others, God will not forgive you.

➢ There is no reward in fasting in such a way that others notice you are hungry. God rewards those who fast in a manner that is not obvious to everyone. God knows our motivation. He knows when we are merely seeking recognition.

➢ Do not make earthly treasures and material wealth your primary focus. You cannot take your possessions with you when you die. You should instead focus on storing up heavenly treasures. Your highest priority should be to please God. *"You cannot serve both God and money"* (Matthew 6:24c).

➢ Do not worry about your daily needs, such as food or clothing. God, the Father, is in control of everything, including your future. He knows all things. He knows your specific needs and will give you exactly what you need—when you need it—if you trust in Him wholeheartedly. Make God your primary focus and stop worrying about the future.

➢ Do not judge others. It will only cause them to judge you. Instead of judging and criticizing others, examine yourself and work on areas in your life that are in need of improvement.

➢ Don't give what is holy to ungodly people. They will not acknowledge or respect it as holy.

➢ Continue asking and it will be given to you. Continue looking and you will find what you are looking for. Continue knocking and the door will be opened. God responds and blesses those who ask in earnest.

➢ Treat others the same way you would like to be treated, for this sums up everything taught in Scripture.

➢ Enter the Kingdom of God through the narrow gate. The wide gate leads to separation from God. Choose the narrow gate, which leads to eternal life with God.

➢ Watch out for people claiming to know God, but who are far from Him. You will know godly people by their actions. A healthy tree produces good fruit, but an unhealthy tree produces bad fruit. In this same way, godly people produce good fruit (godly actions).

➢ Many will call Me their Lord, but will not enter the Kingdom of Heaven, for they have not submitted their lives to My Father's authority. On judgment day, these very same people will claim to have prophesied and performed miracles in My name, *"But I will reply, 'I never knew you. Get away from me, you who break God's laws'"* (Matthew 7:23).

➢ Anyone who hears My message and practices what I preach is like a wise man who builds his house on rock, a solid foundation. Those who hear what I say—but do not take My message to heart—are like a foolish man who builds his house on sand. When rainstorms and floods come, the foolish man's house will fall to the ground.

• Jesus mesmerized the crowds. They had never heard anyone speak with such eloquence, power, and authority.

RECOMMENDED BIBLE READING

Matthew 5:1–12 **The Beatitudes**

Exodus 20:1–21 **The Ten Commandments**

SECTION 3: MIRACLES AND CONFRONTATIONS

Jesus' Healing Miracles: (Matthew 8:5–13; Luke 7:1–17)

- After Jesus finished His sermon, He went back to Capernaum. Shortly afterward, some Jewish leaders asked Him to heal a Roman officer's slave, who was near death. The slave had been very faithful to the Roman officer and was like a member of the officer's own family.

- The religious leaders explained that the Roman officer had been very kind to the Jews. The officer had helped the Jews build their local synagogue.

- As Jesus was on His way to the Roman officer's house, some of the officer's friends met Him on the road with a message from the officer. They told Jesus the Roman officer did not feel worthy enough for Him to enter his house.

- The Roman officer wanted Jesus to heal his slave from a distance, for he knew Jesus could simply speak words and his slave would be healed.

- Impressed by the Roman officer's faith, Jesus said, *"I tell you, I haven't seen faith like this in all Israel!"* (Luke 7:9b). When the officer's friends returned to his house, his slave had been healed.

- Shortly afterward, Jesus and His disciples traveled to the village of Nain. As they reached the entrance to the city, a large funeral procession was passing. A widow's only son had died.

- When Jesus saw the widow in tears accompanied by a large group of mourners, He was overcome with compassion. Jesus touched the coffin and then called out to the dead boy.

- The boy sat up at the sound of Jesus' voice and began talking. Jesus returned the boy to his mother in good health.

- When the people saw the boy was alive and well, they began calling Jesus a mighty prophet of God. The news soon spread about how Jesus brought the dead boy back to life.

Jesus Addresses John's Doubt: (Matthew 11:1–30; Luke 7:18–50)

- While John the Baptist was in prison, his disciples kept him informed about Jesus' ministry.

- One day, John sent his disciples to Jesus with a question. John wanted to know if Jesus was indeed the Messiah or should he (John) expect someone else.

- Jesus answered John's disciples saying, *"Go back to John and tell him what you have seen and heard—the blind see, the lame walk, the lepers are cured, the deaf hear, the dead are raised to life, and the Good News is being preached to the poor. And tell him, 'God blesses those who do not turn away because of me'"* (Luke 7:22–23).

- As John's disciples were leaving, Jesus addressed the crowd saying, *"I tell you, of all who have ever lived, none is greater than John. Yet even the least person in the Kingdom of God is greater than he is!"* (Luke 7:28).

Note: The reports John heard about Jesus' ministry were puzzling and caused him to doubt. John expressed very human concerns. Jesus understood John's concerns and responded in a way that would alleviate his doubts. Jesus told the crowd that John was the greatest prophet who had ever lived; and yet the lowliest person—who accepts God's plan—is greater than John. How can this be? John fulfilled God's plan for his life better than any other who had lived before him. However, John lived and died before God's plan was fully implemented. Jesus had not yet died for our sins. Jesus was saying those who accept God's plan after His death and resurrection would be blessed with greater and clearer spiritual knowledge.

- While Jesus was speaking to the crowd, a Pharisee named Simon interrupted and invited Jesus to his house for dinner. Jesus went and, while there, an immoral woman entered with a jar of expensive perfume.

- The woman knelt at Jesus' feet and began crying. As she cried, her tears fell on Jesus' feet. The woman used her hair to wipe the tears from His feet. She then kissed Jesus' feet and rubbed them with perfume.

- Simon thought to himself, "If Jesus were truly a prophet, He would know the woman was immoral and would not let her touch Him."

- With divine insight, Jesus knew what Simon was thinking. Turning to Simon, Jesus said a man loaned a large sum of money to one person and a smaller amount to another. Neither could repay the man, so he canceled both debts. Jesus then asked Simon which of the two loved the man more for canceling the debt.

- Simon answered saying the one with the larger debt would be more grateful. Jesus told Simon he was correct.

- Turning His attention to the woman still kneeling at His feet, Jesus said she had shown Him a great amount of love ever since she arrived. Simon, on the other hand, had not shown Jesus any of the simplest courtesies.

- Jesus then told the woman her sins were forgiven. Those who heard this wondered who Jesus thought He was, for only God could forgive sins.

More Miracles: (Matthew 8:23–34; Mark 4:35–5:43; Luke 8:22–56)

- One day, Jesus and His disciples got into a boat to cross the lake. While the disciples rowed the boat, Jesus took a nap.

- A violent storm suddenly arose. The waves were so high, the disciples thought they were going to drown. They woke Jesus up with their shouts for help.

- Jesus got up and asked the disciples why they were afraid. He told them their fear demonstrated a lack of faith.

- Looking out into the stormy sea, Jesus commanded the waters to calm down. At Jesus' command, the sea was suddenly peaceful.

- The disciples could hardly believe their eyes. They asked themselves, *"Who is this? Even the wind and the waves obey him"* (Matthew 8:27 CEV).

- When Jesus and the disciples arrived on the other side of the lake, a demon-possessed man hobbled over to them. The man was naked and lived in a nearby cemetery.

- The demons inside the man recognized Jesus as the Son of God and begged Him to leave them alone. When Jesus asked the demons their name, they answered saying their name was Legion, for there were many of them.

- As the demons pleaded for mercy, Jesus forced them out of the man and allowed them to enter a nearby herd of pigs.

- When the demons entered the pigs, they went wild and jumped off the hillside. The pigs fell into the lake below and drowned.

- Although the demon-possessed man was healed, the incident frightened the local people. They went to Jesus and asked Him to leave.

- As Jesus returned to the other side of the lake, a large crowd was already there, waiting for Him. A man named Jairus, a religious leader in the synagogue, was among those in the crowd.

- Jairus begged Jesus to come home with him and heal his only daughter, who was near death.

- As Jesus was leaving with Jairus, a woman, who had been hemorrhaging for twelve years, reached out to touch Him. When she touched the edge of Jesus' robe, the bleeding immediately stopped.

- Jesus recognized someone had touched Him and asked who had received His healing power.

- Trembling, the woman knelt before Jesus and identified herself as the one who had touched Him. Filled with compassion, Jesus explained to her she had been healed because of her faith.

 Touching the edge of Jesus' robe, the woman reached out in faith and was healed. In a prophecy written 400 years earlier, Malachi prophesied about the Messiah's healing power. Malachi wrote, *"But to you who fear My name The Sun of Righteousness shall arise With healing in His wings"* (Malachi 4:2 NKJ).

- Someone then ran over and told Jairus his daughter was dead. Turning His attention to Jairus, Jesus encouraged him, saying there was nothing to fear.

- As Jesus headed for Jairus' house, He urged Jairus to trust Him. When Jesus arrived, a large crowd had gathered and was already in mourning. Jesus said to them, *"The child isn't dead. She is just asleep"* (Luke 8:52 CEV).

- The people laughed at Jesus, for they were sure the girl was dead. When Jesus commanded the girl to get up, life returned to her body. The girl's parents watched in awe as she got up from her deathbed.

- After leaving Jairus' house Jesus came across two blind men. When the blind men realized they were in Jesus' presence, they begged Him for mercy.

- Jesus asked the blind men if they believed He could heal them. When they replied "yes," Jesus touched their eyes and their sight was restored because of their faith.

- Shortly afterward, some people came to Jesus with a demon-possessed man, who was also deaf and mute. Jesus rebuked the demon and the man was suddenly able to speak and hear.

Jesus' Ministry Tour: (Matthew 12:22–50; Mark 3:20–35; Luke 8:1–3; 19–21; 11:14–32)

- Jesus began traveling from town to town throughout Galilee, announcing the Good News of God's Kingdom.

- The twelve disciples traveled with Him. Several women also traveled with Jesus. They were Mary Magdalene, a demon-possessed woman whom Jesus had healed; Joanna, the wife of Herod's manager; Susanna, and many others who helped fund Jesus' ministry.

- On one occasion a large crowd of people had gathered to hear Jesus' message. Jesus was so busy teaching and healing people that neither He nor His disciples had eaten anything all day.

- When Jesus' family heard about this, they decided to go get Him, for they thought He was losing control.

- Meanwhile, Jesus healed a demon-possessed man who had been blind and unable to talk. Those witnessing this miracle thought Jesus might be the Messiah.

- The Pharisees and other religious leaders insisted Jesus' healing miracles were not from God. They claimed Jesus' power came from Satan.

- Countering the religious leaders' accusation, Jesus said a house divided cannot stand. Demons are Satan's cohorts and are opposed to God. Satan would not drive out his own demons because it would defeat his purpose.

- In response, the religious leaders asked Jesus for proof God had sent Him. They wanted Jesus to show them a sign from God.

- Jesus replied, *"Only an evil, adulterous generation would demand a miraculous sign; but the only sign I will give them is the sign of the prophet Jonah. For as Jonah was in the belly of the great fish for three days and three nights, so will the Son of Man be in the heart of the earth for three days and three nights"* (Matthew 12:39–40).

Note: In the Old Testament, God told the prophet Jonah to go to Nineveh in Assyria and tell the people to repent. Jonah did not want the Assyrians to have an opportunity to repent because they were Israel's dreaded enemy. Disobeying God, Jonah ran in a direction opposite of Nineveh. God had a way of getting Jonah's attention. A large fish swallowed Jonah. He was in the fish's belly for three days and three nights. Jonah prayed and God delivered him from the fish's belly. (See Jonah 1–2.) Jesus used this Old Testament story as an analogy. Just as Jonah was in the fish's belly for three days, Jesus would die and lay in the tomb for three days before rising from the dead.

- Someone from the crowd called out to Jesus, saying His mother and brothers were waiting outside to speak to Him.

- Jesus responded, *"My mother and my brothers are all those who hear God's word and obey it"* (Luke 8:21). All who belong to God are related to Jesus.

Note: At first glance, Jesus' response might have appeared to be insensitive. However, Jesus knew His time on earth would be cut short. He understood His true mission was to deliver God's message to all of God's people— His brothers and sisters—in a very short period of time. Jesus loved His mother, as indicated later when, on the cross, He told Apostle John to take care of her. (See John 19:25–27.)

RECOMMENDED BIBLE READING

Luke 7:1–17; 8:40–56 **Jesus' Miracles**

Matthew 12:38–45 **The Sign of Jonah**

Jonah 1:1–2:10 **The Story of Jonah**

SECTION 4: JESUS' PARABLES

Jesus Teaches in Parables: (Matthew 13:1–3; Mark 4:1–2)

- Jesus got into a boat and began teaching the people using parables.

 Note: What is a parable? A parable is a short story with an underlying spiritual meaning. Jesus often used parables as a method of teaching. Jesus knew those who believed in Him would be able to discern the underlying message of His parables, while non-believers—who were blind to the Truth of God—would not be able to understand their true meaning. By using parables, Jesus could teach His disciples in public without getting caught up in lengthy debates with the Pharisees and other religious leaders.

The Farmer's Seed: (Matthew 13:1–23; Mark 4:1–25; Luke 8:4–18)

- Jesus taught His disciples saying:

  ➢ During the planting season, a farmer scattered seed in his field. Some of the seed fell on the road and was immediately eaten by birds. Some fell on shallow rocky soil. Although these seed began to sprout, the seedlings soon wilted in the hot sun because their roots were unable to fully develop. Other seed fell among thorns. As these seed sprouted, they were quickly choked out by weeds. Some seed fell on fertile soil and produced a bumper crop.

- When Jesus finished this parable, He encouraged the disciples to think about its underlying meaning.

- Puzzled, the disciples asked Jesus why He spoke in parables. Jesus answered, *"I have explained the secrets about God's kingdom to you, but for others I can only use stories. These people look, but they don't see, and they hear, but they don't understand"* (Luke 8:10 CEV).

> Jesus' parables fulfilled several Old Testament prophecies. David wrote, *"I will open my mouth in parables, I will utter hidden things, things from of old-"* (Psalm 78:2 NIV). (See Matthew 13:35.) Jesus told His disciples that His parables fulfilled Isaiah's prophecy which says, *"You will listen and listen, but never understand. You will look and look, but never see"* (Isaiah 6:9 CEV). (See Matthew 13:14.)

- Jesus' disciples then asked the meaning of the parable about the farmer's seed. He explained saying the seed represents the Word.

- The seed falling on the road is much like the Word falling on deaf ears. These people hear the Word, but do not perceive its meaning. Satan quickly comes along and removes it from their memory.

- The seed that fell on rocky soil is like the Word people hear and initially accept with great joy. However, they wilt because their roots are not well-developed. These people are not grounded in the Word. They do not know the Word well enough to persevere through adversities.

- The seed that fell among thorns is like the Word people hear and accept; and is later choked out by non-spiritual concerns. These people fail to produce a crop—glorifying God with their actions. They allow themselves to become consumed by fear and human weaknesses.

- The seed falling on fertile soil is like the Word people hear, accept, and then cultivate. These people read, study, and meditate on the Word. They produce a bountiful crop—glorifying God—because they are well-grounded in His Word.

The Wheat Harvest / Weeds among the Wheat / Fishing Net: (Mark 4:26–29; Matthew 13:24–30, 36–43, 47–52)

- Jesus told several parables about Judgment Day saying:

  ➤ The Kingdom of God is like a farmer who planted wheat and then concentrated on his other chores. Over time, the seed sprouted and wheat began growing on its own without any help from the farmer. The wheat continued to grow until it was ready to be harvested. When the farmer returned, he cut the wheat with his sickle and gathered it for the harvest.

 Note: In this parable, Jesus taught that spiritual growth is a gradual process. God plants His Word in our hearts and then it becomes our responsibility to grow spiritually into the image of Jesus. On Judgment Day, Jesus will return and, like the farmer, gather God's people for the harvest.

- Further explaining what will happen on Judgment Day, Jesus said:

  ➤ The Kingdom of Heaven is like a farmer who planted good seed. His enemy came along overnight and planted weeds in his field. After a while, the farmer's servant noticed weeds were growing in the field among the wheat. When he asked the farmer if he should pull up the weeds, the farmer replied "no." He then explained to his servant that he might accidentally damage the wheat as he pulled up the weeds. The farmer told his servant to let the weeds grow with the wheat. He said the wheat would be separated from the weeds during the harvest season. The harvesters would be instructed to burn the weeds and store the wheat in the barn.

- The disciples later asked Jesus to explain the parable about the weeds. Jesus said He is the farmer planting good seed, and Satan is the one sowing weeds. The harvest is the end of the world and the harvesters are God's angels. The angels will separate the wheat (those who believed the Word) from the weeds (those who rejected the Word). Believers will inherit eternal life with God, while non-believers will be eternally separated from God.

- Emphasizing His point about Judgment Day, Jesus said:

  ➤ The Kingdom of Heaven is like a fishing net full of fish. The good fish must be separated from the bad ones. In this same way, angels will come at the end of the world to separate the righteous from the ungodly. The ungodly will forever be separated from God and live in eternal misery.

The Mustard Seed / Yeast: (Matthew 13:31–34; Mark 4:30–34; Luke 13:18–21)

- Jesus gave several illustrations about the Kingdom of Heaven saying:

  ➤ The Kingdom of Heaven is like a mustard seed. It is the smallest of all seeds. When it is planted, it grows to become the largest tree in the garden.

  ➤ The Kingdom of Heaven is like yeast used to make bread dough rise. Although a small amount of yeast is added to a large amount of flour, the yeast works its way through every part of the dough.

 Note: In these parables, Jesus revealed that the Kingdom would start out small—but like the mustard seed or a small amount of yeast—God's Kingdom would soon grow into a vast number of believers. We see this in action today. When a new believer comes to faith and begins growing in Christ, a radical change occurs in his or her life. Soon, family and friends are touched by what they see happening and become more receptive to the gospel message. Before long, another family member or friend comes to faith, and that person influences another. As each family member or friend accepts Jesus as Savior, other lives are touched by His infectious love.

Hidden Treasure / Fine Pearls: (Matthew 13:44–46)

- Jesus used several parables to teach that nothing is as valuable or important as heaven. Jesus said:

  ➤ The Kingdom of Heaven is like a treasure a man found hidden in a field. The man was so excited about the treasure that he sold all his possessions and bought the entire field to search for more treasure. The Kingdom of Heaven is also like a jewelry salesman looking for fine pearls. When he discovers a valuable pearl, he sells everything to buy it.

The Good Samaritan: (Luke 10:25–37)

- A man proficient in Jewish law came to Jesus and asked what a person must do to receive eternal life. Jesus asked the man what Scripture said about this and how did he interpret it.

- The man answered saying a person must love the Lord God whole-heartedly and love his neighbor as he loves himself. Jesus told the man he had answered correctly, and if he did this, he would receive eternal life.

- Since the man was seeking approval to justify his past actions, he probed further, asking Jesus who his neighbor is. Jesus responded with a parable:

  ➤ As a man was traveling to Jericho, robbers attacked him, beat him, and then left him for dead. A priest came along, saw the man lying in the road and passed him by. Afterward, a Levite (a Temple assistant) came along. He saw the man and passed him by also. A Samaritan later came along and saw the man lying in the road. Moved with compassion, the Samaritan stopped to help the man. The Samaritan treated the man's wounds and took him to an inn, where he cared for the man overnight. The next day, the Samaritan gave the innkeeper money to take care of the man. He told the innkeeper he would pay any additional cost needed for the man's care when he returned.

- After telling the parable, Jesus asked the man which of the three—the priest, the Levite, or the Samaritan—was a neighbor to the man attacked by robbers. The man replied saying the one who showed compassion by caring for the man's wounds. Jesus told the man he should demonstrate that same kind of love.

 Note: In the "Parable of the Good Samaritan" Jesus taught what it means to truly love one's neighbor. This parable implied that a Samaritan could know more about love than a priest or a Levite, a clear insult to religious leaders of Jesus' day.

The Rich Fool: (Luke 12:13–33)

- One day as Jesus was teaching, a man in the crowd asked Jesus to tell his brother to give him part of their father's inheritance. Jesus warned against greed and said life is not about possessions. He told a parable to illustrate His point:

  ➤ One year a rich man produced an abundant crop. His barns soon overflowed with excess grain, so he tore them down and built larger ones. He thought to himself, *"You have stored up enough good things to last for years to come. Live it up! Eat, drink, and enjoy yourself."* God interrupted the man's thoughts saying, *"You fool! Tonight you will die. Then who will get what you have stored up?"* (Luke 12:19–20 CEV).

Parable of the Great Feast: (Luke 14:15–24)

- One day, Jesus was dining in the home of a leading Pharisee. A man seated at the table turned to Jesus and said what a blessing it will be to eat bread in God's Kingdom. Jesus replied with a parable:

  ➤ A man prepared a great feast and invited a large number of guests. On the day of the feast, each guest—one by one—began making excuses, saying they would not be able to attend. The host became angry. He told his servant to go into the city streets and alleyways, and invite the poor, who were starving, to come dine at his feast. The servant did as he was told and returned saying there was still room for more. The host then instructed his servant to go throughout the countryside and urge everyone he met to come until the house was full, for none of those who received his initial invitation would be allowed to taste the tiniest morsel of the dinner he had prepared.

 Note: In this parable, Jesus taught the importance of accepting God's invitation to join Him. Jesus came to bring salvation to the entire world, Jews and Gentiles alike. Those who make excuses and reject God's invitation on earth will not be allowed to share in what He has prepared in heaven.

Lost Sheep / Lost Coin / Prodigal Son: (Luke 15:1–32)

- The Pharisees and other religious leaders often complained about Jesus socializing with sinners. On one occasion, Jesus used several parables to explain that everyone—regardless of social status—is important to God. Jesus said:

  ➢ If a man has 100 sheep and loses just one, he will search for his missing sheep. In this same way, God pursues all who are lost because He does not want to lose a single one of His creations.

  ➢ If a woman has ten coins and loses a single one, she will frantically search for the one missing coin. When she finds it, she will jump for joy and share the news with her friends. Jesus then said, *"In the same way, there is joy in the presence of God's angels when even one sinner repents"* (Luke 15:10).

  ➢ A man had two sons. The younger son decided he wanted his inheritance before his father died. He asked for his inheritance and his father agreed to give it to him immediately. The younger son left and spent all his money on wild parties. He was soon broke and starving to death. As he thought about his situation, He said to himself, *"My father's workers have plenty to eat, and here I am, starving to death!"* (Luke 15:17 CEV). He decided to go back home and ask his father for a job. When his father saw him from a distance, he was filled with compassion and held a great celebration for his son. When the older brother realized what was happening, he became angry. He said to his father, *"For years I have worked for you like a slave and have always obeyed you. But you have never even given me a little goat . . . This other son of yours wasted your money on prostitutes. And now that he has come home, you ordered the best calf to be killed for a feast"* (Luke 15:29–30 CEV). The father replied, saying he and his older son had always been close, and everything he owned belonged to his older son. The father explained that the younger son had been lost, but has now been found. Likewise, our Heavenly Father extends forgiveness and love to all who come to Him with repentant hearts.

The Rich Man and Lazarus: (Luke 16:1–31)

- Jesus told another parable to explain to His disciples that they should use their earthly wealth to help others, for God rewards our generosity. The Pharisees scoffed at Jesus' advice, for they loved their money and material possessions. Jesus responded with an illustration to stress the importance of living for God and not material wealth:

  ➢ A certain rich man lived a very extravagant lifestyle. Each day, a sore-infested beggar named Lazarus would sit at the rich man's door longing for a few crumbs to eat. Lazarus finally died and angels took him to be with Father Abraham. When the rich man died, he went to a fiery abyss that burned continuously. The rich man was in agony. He asked Abraham to send Lazarus to him with a cool drink of water. Abraham replied, *"My friend, remember that while you lived, you had everything good, and Lazarus had everything bad. Now he is happy, and you are in pain. And besides, there is a deep ditch between us, and no one from either side can cross over"* (Luke 16:25–26 CEV). The rich man then asked Abraham to send Lazarus to warn his family about the fiery place of torment. Abraham told him Moses and the prophets had already warned his family in Scripture. Abraham then said, *"If they won't pay attention to Moses and the prophets, they won't listen even to someone who comes back from the dead"* (Luke 16:31 CEV).

The Persistent Widow: (Luke 18:1–8)

- One day, Jesus told His disciples a parable to remind them they should be persistent in prayer. Jesus said:

  ➤ There was a judge who feared no one. A woman came to him repeatedly, demanding justice. The judge ignored the woman for a long time. She finally wore him down with her persistence and he granted her request.

- Jesus then said, *"Do you hear what that judge, corrupt as he is, is saying? So what makes you think God won't step in and work justice for his chosen people, who continue to cry out for help? . . . I assure you, he will . . . But how much of that kind of persistent faith will the Son of Man find on the earth when he returns?"* (Luke 18:6–8 MSG).

The Two Men Who Prayed: (Luke 18:9–14)

- Jesus explained that God is not pleased with self-righteous, prideful people. He clarified His point with a parable:

  ➤ A Pharisee and a tax collector went to the Temple to pray. The Pharisee arrogantly prayed, *"Oh, God, I thank you that I am not like other people—robbers, crooks, adulterers, or, heaven forbid, like this tax man. I fast twice a week and tithe on all my income"* (Luke 18:11–12 MSG). The tax collector humbly prayed, *"God, give mercy. Forgive me, a sinner"* (Luke 18:13 MSG).

- Jesus then said God honored the tax collector's prayer, but was displeased with the Pharisee's prayer.

Parable of the Vineyard Workers: (Matthew 20:1–16)

- Further explaining the Kingdom of Heaven, Jesus said:

  ➤ The Kingdom of Heaven is like a land owner who got up early one morning and hired workers for his vineyard. He agreed to pay them a full day's pay for a day's work. He hired more workers later that morning and again in the afternoon. He also hired workers later that evening. At the end of the day, he paid them all the same amount. Those who were hired first assumed they would be paid more than the others, for they had worked longer hours. The land owner said to one of them, *"Friend, I didn't cheat you. I paid you exactly what we agreed on . . . What business is it of yours if I want to pay them the same that I paid you? . . . Why should you be jealous, if I want to be generous?"* (Matthew 20:13–15 CEV).

- Jesus then said the first will be last and the last will be first.

Note: In this parable, Jesus taught that God has prepared a place in heaven for all believers, regardless of how long they have been in His service. A person who accepts Christ on his or her death bed will join others in heaven who might have been long-time believers. God is sovereign and extends His grace to whomever He pleases. When we humble ourselves before Him in repentance, God is eager to forgive all our past sins—no matter how terrible or numerous they might be.

RECOMMENDED BIBLE READING

Matthew 13:1–23 **The Farmer's Seed**

Luke 15:11–32 **The Prodigal Son**

Psalm 78:1–8 **I Will Speak in Parables**

SECTION 5: REJECTION AND OPPOSITION

Rejected in Nazareth: (Matthew 13:53–58; Mark 6:1–6)

- After teaching in other areas of Galilee, Jesus returned to His hometown of Nazareth and taught in the synagogue.

- Although the people of Nazareth were amazed by Jesus' wisdom and healing power, they did not believe He had been sent from God. They knew His family—His mother, brothers, and sisters—and refused to accept Him as the Messiah.

- Jesus performed very few miracles in Nazareth because the people lacked faith.

The Twelve are Sent Out: (Matthew 10:1–42; Mark 6:7–13; Luke 9:1–6)

- Shortly afterward, Jesus began preparing the twelve disciples to help in His ministry. He partnered them together in groups of two and empowered them with the ability to perform healing miracles.

- Jesus explained to His disciples that they would be like sheep among wolves. Jesus told them they would encounter enemies, who would abuse and persecute them. He assured them that the Holy Spirit would give them the right words to say and God would take care of their souls.

- After giving the disciples some final instructions, Jesus sent them out to help in His ministry. The disciples traveled in groups of two from village to village preaching the Good News of God's Kingdom and performing healing miracles.

John the Baptist's Death: (Matthew 14:1–12; Mark 6:14–29; Luke 9:7–9)

- As King Herod's birthday neared, he decided to throw himself a royal party. During the celebration, Herodias' daughter danced magnificently for Herod and his guests.

- Herod was so pleased with the girl's performance that he promised to give her whatever she desired.

- Herodias, the girl's mother, was still fuming over John's criticism of her marriage to Herod. Seizing the opportunity to get revenge, Herodias told her daughter to ask Herod for John the Baptist's head.

- Although Herod was saddened by the girl's request, he kept his promise and ordered John's beheading. Shortly afterward, John's disciples came and buried his body.

Jesus Feeds the 5,000: (Matthew 14:13–36; Mark 6:30–56; Luke 9:10–17; John 6:1–21)

- After Jesus heard the news of John's death, He went away in a boat to be alone. The people noticed Jesus getting into a boat and began following Him by land along the shore.

- When Jesus arrived at His destination, the people were already there waiting for Him. Moved with compassion, Jesus began teaching and healing the sick.

- After a while, Jesus' disciples urged Him to stop teaching so that the people could go into town and buy something to eat before nightfall. (In Jesus' day, local markets did not stay open after dark.)

- Jesus responded saying the disciples should feed the people. The disciples were stunned, for they knew they did not have enough food for such a large crowd. There were 5,000 people, not including the women and children.

- Peter's brother, Andrew, mentioned that a boy in the crowd had five loaves of bread and two fish. Andrew then said, *"But what good is that with this huge crowd?"* (John 6:9b).

- Jesus instructed the disciples to tell the people to sit on the ground in groups of about fifty. Looking up toward heaven, Jesus asked God to bless the five loaves of bread and two fish. He then broke the food into pieces and gave it to His disciples.

- As the disciples distributed the food to the people, Jesus kept giving them more until everyone had eaten as much as they wanted. Jesus fed well over 5,000 people with five loaves of bread and two fish; and there were enough leftovers to fill twelve baskets with food.

- After everyone finished eating, the disciples got in a boat and headed for the other side of the lake. Jesus stayed behind to pray.

- As the disciples were crossing the lake, a terrible storm arose. The disciples suddenly found themselves in grave danger.

- Fearing for their lives, the disciples looked up and saw Jesus walking on water toward them. The sight of Jesus walking on water terrified the disciples even more.

- Jesus reassured the disciples they had nothing to fear. Peter shouted out, *"Master, if it's really you, call me to come to you on the water"* (Matthew 14:28 MSG).

- Calling out to Peter, Jesus said, "Come!" Peter jumped out of the boat and stepped into the water.

- As Peter walked toward Jesus, he suddenly noticed the high waves and began to sink. Terrified, Peter called out to Jesus for help.

- Jesus grabbed Peter's hand and steadied him. Jesus then told Peter he had little faith and asked why he had doubted. As soon as they climbed into the boat, the winds suddenly calmed down.

Jesus Is the Bread of Life: (John 6:22–71)

- After Jesus and His disciples reached the other side of the lake, the people Jesus fed the day before with the five loaves of bread and two fish soon found Him.

- When Jesus saw the people, He said the only reason they were following Him was because He had fed them. He encouraged the people to stop searching for earthly treasures and start seeking God's gift of eternal life.

- The people asked Jesus for a miraculous sign to prove God had really sent Him. They said Moses gave their ancestor's manna from heaven, which proved God sent Moses.

- Correcting the people's misconception, Jesus said, *"I tell you the truth, Moses didn't give you bread from heaven. My Father did. And now he offers you the true bread from heaven . . . I am the bread of life. Whoever comes to me will never be hungry again"* (John 6:32–33, 35a).

As the Bread of Life, Jesus satisfies our spiritual hunger and leads us into righteousness and eternal life with God. In the Old Testament, God sent manna from heaven as bread for the Israelites to eat as they journeyed to Canaan. (See Exodus 16:14–15.) Jesus reminded the people that God—not Moses—was the One who provided manna as sustenance for their ancestors in the desert.

Fourteen hundred years later, God sent spiritual bread in the person of Jesus as our sustenance. Jesus sustains us spiritually in the same way bread sustains us physically.

- When Jesus said, *"I am the bread of life,"* the people did not understand what He meant. They argued among themselves as they tried to envision how Jesus could give them His flesh to eat.

- The disciples told Jesus His words were difficult to understand. In response, Jesus said His words were spirit and life-giving.

- Many of Jesus' followers deserted Him because they thought His words were too harsh and difficult to accept.

- After losing a great number of followers, Jesus asked His twelve disciples if they were going to leave Him, too. Peter answered for all twelve, saying they believed in Him as the Holy One of God.

- Jesus then revealed they had been specifically chosen as His disciples, but one of them was a devil. Jesus was referring to Judas Iscariot, who would later betray Him.

Opposition to Jesus' Ministry: (Matthew 15:1–20; Mark 7:1–23)

- One day as Jesus was teaching, a group of Pharisees and religious teachers asked Him why His disciples did not follow Jewish traditions, such as washing one's hands before eating. Jesus responded calling them hypocrites. He then turned to the crowd and said a man does not become unclean by what goes into his mouth, but by what comes out.

- Peter later asked Jesus what He meant. Jesus answered, saying food is digested and then leaves the body, but words are spoken from the heart. An evil heart produces evil thoughts. Eating with unwashed hands does not make a person unclean or unrighteous before God, but an evil heart does.

Jesus in Tyre, Sidon, and Decapolis: (Matthew 15:21–31; Mark 7:24–37)

- Jesus left the Galilee area and traveled north to minister in the villages of Tyre and Sidon.

- As soon as Jesus arrived in Tyre, a woman of non-Jewish descent fell at His feet and begged Him to heal her demon-possessed daughter. Upset that the Gentile woman had interrupted Jesus, the disciples urged Him to send her away.

- Jesus explained to the woman that God sent Him to the Jews and not to the Gentiles. As the woman continued her pleas for mercy, Jesus said it was not right to take the children's food and toss it to dogs.

- The woman replied, saying even dogs are allowed to eat the crumbs that fall from the master's table. When Jesus heard this, He praised the woman's faith and told her that her daughter had been healed.

Note: Jesus' primary mission was to minister to the Jews. His disciples would later minister to the Gentiles after His death and resurrection. According to present day etiquette, Jesus' statement to the woman would appear to be somewhat harsh. However, when viewed in context—based on Jesus' time period—it becomes clear Jesus was merely calling the disciples "His children" and referring to "non believers" as pet dogs. In Jesus' day, it was common for people's pets to eat table scraps. Jesus was explaining to the woman that His utmost priority while in Tyre was to minister to His disciples (His children). He was not there to be distracted by non believers (pet dogs). The woman's response demonstrated her persistence and faith, so Jesus healed her daughter.

- Jesus later traveled to a region called Decapolis. A large crowd gathered around as He healed those who were sick, crippled, blind, and unable to speak.

Jesus Feeds 4,000 Men: (Matthew 15:32–16:12; Mark 8:1–26)

- Jesus stayed in Decapolis, healing the sick for three days. When the people ran out of food, Jesus wanted to feed them. The disciples told Jesus all they had was seven loaves of bread and a few fish. Jesus thanked God for the food, broke it into pieces, and fed the people.

- The small amount of food miraculously fed 4,000 men, along with the women and children who were present. Everyone ate until they were full and seven large baskets of food were left over.

- When the Pharisees and Sadducees heard Jesus was in the area, they came demanding He show them a miraculous sign to prove His claims.

- Jesus responded, saying the only sign they would get is the sign of Jonah, referring again to His upcoming death and resurrection. Jesus then left.

- As Jesus and His disciples crossed to the other side of the lake, Jesus warned them to beware of the yeast of the Pharisees and Sadducees.

- The disciples did not understand what Jesus meant. He explained that they should watch out for the hypocrisy and false teachings of the Pharisees.

Note: Yeast or leavening is often used in Scripture to represent sin. Yeast causes bread to puff up and similarly, sin causes people to puff up in pride. Unleavened bread—bread without yeast—is used in Scripture to symbolize freedom or the removal of sin. For Scriptures referring to yeast as sin, see Matthew 16:5–12; Mark 8:15; Luke 12:1; and Galatians 5:9.

- When Jesus arrived in Bethsaida, some people brought a blind man to Him. They begged Him to heal their blind friend.

- Taking the blind man to the side, Jesus spit on the man's eyes and then laid His hands on him. After Jesus did this, the man was able to see faint images. The man said the people looked like trees walking around.

- When Jesus laid His hands on the man again, he was suddenly able to see everything clearly.

RECOMMENDED BIBLE READING

Matthew 14:13–33 **Jesus Feeds 5,000 and Walks on Water**

John 6:22–40 **Jesus is the Bread of Life**

Exodus 16:1–36 **Manna and Quail from Heaven**

MEDITATION & PRAYER

Apostle John teaches how to show our love for God:

"And we can be sure that we know him if we obey his commandments. If someone claims, 'I know God,' but doesn't obey God's commandments, that person is a liar and is not living in the truth. But those who obey God's word truly show how completely they love him. That is how we know we are living in him. Those who say they live in God should live their lives as Jesus did . . . Dear friends, let us continue to love one another, for love comes from God. Anyone who loves is a child of God and knows God. But anyone who does not love does not know God, for God is love."

(1 John 2:3–6; 4:7–8)

Dear God,

I thank You for Your love and Your tender mercy. I want to know You in a deeper and more intimate way. Guide me and teach me Your ways. Reveal Yourself and Your Truths to me. Strengthen me through the Holy Spirit to obey Your commandments. I want to live a life firmly grounded in Your Word, abiding by Your Truths. Help me to show others the same kind of love You have for me. Teach me to love more deeply, completely, and unconditionally. You alone are God and You alone are perfect love.

Amen

REVIEW QUESTIONS

1. What were some of the major themes of Jesus' teachings during His "Sermon on the Mount?"

    _____

    _____

    _____

    _____

2. Why was Jesus unable to perform miracles in His hometown of Nazareth? What is required for miracles to occur?

    _____

    _____

    _____

    _____

3. Why did the Jews of Jesus' day despise tax collectors, calling them sinners? How did Jesus address the Pharisee's complaint about His socializing with sinners? (See Matthew 9:12–13.)

    _____

    _____

    _____

    _____

4. How did Jesus respond when religious leaders' accused Him of blasphemy? (See John 31–47.)

    _____

    _____

    _____

    _____

5. Why did the Pharisees and other religious leaders object to Jesus healing and picking grain on the Sabbath? How did Jesus counter their objections? (See Mark 2:27–28.)

_____

_____

_____

_____

6. Why did Jesus call the Pharisees hypocrites? What did they do that was hypocritical?

_____

_____

_____

_____

7. What did Jesus mean when He said, *"I am the bread of life?"*

_____

_____

_____

_____

8. What is a parable? Why did Jesus teach in parables?

_____

_____

_____

_____

PERSONAL REFLECTIONS

9. What did you learn about leadership from how Jesus interacted with His disciples?

_____

_____

_____

_____

_____

10. What did you learn from Jesus about socializing with those whose lifestyles are immoral or ungodly? How should they be treated?

_____

_____

_____

_____

_____

11. The Pharisees practiced their religion in a very strict manner. Jesus said they did not know God. In your opinion, what is the difference between practicing a religion and developing a personal relationship with God?

_____

_____

_____

_____

_____

12. Read "The Beatitudes" in Matthew 5:3–12. Which of the people blessed in these verses describes you? Why? Which of these areas do you need to work on improving? What specific steps can you take to improve in that area?

_____

_____

_____

_____

_____

13. Jesus said the seed falling on fertile soil is like the Word people hear, accept, and then cultivate. What additional steps can you take to ensure the Word of God is firmly planted in your heart and demonstrated by your actions?

_____

_____

_____

_____

_____

14. Jesus prayed in solitude all night before choosing the twelve disciples. What major decision(s), challenge(s), or struggle(s) are you facing? Do what Jesus did. Write a prayer asking God for guidance and His special favor.

_____

_____

_____

_____

CLOSING PRAYER

Isaiah prophesies about God's Servant, Who will reveal truth to the nations:

"BEHOLD MY Servant, Whom I uphold, My elect in Whom My soul delights! I have put My Spirit upon Him; He will bring forth justice . . . and reveal truth to the nations. He will not cry or shout aloud or cause His voice to be heard in the street. A bruised reed He will not break, and a dimly burning wick He will not quench; He will bring forth justice in truth. He will not fail or become weak or be crushed and discouraged till He has established justice in the earth; and the islands and coastal regions shall wait hopefully for Him and expect His direction and law."

(Isaiah 42:1–4 AMP)

Lord God,

I thank You for Your Servant Jesus! He came bringing justice and revealing Truth to the world. Jesus is Your Elect One in Whom You delight! In obedience, He so perfectly executed Your will. He is the Bread of Life, the source of my strength. Here I am. Use me. I stand waiting for Your direction. Teach me Your justice, Your righteousness, and Your Truth. I want to be in the center of Your will and become one in whom You delight.

Amen

CHAPTER 3

FINAL PHASE OF JESUS' MINISTRY

OPENING PRAYER

Dear Lord,

All praise and glory belong to You. I thank You for Your abundant love and compassion. Open the eyes of my understanding as I read about the final phase of Jesus' ministry. Help me envision Scripture as it unfolds. I want to experience Scripture in a more meaningful way. Give me insight into Jesus' message and His mission. Help me understand the pain and agony Jesus endured during His final days on earth. Increase my spiritual understanding and draw me ever closer to You!

Amen

CHAPTER SUMMARY

FINAL PHASE OF JESUS' MINISTRY

(Matthew, Mark, Luke, and John)

During the last year of Jesus' life, opposition to His ministry significantly increased. The Pharisees, Sadducees, and other religious leaders criticized Jesus for failing to keep their Jewish traditions and man-made rules. They accused Him of the following:

- Associating with tax collectors and other sinners.

- Performing healings and other kinds of work on the Sabbath.

- Claiming to be God (blaspheming).

Jesus responded to these accusations, outwitting the religious leaders with His spiritual insight and wisdom. He called them hypocrites, saying they enjoyed praising each other more than glorifying God. The religious leaders' interpretation of Jewish law included burdensome restrictions, while Jesus emphasized love and compassion.

One day, Jesus took Peter, James, and John with Him to the top of a mountain to pray. After they reached the top, the three disciples were astonished by an amazing sight. The prophets—Moses and Elijah—suddenly appeared, standing next to Jesus. In an event commonly referred to as the "Transfiguration," Jesus' appearance suddenly changed to a radiant glow. The three disciples watched in awe as Moses and Elijah talked to Jesus.

As time progressed, Jesus changed His focus from teaching large crowds to mentoring His disciples. Jesus told them He would soon experience great pain and suffering at the hands of His adversaries. Jesus explained He would die and be raised from the dead on the third day. Although Jesus tried to prepare the disciples for what lay ahead, they did not fully understand what He meant. Shortly after predicting His death, the disciples began arguing among themselves about which of them would receive the greatest honor in God's Kingdom.

During the final six months of Jesus' ministry, He traveled with His disciples throughout Judea and Perea, teaching and performing miracles. According to Apostle John, Jesus made the journey to Jerusalem at least three times during the final six months of His life. He visited Jerusalem in the September/October timeframe to celebrate the Festival of Shelters (also known as the Feast of Tabernacles or Festival of Booths). He returned to Jerusalem in the November/December timeframe for the Feast of Dedications (also known as Hanukkah). His final visit to Jerusalem was for the Passover celebration, which occurred in the March/April timeframe.

Shortly before His final visit to Jerusalem, Jesus' dear friend, Lazarus, became gravely ill and died. Jesus went to Lazarus' hometown of Bethany and miraculously raised him from the dead. As news of this miracle spread, many people began believing in Jesus as the Messiah. Concerned about losing their religious authority and social status, the Pharisees and other religious leaders decided Jesus must die.

On several occasions, the Pharisees and other religious leaders heard Jesus describe various aspects of His divinity using the words, "I AM." In Jesus' day, every Jew recognized this as God's Hebrew name, *Yahweh*, translated "I AM" in English. This name of God was so sacred that Jews would not say it out loud. When Jesus used the name "I AM" in reference to Himself, it was clear to everyone He was claiming to be God. In John's gospel, Jesus described Himself using the words "I AM" on seven separate occasions. The Pharisees and other religious leaders were outraged by Jesus' references to His divinity. They accused Him of blasphemy and wanted Him put to death.

Jesus' Seven "I AM" Statements

"I AM" Statement	Scripture	Role	Meaning
I am the Bread of Life.	John 6:35, 48	Sustainer	Jesus sustains us spiritually in the same way bread sustains us physically. Jesus is our sustenance and provides everything we need.
I am the Light of the World.	John 8:12; 9:5	Illuminator	Jesus illuminates God's Word. He leads us out of darkness into the light, guiding us to the Truth of God.
I am the Gate (Door).	John 10:7, 9	Intercessor	Jesus intercedes for us with God. He is our gate (door), providing access to God. We enter into God's presence through Jesus Christ.
I am the Good Shepherd.	John 10:11, 14	Caregiver	Jesus takes care of all the needs of His flock. Jesus feeds, calms, leads, renews, guides, accompanies, protects, comforts, and so much more.
I am the Resurrection and the Life.	John 11:25	Giver of Life	Jesus gives meaning and purpose to life on earth; and makes eternal life possible. Jesus' resurrection gives us hope of eternal life with God.
I am the Way, the Truth, and the Life.	John 14:6	Guide	Jesus accompanies us through life, showing us the way to Truth and more abundant life. We can depend on Jesus to guide us successfully through life's difficult challenges.
I am the True Vine.	John 15:1, 5	Nurturer	Jesus nurtures us and helps us to grow spiritually so that we can do God's work. He helps us to become productive members of God's Kingdom.

	Approximate Timeline	Location	Biblical Scriptures	Author
Mentoring the Disciples	29 A.D.	Caesarea Philippi, Capernaum, Galilee	Matthew 16:13–18:35 Mark 8:27–9:50 Luke 9:18–9:50	Matthew Mark Luke
Conflict with Religious Leaders	29 A.D.	Galilee, Jerusalem, Judea	John 7:1–10:42	John
Preparing the Disciples	29 A.D.	Samaria, Bethany, Judea	Luke 9:51–14:6; 14:25–35; 17:1–10	Luke
One Man Should Die	29 A.D.	Bethany, Judea, Galilee, Samaria, Perea	Matthew 19:1–15 Mark 10:1–16 Luke 17:11– 8:30 John 11:1–57	Matthew Mark Luke John
On the Way to Jerusalem	29 A.D.	Bethany, Jericho, Judea	Matthew 20:17–34; 26:6–13 Mark 10:32–52; 14:3–9 Luke 18:31–19:27 John 12:1–11	Matthew Mark Luke John

MAP OF KEY LOCATIONS

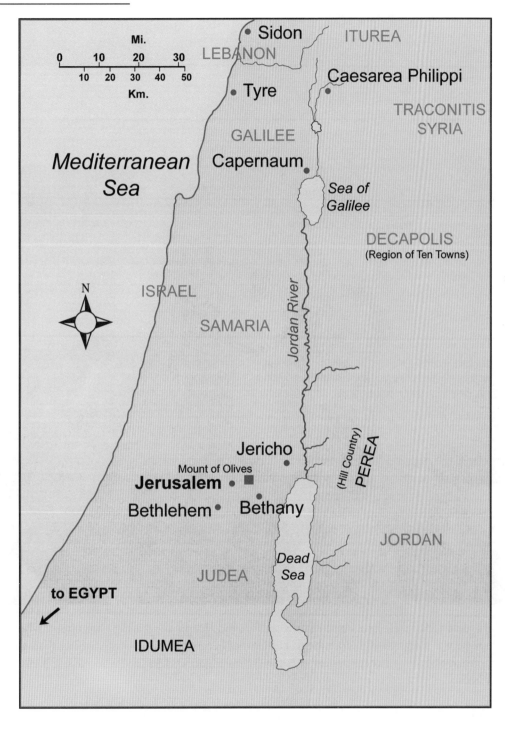

THE TRANSFIGURATION

"After six days Jesus took Peter, James and John with him and led them up a high mountain, where they were all alone. There he was transfigured before them. His clothes became dazzling white, whiter than anyone in the world could bleach them. And there appeared before them Elijah and Moses, who were talking with Jesus." (Mark 9:2–4 NIV)

SECTION 1: MENTORING THE DISCIPLES

Jesus Predicts His Death: (Matthew 16:13–28; Mark 8:27–9:1; Luke 9:1–27)

- Jesus and His disciples left Bethsaida and went to the town of Caesarea Philippi. When they arrived, Jesus asked His disciples, *"Who do people say I am?"* (Mark 8:27b).

- The disciples answered, saying some people think you are John the Baptist while others say you are Elijah or some other prophet come back to life. Jesus then asked, *"But who do you say I am?"* (Mark 8:29a).

- Peter answered, *"You are the Messiah, the Son of the living God"* (Matthew 16:16). Jesus pointed out that God had blessed Peter with this revelation. Jesus then said to Peter, *"Now I say to you that you are Peter (which means 'rock'), and upon this rock I will build my church, and all the powers of hell will not conquer it"* (Matthew 16:18).

- Preparing His disciples for what lay ahead, Jesus informed them that He would be killed in Jerusalem, but would come back to life again on the third day.

- As Jesus was speaking, Peter interrupted and took Him aside. Peter then told Jesus He shouldn't say such things. Turning back toward the disciples, Jesus reprimanded Peter saying, *"Get away from me, Satan! . . . You are seeing things merely from a human point of view, not from God's"* (Mark 8:33b).

Note: Jesus recognized Satan was trying to prevent Him from fulfilling His mission by using Peter to speak against God's will. Although Peter had good intentions, he did not understand Jesus' role in fulfilling God's plan for humanity.

The Transfiguration: (Matthew 17:1–27; Mark 9:2–32; Luke 9:28–45)

- One day, Jesus took Peter, James, and John with Him up a mountain to pray. While praying, Jesus' appearance supernaturally changed. His face and clothes became bright as the sun.

- The prophets Elijah and Moses suddenly appeared and began talking to Jesus. When the three disciples saw this, they were terrified. Confused and bewildered, Peter impulsively suggested they build three shrines to honor Jesus, Elijah, and Moses.

- After Peter said this, a cloud appeared, completely engulfing them. The disciples heard a voice from the cloud say, *"This is my Son, Whom I love; with Him I am well pleased. Listen to Him"* (Matthew 17:5 NIV).

- Jesus instructed His disciples not to discuss what they had seen with anyone until after He had risen from the dead. Peter, James, and John wondered what Jesus meant by this.

- Although Jesus had previously mentioned His death and resurrection, his disciples did not understand what He meant by "rising from the dead." As they walked down the mountainside, the disciples asked Jesus why religious leaders taught that Elijah must first return before the Messiah would appear.

- Jesus replied saying Elijah had already come and was not recognized. Peter, James, and John suddenly realized Jesus was referring to John the Baptist as the Elijah people failed to recognize.

- When the foursome finally reached the bottom of the mountain, a man came to Jesus begging Him to heal His demon-possessed son. The man explained that Jesus' disciples had tried, but were unable to heal his son.

- As the man pleaded, Jesus said to him, *"Everything is possible for him who believes"* (Mark 9:23b NIV). The man affirmed his belief and asked Jesus to help him overcome his doubts. Jesus then commanded the evil spirit to leave and the boy was healed.

- Jesus' disciples later asked why they could not heal the boy. Jesus explained that the boy's case—and those like it—could only be healed through prayer.

- In order to spend more time alone with the disciples, Jesus deliberately avoided the crowds. He again predicted His death, saying He would be betrayed and killed; but would rise from the dead three days later.

Jesus Teaches His Disciples: (Matthew 17:24–18:35; Mark 9:33–50; Luke 9:46–50)

- Jesus traveled to Capernaum. While there, a tax collector asked Peter if Jesus planned to pay the Temple tax. Peter instinctively said "yes" and then went to discuss the matter with Jesus. Before Peter could say anything, Jesus told him they should obey the authorities and pay the tax.

- Jesus instructed Peter to cast his fishing pole into the lake. Jesus then said the first fish Peter caught would have a coin in its mouth which he should use to pay the tax. Following Jesus' instructions, Peter found the coin in the mouth of the first fish he caught and paid the tax.

- Shortly afterward, Jesus' disciples began arguing among themselves about which one of them would be the greatest in the Kingdom of Heaven. Jesus told them they must first become as humble as a little child if they wanted to be great in God's Kingdom.

- John later stopped a man from casting out demons in Jesus' name because the man was not one of Jesus' disciples. When John mentioned what he had done, Jesus told him he should not have stopped the man, for anyone who is not against them is for them.

- One day as Jesus was teaching His disciples, He said anyone who causes others to lose faith will be held accountable on Judgment Day. Do not look down on anyone, for angels are standing in God's presence ready to protect the downtrodden.

- Jesus explained how to confront those who hurt or offend us. If a person offends you, discuss the matter with him privately. If he does not apologize, discuss the matter with him again in the company of two or three friends. If he still fails to acknowledge wrongdoing, take the matter to the church. If he refuses the church's advice, he should be treated as a sinner.

- Jesus then said, *"I promise that when any two of you on earth agree about something you are praying for, my Father in heaven will do it for you. Whenever two or three of you come together in my name, I am there with you"* (Matthew 18:19–20 CEV).

- Peter interrupted Jesus and asked how many times a person should forgive an individual who has wronged him. When Peter suggested "seven" as the correct number, Jesus replied we should forgive a person seventy times seven times. Jesus explained that God mercifully forgives all who come to Him with a repentant heart. We should forgive in the same way God forgives us.

 Note: Jesus was not saying we should forgive 490 times, but that we should not keep count at all. We should always be willing to forgive.

RECOMMENDED BIBLE READING

Matthew 16:13–28 **Jesus Predicts His Death**

Luke 9:28–36 **The Transfiguration**

Malachi 4:1–5 **The Sun of Righteousness**

SECTION 2: CONFLICT WITH RELIGIOUS LEADERS

Jesus Attends the Festival of Shelters: (John 7:1–53)

- Since Jesus knew religious leaders were trying to kill Him, He stayed away from Jerusalem and limited His travels to areas in Galilee.

- As time drew near for the Festival of Shelters, Jesus' brothers urged Him to stop hiding and go with them to Jerusalem for the holiday celebration.

- Jesus' brothers did not believe in Him. They mocked Him, saying He should prove His incredible claim to the world. Jesus told His brothers the time was not yet right for Him to attend the festival.

- Shortly after His brothers left for the festival, Jesus secretly went to Jerusalem, but initially stayed out of sight.

 Note: Jesus attended the Festival of Shelters about six months before His death.

- About midway through the festival, Jesus came out of seclusion. He went into the Temple and began teaching. A large crowd of people gathered to hear Him.

- Some people thought Jesus was the Messiah. They said only the Messiah would be able to perform such wonderful miracles. Others called Jesus a prophet.

- Infuriated by the people's remarks, the religious leaders said the people were ignorant, for the Scriptures never spoke of a prophet coming from Galilee.

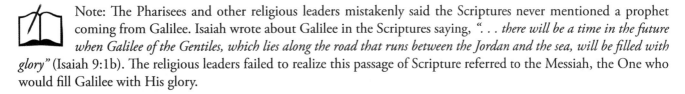 Note: The Pharisees and other religious leaders mistakenly said the Scriptures never mentioned a prophet coming from Galilee. Isaiah wrote about Galilee in the Scriptures saying, *". . . there will be a time in the future when Galilee of the Gentiles, which lies along the road that runs between the Jordan and the sea, will be filled with glory"* (Isaiah 9:1b). The religious leaders failed to realize this passage of Scripture referred to the Messiah, the One who would fill Galilee with His glory.

Jesus Is the Light of the World: (John 8:1–59)

- Shortly afterward, the religious leaders came to Jesus with a woman who had been caught in adultery. They said the woman should be stoned to death in accordance with the law of Moses.

- In an attempt to trap Jesus, the religious leaders asked for His opinion. They wanted Jesus to contradict the law, so they would have a reason to arrest Him.

- Jesus did not answer. Instead, He stooped down and began writing on the ground with His finger.

- The religious leaders began shouting at Jesus, demanding a response. After they kept insisting that He answer them, Jesus stood up and said the person without sin should throw the first stone. Jesus then stooped back down and continued writing on the ground.

- After Jesus said this, the woman's accusers began walking away—one by one—starting with the oldest until everyone was gone except Jesus and the woman.

- Jesus stood up and asked the woman if anyone had condemned her. When she answered "no," Jesus said He did not condemn her either. Jesus told the woman to go and begin living life anew in righteousness.

- Jesus then declared, *"I am the light of the world. Whoever follows me will never walk in darkness, but will have the light of life"* (John 8:12 NIV).

As the Light of the World, Jesus illuminates God's Word, giving us spiritual understanding and insight into God's Word. Darkness represents life spiritually separated from God. Those walking in darkness lack spiritual understanding and knowledge of God's Word. Light symbolizes life with God. When we accept Jesus as our Lord and Savior, we step out of darkness and into God's glorious light.

God spoke through the prophet Isaiah saying, *"The people who walk in darkness will see a great light. For those who live in a land of deep darkness, a light will shine"* (Isaiah 9:2). Isaiah also wrote, *"The earth and its people are covered with darkness, but the glory of the LORD is shining upon you. Nations and kings will come to the light of your dawning day"* (Isaiah 60:2–3 CEV).

- When Jesus declared Himself to be the Light of the World, the Pharisees and other religious leaders were furious. They said Jesus' claims were unsubstantiated and false.

- Jesus responded, *"You are from below; I am from above. You belong to this world; I do not . . . unless you believe that I Am who I claim to be, you will die in your sins"* (John 8:23).

- Outraged, the Pharisees and other religious leaders demanded to know who Jesus was. Jesus told them His mission in life was to do what pleases the One who sent Him.

- Addressing the crowd, Jesus said, *"If you keep on obeying what I have said, you truly are my disciples. You will know the truth, and the truth will set you free"* (John 8:31–32 CEV).

- The people responded, saying they were Abraham's descendants and had never been slaves. They wanted to know how Jesus was going to set them free if they were already free.

- Jesus explained, saying they were slaves to sin. He added that they were indeed Abraham's descendants, but some were not following Abraham's righteous example.

- Jesus then said anyone who obeyed His teachings will never die. When the people heard this, they sneered and said everyone who has ever lived has died, including Abraham and all the prophets.

- Jesus replied, *"Your father Abraham rejoiced as he looked forward to my coming. He saw it and was glad"* (John 8:56a). Puzzled by Jesus' statement, the people told Him that He was too young to have known Abraham.

- Jesus then declared He existed before Abraham was born. When the people heard this, they tried to stone Jesus, but He escaped.

Jesus Heals a Man Born Blind: (John 9:1–41)

- Jesus later met a man who had been born blind. The disciples asked Jesus who had sinned, the man or his parents. They thought the man's birth defect had been the result of sin.

- Jesus answered, saying neither the blind man nor His parents had sinned. Jesus told them it happened so God could be glorified through the man's life.

- Jesus then mixed some dirt with His saliva and made a muddy paste. He smeared it on the man's eyes and told him to wash in the pool of Siloam, located at the south end of Jerusalem. The word *Siloam* means "sent."

- After the blind man washed in the pool, he was able to see for the first time in his life. Those who knew him were amazed. They found it difficult to believe he was the same man who had been blind all his life.

 Note: Apostle John pointed out the symbolism of this healing by letting his readers know the word Siloam means "sent." (See John 9:7.) Jesus sent the blind man to the pool of Siloam to wash in its waters—a symbolic cleansing of sin. Jesus was the One "sent" by God to cleanse us of sin—the real life application of the same spiritual truth.

- When the Pharisees heard about the man's healing, they were upset because it occurred on a Sabbath. They interrogated the man and discovered Jesus was the One responsible for the healing.

- This miracle created a division among the Jewish leaders. Some thought Jesus had been sent from God because only God could heal a man blind from birth. Others felt Jesus could not be from God because He healed the man on the Sabbath.

- The Jewish leaders decided to ask the man's parents if he had been born blind and if so, who had healed him. The man's parents confirmed their son had been blind from birth, but said they did not know who had healed him.

- Since the Jewish leaders had previously threatened to excommunicate anyone acknowledging Jesus as the Messiah, the man's parents did not want to discuss the matter any further. They said their son was old enough to speak for himself.

- The Jewish leaders asked the man again who had healed him. They urged him to tell the truth because Jesus—a sinner—could not have healed him.

- The man replied, *"I don't know if he is a sinner or not. All I know is that I used to be blind, but now I can see!"* (John 9:25 CEV). When the man said this, the Jewish leaders became so frustrated that they threw him out of the synagogue.

- Jesus later found the man and asked if he believed in the Son of Man. The man answered, *"Sir, if you will tell me who he is, I will put my faith in him"* (John 9:36 CEV).

- Jesus replied, *"You have already seen him . . . and right now he is talking with you"* (John 9:37 CEV). The man told Jesus he believed and began praising Him.

Jesus Is the Gate (Door) and the Good Shepherd: (John 10:1–21)

- Some people overheard Jesus talking to the man. Turning to the people, Jesus said, *"I tell you for certain that I am the gate for the sheep . . . I am the gate. All who come in through me will be saved . . . A thief comes only to rob, kill, and destroy. I came so that everyone would have life, and have it in its fullest"* (John 10:7–10 CEV).

 As the Gate (Door), Jesus is our Intercessor. He intercedes for us as our entryway to God, the Father. He opens the gate, which separates us from God and allows us to enter into God's presence. He is our entryway to eternal life with God in heaven.

Old Testament Scripture depicts the gate as an entryway, which provides access to God, *"Open to me the gates of righteousness; I shall enter through them, I shall give thanks to the LORD. This is the gate of the LORD; The righteous will enter through it"* (Psalm 118:19–20 NASB). (See also Isaiah 26:2.)

- After declaring Himself to be the Gate, Jesus said, *"I am the good shepherd. The good shepherd sacrifices his life for the sheep . . . I know my own sheep, and they know me"* (John 10:11, 14).

As the Good Shepherd, Jesus is our Caregiver. Old Testament Scripture often portrayed God as a shepherd. In Psalm 23, David refers to God as *Jehovah-Raah*, meaning "The LORD Is My Shepherd." God spoke to the prophet Ezekiel about the Messiah saying, *"I'll appoint one shepherd over them all: my servant David. He'll feed them. He'll be their shepherd. And I, God, will be their God. My servant David will be their prince. I, God, have spoken"* (Ezekiel 34:23–24 MSG).

Jesus is the shepherd from David's lineage appointed by God to care for His sheep. As our Caregiver, Jesus feeds us, calms us, leads us, renews us, guides us, accompanies us, protects us, comforts us, befriends us, invites us, welcomes us, and more.

- As Jesus elaborated on His roles as the Gate and the Good Shepherd, the people did not know what to think. Some thought Jesus was demon-possessed. Others said He could not be demon-possessed because a demon could not have given sight to a man born blind.

Jesus Attends the Festival of Dedication (Hanukkah): (John 10:22–42)

 Note: Jesus attended the Feast of Dedications—also known as Hanukkah—about four months before His death.

- One day while Jesus was in the Temple for the annual Hanukkah services, a group of religious leaders cornered Him. They asked if He claimed to be the Messiah.

- Jesus answered saying, *"I have already told you, and you don't believe me. The proof is the work I do in my Father's name. But you don't believe me because you are not my sheep. . . . The Father and I are one"* (John 10:25–26, 30).

 Note: The most direct statement Jesus ever made about His divinity is documented in John 10:30, *"The Father and I are one."* Other statements Jesus made about His divinity are in John 12:44–45; 14:8–11; and 17:21–24.

- When Jesus said He and the Father were One, the religious leaders were enraged. As they began picking up stones to throw at Him, Jesus asked, *"At my Father's direction I have done many good works. For which one are you going to stone me?"* (John 10:32).

- The religious leaders replied, *"We are not stoning you because of any good thing you did. We are stoning you because you did a terrible thing. You are just a man, and here you are claiming to be God!"* (John 10:33 CEV).

- The religious leaders tried to arrest Jesus, but He escaped and traveled to an area just beyond the Jordan River.

RECOMMENDED BIBLE READING

John 9:1–41   **Jesus Heals the Man Born Blind**

John 10:1–21   **Jesus is the Good Shepherd**

Ezekiel 34:11–24   **Prophecy about the Good Shepherd**

SECTION 3: PREPARING THE DISCIPLES

Jesus Teaches about the Cost of Discipleship: (Luke 9:51–62)

- After ministering in Galilee for a while, Jesus began His final journey to Jerusalem. As Jesus and the disciples approached a Samaritan village, He sent messengers ahead to prepare the people for His arrival.

- The people refused to welcome Jesus to their village. When James and John found out about this, they asked Jesus if they should command fire to come down from heaven and destroy the town. Jesus rebuked the two brothers for suggesting such a thing and then He and His disciples by-passed the village.

The Commissioning of Seventy-two Disciples: (Luke 10:1–24)

- Jesus later chose seventy-two other disciples. He partnered them together in groups of two and sent them ahead to all the villages He planned to visit. They were sent as messengers to prepare the people for His arrival.

- When the seventy-two disciples returned from their mission, they were overjoyed by what they had accomplished. They told Jesus that demons obeyed when they used His name.

- Pleased by their report, Jesus said to them, *"I saw Satan fall from heaven like lightning! Look, I have given you authority over all the power of the enemy. . . . don't rejoice because evil spirits obey you; rejoice because your names are registered in heaven"* (Luke 10:18–20).

Jesus Visits Mary and Martha: (Luke 10:38–42)

- While on the way to Jerusalem, Jesus and His disciples came to the town of Bethany. A woman named Martha lived there with her sister, Mary, and her brother, Lazarus. All three were close friends of Jesus.

- Martha invited Jesus and His disciples to her home for dinner. While Martha was busy preparing the meal, her sister sat near Jesus' feet, intently listening to His every word.

- Frustrated, Martha asked Jesus to tell Mary to help her with the meal. Jesus replied, *"My dear Martha, you are worried and upset over all these details! There is only one thing worth being concerned about. Mary has discovered it, and it will not be taken away from her"* (Luke 10:41–42).

Warning to the Religious Leaders: (Luke 11:37–54)

- A Pharisee later invited Jesus to his home for dinner. The Pharisee was shocked when Jesus sat down to eat without washing his hands as required by Jewish law.

- Jesus declared, *"Now then, Pharisees clean the outside of the cup and dish, but inside you are full of greed and wickedness"* (Luke 11:39 NIV).

- Appalled, an expert in religious law attending the dinner told Jesus He had insulted them. Jesus replied, *"Yes . . . what sorrow also awaits you experts in religious law! For you crush people with unbearable religious demands, and you never lift a finger to ease the burden."* (Luke 11:46).

- The religious leaders were outraged. They began looking for a reason to have Jesus arrested.

Jesus Teaches About the Kingdom of God: (Luke 12:35–13:30)

- One day while Jesus was teaching, He encouraged the people to stay focused on God and be prepared for His return. Someone later asked if only a few people will be saved. Jesus replied that heaven's doorway is very narrow.

- Admonishing the people to be true followers, Jesus said, *"Work hard to enter the narrow door to God's Kingdom, for many will try to enter but will fail. When the master of the house has locked the door, it will be too late. You will stand outside knocking and pleading, 'Lord, open the door for us!' But he will reply, 'I don't know you or where you come from . . .'"* (Luke 13:24–25).

- As Jesus was teaching, He said some people who appear to be lowly and unimportant will be great in God's Kingdom; and some who are great by earthly standards will be least important in God's Kingdom.

Jesus Teaches About Discipleship: (Luke 14:1–6; 25–35; Luke 17:1–10)

- One Sabbath day, a leading Pharisee invited Jesus to his home. When Jesus arrived, a man sick with dropsy (edema) was already there. The man's arms and legs were swollen from the disease.

- Everyone at the Pharisee's home watched closely to see if Jesus would heal the man. Turning to the Pharisees, Jesus asked if the law permitted healing miracles on the Sabbath. The Pharisees would not answer, so Jesus healed the man.

- Jesus then asked the Pharisees, *"Which of you doesn't work on the Sabbath? If your son or your cow falls into a pit, don't you rush to get him out?"* (Luke 14:5). Again, the Pharisees refused to answer.

- When Jesus got up to leave, crowds of people followed Him. Jesus explained to the people that they must love God more than anything else and be willing to give up everything to follow Him.

- Jesus advised the people to carefully consider everything involved in being one of His disciples before deciding to join Him.

- Jesus later explained the power of faith to His disciples. He said, *"If you had faith even as small as a mustard seed, you could say to this mulberry tree, 'May you be uprooted and thrown into the sea,' and it would obey you!"* (Luke 17:6).

RECOMMENDED BIBLE READING

Luke 10:38–42   **Jesus' Visit with Martha and Mary**

Luke 11:37–53   **Jesus Criticizes the Pharisees**

Psalm 37:1–6   **The Wicked and the Righteous**

SECTION 4: ONE MAN SHOULD DIE

Jesus Raises Lazarus from the Dead: (John 11:1–57)

- One day, Mary and Martha's brother, Lazarus, became very sick. Since Jesus was a close friend of the family, Mary and Martha sent a message to Him about their brother's illness.

- When Jesus received the sisters' message, He said to the disciples, *"This sickness will not end in death. No, it is for God's glory so that God's Son may be glorified through it"* (John 11:4 NIV).

- Although Jesus cared deeply for Lazarus, He did not leave right away for Bethany, Lazarus' hometown. After two days had passed, Jesus informed His disciples it was time to go see about Lazarus.

- The disciples warned Jesus about going to Bethany. They reminded Him it was in Judea that religious leaders had recently tried to kill Him. Jesus responded, *"Our friend Lazarus has fallen asleep, but now I will go and wake him up"* (John 11:11).

- When the disciples heard Jesus say Lazarus had fallen asleep, they thought Lazarus was merely resting. They did not understand Jesus meant Lazarus had died. Realizing the disciples were confused, Jesus very explicitly stated that Lazarus was dead. They then headed for Bethany.

- A large crowd of mourners were gathered at the sisters' house. When someone in the crowd said Jesus was nearby, Martha ran out to meet Him.

- As soon as Martha saw Jesus, she cried out, *"Lord, if only you had been here, my brother would not have died"* (John 11:21).Jesus responded, *"I am the resurrection and the life. Anyone who believes in me will live, even after dying"* (John 11:25).

 As the Resurrection and the Life, Jesus is the Giver of Life. Jesus was with God from the beginning as the Creator of Life and was the first to rise from the dead as the Conqueror of Death. He has the power over life and death. As the Giver of Life, Jesus holds the keys to peace with God and eternal life. Those who believe in Him will rise from the dead—just like He did—and live with God forever.

- Jesus asked Martha if she believed those who trusted in Him will never die. Martha answered saying she believed and declared Jesus to be the Messiah.

- After talking to Jesus, Martha walked back to the house and went inside. In a private conversation, Martha told Mary Jesus was outside and wanted to see her.

- Mary jumped up and ran out to meet Jesus. The people, who were comforting the sisters, thought Mary was going to Lazarus' gravesite. Concerned for Mary's welfare, they decided to follow her.

- With tears in her eyes, Mary fell down at Jesus' feet. The first words out of her mouth were the same as her sister's, *"Lord, if only you had been here, my brother would not have died"* (John 11:32).

- When Jesus saw Mary and the other mourners' tears, He was deeply moved with compassion. He asked about Lazarus' gravesite and then began to weep.

- The sisters and other mourners led Jesus to Lazarus' gravesite. Lazarus' body was in a cave with a stone in front of the entrance. When they arrived, Jesus told the people to remove the stone from the entrance.

- Martha reminded Jesus that Lazarus had been in the cave for four days and his body had started to decay. She said the smell would be too terrible to bear. Turning to Martha, Jesus said, *"Didn't I tell you that you would see God's glory if you believe?"* (John 11:40). After Jesus said this, the mourners obediently removed the stone from Lazarus' gravesite.

- Jesus gave thanks to God and then shouted, *"Lazarus, come out!"* (John 11:43). Lazarus came out of the cave—wrapped in burial garments. Lazarus was alive!

- The people gathered at the gravesite began spreading the news. As a result of this miracle, many believed Jesus was the Messiah.

- When the leading priests and Pharisees heard about the miracle, they were upset. They held a meeting of the high council to discuss the situation. As the priests and Pharisees debated the matter, one of them said, *"If we allow him to go on like this, soon everyone will believe in him. Then the Roman army will come and destroy both our Temple and our nation"* (John 11:48).

- Caiaphas, the high priest, responded, *"You don't know what you're talking about! You don't realize that it's better for you that one man should die for the people than for the whole nation to be destroyed"* (John 11:49–50). After Caiaphas said this, they all decided Jesus must die.

- Jesus knew the religious leaders were plotting His death, so He left Judea and headed north.

Jesus Heals Ten Lepers: (Luke 17:11–19)

- As Passover drew near, Jesus and the disciples journeyed back south. When they reached a village between Galilee and Samaria, ten lepers cried out to Jesus for help.

- Keeping their distance, the lepers asked Jesus to heal them. Jesus instructed them to find a priest and submit to an examination for signs of leprosy.

- As the lepers hurried to find a priest, their leprosy began to disappear. One of the lepers—a Samaritan—suddenly realized he had been healed and went back to thank Jesus for the miracle.

- Jesus asked the Samaritan about the other lepers saying, *"Where are the other nine? Has no one returned to give glory to God except this foreigner (the Samaritan)?"* (Luke 17:17b–18).

- Stressing the importance of faith, Jesus said to the Samaritan, *"Your faith has healed you"* (Luke 17:19b).

Jesus Teaches About His Second Coming: (Luke 17:20–37)

- One day, Jesus talked to His disciples about His second coming. Jesus said He would return to earth one day and suddenly appear in the sky with no warning.

- Describing the day of His return, Jesus said, *"On that Day, two men will be in the same boat fishing—one taken, the other left. Two women will be working in the same kitchen—one taken, the other left"* (Luke 17:34–35 MSG).

 Note: Jesus' return is often called "the Second Coming" or "Second Appearance." Those who are prepared for His return will immediately join God in heaven. Preparation for Jesus' return means accepting Him as God's Plan of Redemption and Salvation. (See Appendices 8 and 9.)

Jesus Teaches about Divorce: (Matthew 19:1–12; Mark 10:1–12)

- Some Pharisees later came to Jesus asking questions designed to trap Him. When the Pharisees asked about the legality of divorce, Jesus said, *"No one should separate a couple that God has joined together"* (Matthew 19:6b CEV).

- The Pharisees then asked why Moses allowed husbands to divorce their wives. Jesus answered saying, *"Moses permitted divorce only as a concession to your hard hearts, but it was not what God had originally intended. And I tell you this, whoever divorces his wife and marries someone else commits adultery—unless his wife has been unfaithful"* (Matthew 19:8–9).

Jesus Blesses Infant Children: (Matthew 19:13–15; Mark 10:13–16; Luke 18:15–17)

- One day, some parents brought their infants to Jesus for Him to touch and bless. The disciples disapproved, saying the people were bothering Jesus with small children.

- Overruling the disciples, Jesus said, *"Let the children come to me! Don't try to stop them. People who are like these children belong to God's kingdom. You will never get into God's kingdom unless you enter it like a child!"* (Luke 18:16–17 CEV).

Discussion with a Rich Young Man: (Luke 18:18–30)

- One day, a leading official came to Jesus wanting to know what he must do to receive eternal life. Jesus answered, *"You know the commandments, don't you? No illicit sex, no killing, no stealing, no lying, honor your father and mother"* (Luke 18:20 MSG).

- The young man answered, saying he had obeyed these commandments throughout his life—from childhood to the present day.

- Jesus listened and then said to the man, *"Then there's only one thing left to do: Sell everything you own and give it away to the poor. You will have riches in heaven. Then come, follow me"* (Luke 18:22 MSG).

- When the young man heard Jesus' advice, he became sad. He was very rich and did not want to give up his wealth.

- As the young man walked away, Jesus turned to His disciples and said, *"Do you have any idea how difficult it is for people who have it all to enter God's kingdom? I'd say it's easier to thread a camel through a needle's eye than get a rich person into God's kingdom"* (Luke 18:24–25 MSG).

 Note: In this story, Jesus was not teaching that we must sell everything we own to receive eternal life. Jesus was pointing out that Christ-followers must be willing to give up whatever is most important to them; i.e., job, friends, fame, power, or money. These can be stumbling blocks that prevent spiritual growth.

RECOMMENDED BIBLE READING

John 11:1–44 **Jesus Raises Lazarus from the Dead**

1 Kings 17:8–24 **Elijah Raises a Young Boy from the Dead**

SECTION 5: ON THE WAY TO JERUSALEM

A Mother's Request: (Matthew 20:17–28; Mark 10:32–45; Luke 18:31–34)

- One day, Jesus called His disciples together and said, *"Listen, we're going up to Jerusalem, where all the predictions of the prophets concerning the Son of Man will come true. He will be handed over to the Romans, and he will be mocked, treated shamefully, and spit upon. They will flog him with a whip and kill him, but on the third day he will rise again"* (Luke 18:31–33).

- James and John's mother later came to Jesus and asked Him to give her sons honored positions—seats on His right and His left—in His Kingdom. Jesus explained to the mother that her sons must be able to drink from the same cup He would soon drink, a cup of great suffering.

- After both brothers said they were able, Jesus said, *"You will indeed drink from my bitter cup. But I have no right to say who will sit on my right or my left. My Father has prepared those places for the ones he has chosen"* (Matthew 20:23). When the other disciples heard about the request, they were upset. Jesus explained to them that those wanting to be great in God's Kingdom must become a servant, for He came to serve, not be served.

Jesus Enters Jericho: (Matthew 20:29–34; Mark 10:46–52; Luke 18:35–19:10)

- Jesus and His disciples traveled south until they reached the outskirts of Jericho. As usual, a large crowd was following Jesus.

- A blind man named Bartimaeus was begging on the side of the road. Bartimaeus heard the commotion and asked what was going on. Someone told him Jesus of Nazareth was passing by. When the blind man heard this, he frantically called out, *"Jesus, Son of David, have mercy on me!"* (Mark 10:47).

- Some people in the crowd tried to silence the man. When they told him to be quiet, he shouted even louder, *"Son of David, have mercy on me!"* (Mark 10:48b). Hearing the man's cries, Jesus went to him and asked what he needed. Without hesitation, the man said he wanted to see.

- Jesus said, *"All right, receive your sight! Your faith has healed you"* (Luke 18:42). With these words, the blind man's sight was restored. Praising God for his healing, the man got up and followed Jesus along with the others.

- As Jesus entered the city of Jericho, the people were rejoicing and praising God. A man named Zacchaeus was among those in the crowd.

- Zacchaeus was a very wealthy man, who made his fortune collecting taxes from his fellow Jews for the Roman government. He wanted a good look at Jesus, but was too short to see through the crowd.

- Determined to find a better view, Zacchaeus ran ahead and climbed a sycamore tree along the path where Jesus would soon travel. Perched high in the tree, Zacchaeus waited for Jesus to pass by.

- As Jesus approached the sycamore tree, He looked up and said, *"Zacchaeus, come down immediately. I must stay at your house today"* (Luke 19:5 NIV).

- Zacchaeus quickly climbed down and invited Jesus to his home for dinner. While Zacchaeus was overjoyed, others in the crowd criticized Jesus for socializing with sinners.

- With heartfelt sorrow, Zacchaeus repented, saying he would donate half of his wealth to the poor. He also promised to reimburse those he had cheated, giving them four times the amount he had overtaxed them.

- Filled with compassion, Jesus announced to the crowd, *"Salvation has come to this home today . . . For the Son of Man came to seek and save those who are lost"* (Luke 19:9–10).

Parable about Ten Servants: (Luke 19:11–27)

- As Jesus approached Jerusalem, He sensed His followers thought the Kingdom of God was about to begin. He stopped and told the following short story to correct this misconception:

  ➢ A certain prince was going to a distant city to be crowned king. Before leaving, the prince gave money to each of his ten servants and instructed them to run his business while he was away. The local people did not want the prince as their king. When the newly-crowned king returned, he asked his servants how they had invested his money. The first servant had ten times more than the original amount. The second servant had five times as much. The newly-crowned king rewarded each of them for wisely investing his money. The king soon discovered the third servant still had the original amount. Instead of investing the money, he dug a hole and hid it. The newly-crowned king said, *"You wicked servant! . . . Why didn't you deposit my money in the bank? At least I could have gotten some interest on it."* Turning to the others, he said, *". . . Take the money from this servant, and give it to the one who has ten pounds. . . . Those who use well what they are given, even more will be given. But from those who do nothing, even what little they have will be taken away. And as for these enemies of mine who didn't want me to be their king—bring them in and execute them right here in front of me"* (Luke 19:22–24, 26–27).

 Note: Jesus told His followers this parable to help them understand He was going away, but would return at a future date. In the meantime, Christ-followers should do good works to advance God's Kingdom. God is not pleased with nonproductive citizens of His Kingdom.

Mary Anoints Jesus' Feet—(Saturday, Six Days Before Passover): (Matthew 26:6–13; Mark 14:3–9; John 12:1–11)

- Six days before Passover, Jesus visited Lazarus and his sisters in Bethany. They hosted a dinner party in which Jesus was the guest of honor.

- As Martha was serving, Mary came in with a very expensive bottle of perfumed oil. She rubbed the oil on Jesus' feet and then wiped his feet with her hair. When Judas Iscariot saw what was happening, he was outraged. Judas chastised Mary, saying the oil should have been donated to Jesus' ministry.

- Judas added that they could have sold the oil and given the money to the poor. As Judas complained, the disciples were unaware of his intentions. In hindsight, Apostle John said, *"He (Judas) did not say this because he cared about the poor but because he was a thief; as keeper of the money bag, he used to help himself to what was put into it"* (John 12:6 NIV).

- Jesus defended Mary's actions, saying to Judas, *"Leave her alone! She has kept this perfume for the day of my burial. You will always have the poor with you, but you won't always have me"* (John 12:7–8 CEV).

- When people in the area realized Jesus was in Bethany, they came to see Him. Still amazed, they wanted to hear from the Man who had raised Lazarus from the dead.

RECOMMENDED BIBLE READING

Luke 18:31–34 **Jesus Predicts His Death**
Luke 18:35–19:9 **Jesus' Entry Into Jericho**
Psalm 22:1–22 **Prophetic Prediction of Jesus' Death**

MEDITATION & PRAYER

Apostle Paul exhorts us to imitate God as children of light:

"Therefore be imitators of God as dear children. And walk in love, as Christ also has loved us and given Himself for us, an offering and a sacrifice to God for a sweet-smelling aroma. But fornication and all uncleanness or covetousness, let it not even be named among you, as is fitting for saints; neither filthiness, nor foolish talking, nor coarse jesting, which are not fitting, but rather giving of thanks . . . For you were once darkness, but now you are light in the Lord. Walk as children of light (for the fruit of the Spirit is in all goodness, righteousness, and truth), finding out what is acceptable to the Lord."

(Ephesians 5:1–4; 8–10 NKJ)

Dear Lord,

I thank You for loving me as one of Your dear children. It is my desire to be more like Jesus. He is my model and my guide. I want to walk in love as Jesus did, so the world will see Him in my life. Forgive me for the times I've been selfish, prideful, and foolish. Help me through the Holy Spirit to overcome my weaknesses. Strengthen me and make me holy. Help me to show others Your goodness, righteousness, and truth. I want to walk as a child of light, glorifying You always!

Amen

REVIEW QUESTIONS

1. The Pharisees and other religious leaders had three major complaints against Jesus. What were they?

    _____

    _____

    _____

    _____

2. What were some things Jesus did to prepare the disciples for His death and resurrection?

    _____

    _____

    _____

    _____

3. Jesus healed a man who was born blind. Why was this particular miracle so controversial? Why wouldn't the blind man's parents admit Jesus healed their son?

    _____

    _____

    _____

    _____

4. Jesus said, *"I am the Gate (Door)."* What did Jesus mean by this?

    _____

    _____

    _____

    _____

5. Jesus said, *"I am the Good Shepherd."* What does this mean?

    _____

    _____

    _____

    _____

6. Before entering Jerusalem, Jesus told a parable about "Ten Servants." (See Luke 19:11–27.) What is the meaning of this parable? Why did Jesus tell this parable before entering Jerusalem?

    _____

    _____

    _____

    _____

7. Why were the Pharisees and religious leaders upset when Jesus raised Lazarus from the dead? In what way was this miracle a major turning point?

    _____

    _____

    _____

    _____

PERSONAL REFLECTIONS

8.   Jesus said, *"I am the Light."* What does this mean to you? In what way has Jesus been a light in your life?

_____

_____

_____

_____

_____

9.   What does it mean to forgive? Why is it important to forgive others? How do you forgive when you've been severely hurt?

_____

_____

_____

_____

_____

10. Martha was busy preparing a meal, while Mary sat at Jesus' feet listening to His every word. Is your life more like Martha's or Mary's? What spiritual growth lesson did you learn from Martha and Mary's story?

_____

_____

_____

_____

_____

11. What lessons have you learned from Jesus' teachings and discussions with the Pharisees? How will you apply these lessons in your life?

_____

_____

_____

_____

_____

12. Jesus said, *"I am the resurrection and the life."* What does this mean to you?

_____

_____

_____

_____

_____

13. When Jesus healed ten lepers, only one went back to thank Him. What has God done for you lately? Take a few moments to write a prayer thanking God for everything He has done for you recently. The next time you need to trust God to answer a prayer, remember to read your thank you prayers. It will remind you that God loves you and help you to overcome your doubts.

_____

_____

_____

_____

CLOSING PRAYER

Isaiah explains that the Lord has called us in righteousness:

"This is what God the LORD says—
    he who created the heavens and stretched them out,
    who spread out the earth and all that comes out of it,
    who gives breath to its people,
    and life to those who walk on it:

I, the LORD, have called you in righteousness;
    I will take hold of your hand.
    I will keep you and will make you
    to be a covenant for the people
    and a light for the Gentiles . . .

        Sing to the LORD a new song,
            his praise from the ends of the earth,
            you who go down to the sea, and all that is in it,
            you islands, and all who live in them."

                            (Isaiah 42:5–6, 10 NIV)

Heavenly Father,

You are the Creator, the One who created the heavens and earth; and everything in it. You breathed and gave life to the world. You are the One who wakes me up each morning and gives me strength to start my day. I praise and glorify Your Holy Name. Hold my hand and keep me in Your righteousness. Help me to demonstrate Your love and tender mercy. It is my desire to be a reflection of You and a light to the world. I will sing a new song, praising Your name all the days of my life.

                                                    Amen

CHAPTER 4

JESUS' DEATH AND RESURRECTION

OPENING PRAYER

Dear Lord,

Thank You for Your abundant love and grace. As I read about Jesus' last days on earth, open my eyes and heart to receive Your Word. Reveal Yourself and Your Truth to me. Give me deeper spiritual insight into the meaning of Jesus' death and resurrection. Help me to more clearly see how high, wide, and deep Your love is for me. You gave Your Son and Your Son gave His life so that I can live with You eternally. All praise be to You forever.

Amen

CHAPTER SUMMARY

JESUS' DEATH AND RESURRECTION

(Matthew, Mark, Luke, and John)

According to John's gospel, Jesus arrived in Bethany on the Sabbath (Saturday), six days before Passover. When people heard Jesus was there, they came to see the Man who had raised Lazarus from the dead.

On Sunday, Jesus rode into Jerusalem seated on a donkey. A large number of people followed close behind, cheering and praising Him. The Pharisees and other religious leaders watched in anguish as the people declared Jesus as their King.

On Monday, Jesus found merchants in the Temple selling animals for the Passover celebration. Outraged by the lack of respect for God's house, Jesus knocked over the merchants' tables and chased them out of the Temple. Afterward, Jesus taught for a while and then returned to Bethany.

On Tuesday, Jesus traveled the two miles back to Jerusalem. When He entered the Temple, the religious leaders cornered Him, asking who had given Him authority to run the merchants out of the Temple. Jesus condemned the religious leaders, calling them hypocrites. Jesus said they only pretended to know God, but were far from Him. Jesus later met with His disciples and predicted the destruction of the Temple. He also described events which would occur at the end of time.

In the meantime—on either Tuesday or Wednesday—the high priest held a meeting with religious leaders to strategize plans for Jesus' death. Judas joined their meeting and agreed to betray Jesus.

On Thursday, Jesus and the disciples met in an upstairs room to celebrate Passover. Jesus gave His disciples and all future disciples instructions on how they were to remember Him. Luke writes, *"He [Jesus] took bread, gave thanks and broke it, and gave it to them, saying, 'This is my body given for you; do this in remembrance of me.' In the same way, after the supper he took the cup, saying, 'This cup is the new covenant in my blood, which is poured out for you'"* (Luke 22:19–20 NIV).

After the meal, Jesus spent time talking to His disciples in a farewell address. John's gospel provides the most detailed information about Jesus' last words to His disciples while in the upstairs room. Late Thursday night—after the Passover meal—they went to the Mount of Olives in a garden grove called Gethsemane. Shortly after their arrival, Judas showed up with Roman soldiers. Judas identified Jesus, betraying Him with a kiss. The soldiers then arrested Jesus and carried Him away to the residence of the high priest.

Early Friday morning, Jesus endured several trials and severe beatings. He was initially questioned by Annas, father-in-law of Caiaphas. Annas sent Jesus to Caiaphas, who quickly assembled the religious leaders and held a trial. They charged Jesus with blasphemy and ordered guards to carry Him away to Pilate. After listening to Jesus' accusers, Pilate said the charges against Jesus did not warrant the death penalty. Having heard that Jesus was a Galilean, Pilate sent Him to Herod for a verdict. When Jesus appeared before Herod, He was questioned and mocked, but remained silent. Herod eventually became disinterested and returned Jesus to Pilate.

Pilate announced to the crowd that he did not find Jesus guilty of anything and neither did Herod. Pilate said he would have Jesus flogged and then released. When Jesus' accusers heard this, they incited the crowd to ask for Jesus' death. Fearing a riot, Pilate gave in to the people's demands and ordered Jesus' death. Jesus was nailed to a cross on Friday morning at about 9:00 A.M. By 3:00 P.M., He was dead. Jesus was buried—on that same Friday—in a tomb. On Saturday morning, Roman soldiers were posted to guard the tomb. On Sunday morning, the tomb was empty! Jesus had risen from the dead and later made several resurrection appearances.

Jesus' Resurrection Appearances

Appeared To:	Scriptural Reference
Mary Magdalene at Jesus' tomb	Mark 16:9–11; John 20:11–18
The other women running from the tomb	Matthew 28:8–10
Two of Jesus' followers on the road	Mark 16:12–13; Luke 24:13–31
Peter in Jerusalem	Luke 24:33–34; 1 Corinthians 15:5
Ten disciples in Jerusalem (Thomas absent)	Mark 16:14; Luke 24:36–43; John 20:19–25
Eleven disciples in Jerusalem (Thomas present)	John 20:26–31; 1 Corinthians 15:5
Seven disciples while fishing in Galilee	John 21:1–23
Eleven disciples on a mountain in Galilee	Matthew 28:16–20; Mark 16:15–18
Disciples who witnessed Jesus' ascension	Luke 24:44–51; Acts 1:1–12
Five hundred followers at one time	1 Corinthians 15:6
James (Jesus' half-brother)	1 Corinthians 15:7
Apostle Paul	Acts 9:3–16; 1 Corinthians 15:8
Apostle John	Revelation 1:10–3:22

	Approximate Timeline	Location	Biblical Scriptures	Author
Entering Jerusalem	30 A.D.	Jerusalem, Bethany	Matthew 21:1–17 Mark 11:1–19 Luke 19:28–48 John 12:12–50	Matthew Mark Luke John
Debates and Warnings	30 A.D.	Jerusalem	Matthew 21:18–26:16 Mark 11:20–14:11 Luke 20:1–22:6	Matthew Mark Luke
Jesus' Farewell	30 A.D.	Jerusalem	Matthew 26:1–46 Mark 14:12–42 Luke 22:7–46 John 13:1–17:26	Matthew Mark Luke John
Arrest and Trial	30 A.D.	Jerusalem	Matthew 26:47–27:31 Mark 14:43–15:20 Luke 22:47–23:25 John 18:1–19:16	Matthew Mark Luke John
Crucifixion and Resurrection	30 A.D.	Jerusalem, Galilee	Matthew 27:32–28:20 Mark 15:21–16:20 Luke 23:26–24:53 John 19:17–21:25	Matthew Mark Luke John

MAP OF KEY LOCATIONS

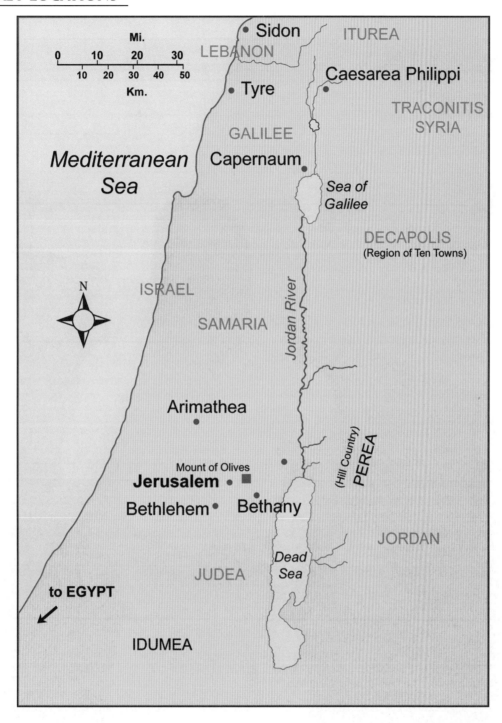

THE RESURRECTION

"Jesus told her, 'I am the resurrection and the life. Anyone who believes in me will live, even after dying.'"
(John 11:25)

SECTION 1: ENTERING JERUSALEM

Jesus Rides Into Jerusalem on a Donkey—(Sunday): (Matthew 21:1–11; Mark 11:1–11; Luke 19:28–44; John 12:12–19)

- After spending the night in Bethany, Jesus and His disciples set out for Jerusalem. As they approached the Mount of Olives, Jesus sent two of His disciples into the village to find a certain young donkey.

- The disciples found the donkey and brought it to Jesus. Using the disciples' cloaks as a makeshift saddle, Jesus mounted the animal and rode toward Jerusalem. The twelve disciples and others followed close behind.

- When people heard Jesus was on His way to Jerusalem, large crowds gathered along the roadside. The crowd was filled with emotion as they waited for Him to pass by.

- Many in the crowd had witnessed Jesus raise Lazarus from the dead. In their excitement, some people lined the road with palm branches, while others took off their cloaks and laid them in front of the processional.

- As Jesus passed by, the people enthusiastically cried out, *"Hosanna! Blessed is he who comes in the name of the Lord! Blessed is the King of Israel!"* (John 12:13 NIV). Their shouts and praises could be heard for miles.

 Note: *Hosanna* is a Hebrew word that means, "Save us now!" This expression is similar to contemporary sayings as "God Bless the King" or "Hail to the Chief." The people were proclaiming Jesus as the Messiah and King of Israel. Today, this event is called "The Triumphal Entry," and is celebrated on the holiday known as "Palm Sunday." Five days later, these same people rejected Jesus as their King. Ironically, their praises turned into demands for His crucifixion.

During the months before Passover, Jesus deliberately stayed away from Jerusalem. On the Sunday before His death, He came out of seclusion, riding into Jerusalem on a donkey. This fulfilled Zechariah's prophecy written over 500 years earlier. Zechariah wrote, *"Rejoice, O people of Zion! Shout in triumph, O people of Jerusalem! Look, your king is coming to you. He is righteous and victorious, yet he is humble, riding on a donkey—riding on a donkey's colt"* (Zechariah 9:9).

In Jesus' day, kings proclaimed victory by riding through the city on a horse. In a display of humility, Jesus proclaimed victory seated on a donkey. This symbolically pictured Jesus as a humble King, coming to declare peace. The crowd's shouts of praise fulfilled another prophecy, *"I have seen what they do, but I will heal them anyway! I will lead them. I will comfort those who mourn, bringing words of praise to their lips"* (Isaiah 57:18–19). The people praised Jesus for healing their physical bodies, but failed to realize He was the One who would bring spiritual healing as well.

- The Pharisees watched in anguish as the people praised Jesus. Feeling defeated, they tried to stop the people from declaring Jesus the King of Israel.

- Jesus called out to the Pharisees saying, *"If they (the people) keep quiet, these stones will start shouting"* (Luke 19:40 CEV).

 Note: In effect, Jesus' words about the stones shouting out came true. (See Luke 19:40.) When Jesus was arrested, the people stopped praising Him; and His disciples were silent and in seclusion. In the middle of this profound silence, an earthquake occurred, causing the stones to shout out in praise.

- As the city of Jerusalem came into view, Jesus looked up and was saddened. Jesus said *"It is too bad that today your people don't know what will bring them peace! . . . Jerusalem, the time will come when your enemies will build walls around you to attack you . . . They will level you to the ground and kill your people. Not one stone in your buildings will be left on top of another. This will happen because you did not see that God had come to save you"* (Luke 19:42–44 CEV).

Note: Jesus' prediction about the destruction of Jerusalem came true about forty years after His death. In 66 A.D., the Jews revolted against Rome. In response to this uprising, Roman soldiers came and attacked Jerusalem. After holding the city under siege for several years, the Romans finally broke through its walls in 70 A.D. They set Jerusalem on fire, destroying everything. Titus, the Roman emperor's son, ordered his men to strip the Temple of its gold. As they stripped each stone for its gold, Jesus' prophecy came true—*"Not one stone in your buildings will be left on top of another."*

- When Jesus arrived in Jerusalem, He went into the Temple for a short while and then returned to Bethany for the night.

Jesus Clears the Temple Again—(Monday): (Matthew 21:12–17; Mark 11:12–19; Luke 19:45–48; John 12:20–50)

- The next morning, Jesus and His disciples got up and began the journey back to Jerusalem.

- As they were traveling, Jesus became hungry and noticed a fig tree along the path. Jesus walked over to the tree in search of some fruit. Although there were plenty of green leaves, the tree had no figs, for it was not yet fruit-bearing season. Jesus cursed the tree saying no one would ever eat its fruit again.

Note: Why did Jesus curse the fig tree? This incident serves as a reminder to those who have accepted Jesus as their Savior. When we accept Jesus' offer of salvation, He gives us new life—like the green leaves on the fig tree. Jesus then expects those who believe in Him to bear fruit—grow spiritually—actively demonstrating God's love to the world.

- When Jesus and His disciples reached Jerusalem, they went to the Temple. Merchants were selling animals to prospective customers for Passover.

- In a fit of righteous indignation, Jesus knocked over the merchants' tables and chased them out of the Temple.

- Outraged by the lack of respect, Jesus shouted, *"The Scriptures declare, 'My Temple will be called a house of prayer for all nations,' but you have turned it into a den of thieves"* (Mark 11:17). (See Isaiah 56:7 and Jeremiah 7:11 for cross-references.)

- Afterward, Jesus began teaching in the Temple. People from many different countries were in Jerusalem for Passover. Some Greeks, who were in Jerusalem for the celebration, asked Philip to introduce them to Jesus.

- Andrew went with Philip to tell Jesus about the men's request. Jesus said to His two disciples, *"Anyone who wants to be my disciple must follow me, because my servants must be where I am. And the Father will honor anyone who serves me"* (John 12:26).

- Troubled by His impending death for the sins of the world, Jesus added, *"Now my soul is deeply troubled. Should I pray, 'Father, save me from this hour'? But this is the very reason I came! Father, bring glory to your name"* (John 12:27–28a).

- As soon as Jesus finished speaking, a thunderous voice spoke from heaven saying, *"I have already brought glory to my name, and I will do so again"* (John 12:28b).

- When the people heard this, they did not know what to think. Jesus explained that the words were spoken for their benefit and not His.

- Jesus then said, *"When I am lifted up from the earth, I will draw everyone to myself"* (John 12:32).

- When the crowd realized Jesus was speaking of His death, they were confused. The people shouted out that the Messiah is supposed to live forever.

 Note: How did the people know the Messiah would live forever? In Jesus' day, Jewish children studied the Scriptures—the Old Testament—in the same way children study textbooks today. Having learned Scripture from childhood, they were very much aware of Old Testament prophecies. (For Old Testament prophecies about the Messiah's eternal reign, see Isaiah 9:6–7, Ezekiel 37:25, and Daniel 7:13–14. For prophecies about the Messiah's death, see Psalm 22, Isaiah 53, and Daniel 9:6.)

- As the people mumbled and complained about Jesus' gloomy message, He turned to them and said, *"My light will shine for you just a little longer. Walk in the light while you can, so the darkness will not overtake you"* (John 12:35).

- After addressing the crowd, Jesus returned to Bethany with the disciples for the evening.

- Many of Jesus' followers became disillusioned and stopped believing in Him. Those who still believed would not admit it publicly, for fear of being excommunicated.

Jesus' words and actions did not match the people's expectations. Jesus came to shed light—the Truth of God—yet most chose to continue in darkness. The prophet Isaiah explained this phenomena saying, *"Then the LORD told me to go and speak this message to the people: 'You will listen and listen, but never understand. You will look and look, but never see . . . Make these people stubborn! Make them stop up their ears, cover their eyes, and fail to understand. Don't let them turn to me and be healed'"* (Isaiah 6:9–10 CEV).

The people had not truly accepted God's will and His ways in their heart. They were consumed with their internal struggles with Rome and refused to accept God's Plan of Redemption and Salvation.

RECOMMENDED BIBLE READING

Luke 19:28–48 **The Triumphal Entry**

Zechariah 9:9–17 **The King's Coming**

SECTION 2: DEBATES AND WARNINGS

Religious Leaders Challenge Jesus' Authority—(Tuesday): (Matthew 21:18–27; Mark 11:20–33; Luke 20:1–8)

- The next morning, Jesus and His disciples traveled back to Jerusalem. When they came across the fig tree Jesus had cursed the previous morning, Peter pointed out that the fig tree had withered.

- As the disciples looked at the fig tree in awe, Jesus said, *"Have faith in God! If you have faith in God and don't doubt, you can tell this mountain to get up and jump into the sea, and it will. Everything you ask for in prayer will be yours, if you only have faith"* (Mark 11:22–24 CEV).

- When they reached Jerusalem, the religious leaders were waiting for Jesus as He entered the Temple. They asked who had given Him authority to chase the merchants out of the Temple.

- In response to the religious leaders' question, Jesus said they must first answer one of His questions. Jesus then asked if John the Baptist had been sent from God.

- The religious leaders were dumbfounded. Although they thought John was a false prophet, they knew the crowd believed John was a true prophet from God.

- Concerned the crowd would mob them if they expressed their true feelings, the religious leaders would not answer Jesus' question. Since they chose to remain silent, Jesus refused to answer their question.

Jesus' Parables in the Temple—(Tuesday): (Matthew 21:28–22:14; Mark 12:1–12; Luke 20:9–19)

- Addressing the religious leaders, Jesus told a parable:

  ➤ *"A man with two sons told the older boy, 'Son, go out and work in the vineyard today.' The son answered, 'No, I won't go,' but later he changed his mind and went anyway. Then the father told the other son, 'You go,' and he said, 'Yes, sir, I will.' But he didn't go"* (Matthew 21:28–30).

- Jesus then asked the religious leaders which one of the sons obeyed His father. They quickly responded saying the first son obeyed his father and the second one did not.

- Alluding to the message of His parable, Jesus said tax collectors and prostitutes would make it to heaven before the religious leaders.

- Jesus explained, *"For John the Baptist came and showed you the right way to live, but you didn't believe him, while tax collectors and prostitutes did. And even when you saw this happening, you refused to believe him and repent of your sins"* (Matthew 21:32).

Note: In this parable about the two sons, Jesus pointed out that some people—like the first son—initially reject God, but later change their minds and choose to obey Him. Other people—like the second son—claim to belong to God, but refuse to obey Him. The Pharisees and other religious leaders were like the second son. They professed allegiance to God, but rejected God's messengers.

- In another parable, Jesus said to the religious leaders:

  ➤ A landowner planted a vineyard and then left it in the care of tenant farmers. The landowner later sent a few of his servants to harvest the grapes. When the servants arrived, the tenant farmers killed them. Hearing this news, the landowner sent a much larger contingency of servants to his vineyard, but they were also killed. Finally, the landowner sent his son. He thought the farmers would certainly respect his son. But, the farmers murdered the landowner's son as well.

- After telling this parable, Jesus asked the religious leaders what they thought the landowner would do to the farmers who killed his son.

- When the religious leaders did not answer, Jesus said, *"I tell you, the Kingdom of God will be taken away from you and given to a nation that will produce the proper fruit"* (Matthew 21:43).

- Realizing they had been portrayed as the tenant farmers in Jesus' parable, the religious leaders wanted to kill Him right there on the spot. They did not because many people in the crowd believed Jesus was a great prophet.

  Note: In the parable about the tenant farmers, God is the landowner who planted the vineyard. The tenant farmers represent those who say they are doing God's work, but refuse to act in accordance to God's will. God sent His prophets—the servants in Jesus' parable—time and time again. The true prophets of God were often threatened, abused, and many lost their lives. God finally sent His Son, Jesus. He, too, was rejected and killed.

Religious Leaders Question Jesus—(Tuesday): (Matthew 22:15–46; Mark 12:13–37; Luke 20:20–44)

- When Jesus finished His parables, the religious leaders walked away to gather their thoughts. They devised a plan to trap Jesus into saying something against the Roman government so that they could have Him arrested.

- After rehearsing their plan, the Pharisees sent a group of their students and some of Herod's supporters to Jesus with a trick question. They asked Him if it is right for Jews to pay taxes to Caesar.

- Seeing through their deception, Jesus asked whose picture was stamped on the coin. They answered saying Caesar's face appeared on Roman coins. Jesus then said, *"Give to Caesar what belongs to Caesar, and give to God what belongs to God"* (Luke 20:25).

- After Jesus silenced the Pharisees, a group of Sadducees—a religious sect who did not believe in life after death—tried to trap Jesus with a question.

- The Sadducees posed a question about marriage in heaven. They painted a scenario in which a woman was married to a man who died before they had children. In accordance with Jewish law, the deceased man's brother married the woman, but also died before having children. This pattern continued until the woman had married all six of her first husband's brothers.

- The Sadducees concluded their story saying the woman finally died. They then asked Jesus which brother would be married to the woman in the afterlife.

- Jesus answered saying, *"Marriage is for people here on earth . . . those worthy of being raised from the dead will neither marry nor be given in marriage . . . In this respect they will be like angels"* (Luke 20:34–36).

- Addressing the issue of life after death, Jesus said, *"But now, as to whether the dead will be raised—even Moses proved this. Long after Abraham, Isaac, and Jacob had died, he referred to the Lord as 'the God of Abraham, the God of Isaac, and the God of Jacob.' So he is the God of the living, not the dead, for they are all alive to him"* (Luke 20:37–38).

- When the Pharisees realized Jesus had outsmarted the Sadducees, they quickly huddled to come up with another question. One of the Pharisees finally asked Jesus which of the commandments was the most important of the law of Moses.

- Jesus answered saying, *"You must love the LORD your God with all your heart, all your soul, and all your mind. This is the first and greatest commandment. A second is equally important: 'Love your neighbor as yourself.' The entire law and all the demands of the prophets are based on these two commandments"* (Matthew 22:37–40).

Jesus Condemns the Pharisees—(Tuesday): (Matthew 23:1–39; Mark 12:38–44; Luke 20:45–21:4)

- Turning to the crowd and His disciples, Jesus said, *"Beware of these teachers of religious law! For they like to parade around in flowing robes and love to receive respectful greetings as they walk in the marketplaces. And how they love the seats of honor in the synagogues and the head table at banquets. Yet they shamelessly cheat widows out of their property and then pretend to be pious by making long prayers in public. Because of this, they will be severely punished"* (Luke 20:46–47).

- Jesus called the Pharisees hypocrites, blind guides, and fools. He chastised them for making people follow their man-made rules and traditions instead of God's Word.

- Jesus said the Pharisees pretended to be righteous—but in essence—they were thieves, robbing the people of their money and the true knowledge of God.

- As Jesus blasted the Pharisees and religious teachers, He repeatedly shouted out, *"Woe to you, scribes and Pharisees, hypocrites!"* (Matthew 23:13–16, 23, 25, 27, 29 NKJ).

 Note: Jesus' speech about the corruption that existed among the Pharisees is often referred to as the "seven woes." (See Matthew 23:1–30.) This is because Jesus' warnings are translated as seven "woes" in the King James Version of the Bible. Jesus systematically pronounced God's judgment against seven sins commonly practiced by the Pharisees and other religious leaders. The seven sins that Jesus condemned were: keeping people in the dark with false teachings; leading people away from God; making people follow their rules instead of God's Word; seeking prestige; ignoring justice and mercy; pretending to be righteous; and covering up their secret sins.

- After speaking out against the Pharisees, Jesus walked over to the collection box in the Temple and sat down. As people passed by with donations, Jesus noticed a poor widow who dropped two pennies into the box.

- Calling His disciples together, Jesus praised the widow saying, *"I tell you the truth, this poor widow has given more than all the others who are making contributions. For they gave a tiny part of their surplus, but she, poor as she is, has given everything she had to live on"* (Mark 12:43–44).

Jesus Tells About Future Events—(Tuesday): (Matthew 24:1–51; Mark 13:1–37; Luke 21:5–38)

- Afterward, Jesus and His disciples left the Temple and headed for the Mount of Olives. When they reached the Mount of Olives, the disciples asked Jesus about the future and how they would know His prophecies were about to be fulfilled.

- Jesus admonished the disciples to keep their eyes open for false messiahs and prophets who would try to mislead them.

- Jesus then described the end of time saying, *"In those days, right after that time of suffering, 'The sun will become dark, and the moon will no longer shine. The stars will fall, and the powers in the sky will be shaken.' Then the Son of Man will be seen coming in the clouds with great power and glory. He will send his angels to gather his chosen ones from all over the earth"* (Mark 13:24–27 CEV).

- Jesus assured the disciples that everything He had described would take place.

 Note: Jesus' prophecy about the end of time is the same as the prophet Joel's description of "The Day of the Lord." (See Joel 2:10–11; 30–32; 3:14–16.)

Jesus' Parables About the Kingdom of Heaven—(Tuesday): (Matthew 25:1–46)

- Jesus then told His disciples a parable as a reminder that believers should always be prepared for His second coming:

> ➤ Ten bridesmaids sat waiting for the bridegroom. As they waited with their oil lamps for the celebration, five of the bridesmaids ran out of oil. While these five were out buying oil for their lamps, the bridegroom arrived. The five bridesmaids, who came prepared with enough oil, entered the banquet hall with the bridegroom. When the other five bridesmaids finally returned with the oil they had purchased, they were not allowed into the banquet hall.

Judas' Decision To Betray Jesus—(Tuesday or Wednesday): (Matthew 26:1–16; Mark 14:1–11; Luke 22:1–6)

- In the meantime, Caiaphas, the high priest, held a secret meeting with the religious leaders. They discussed various ways to bring charges against Jesus.

The Pharisees and other religious leaders refused to believe Jesus was the Messiah. Although they were well-versed in Old Testament Scripture, they failed to see Messianic prophecy unfolding before their very eyes. The religious leaders rejected God's most important gift to humanity.

The prophet Isaiah wrote about the people's rejection of the Messiah saying, "*Who has believed our message? To whom has the LORD revealed his powerful arm? My servant grew up in the LORD's presence like a tender green shoot, like a root in dry ground. There was nothing beautiful or majestic about his appearance, nothing to attract us to him. He was despised and rejected— a man of sorrows, acquainted with deepest grief. We turned our backs on him and looked the other way. He was despised, and we did not care*" (Isaiah 53:1–3).

- After hearing about the religious leaders' secret meeting, Judas Iscariot went to the priests and agreed to betray Jesus.

- The religious leaders were excited that one of Jesus' disciples would participate in a plot to capture Him. They promised to give Judas a handsome reward as soon as Jesus was arrested.

- After the meeting, Judas began looking for an opportunity to betray Jesus. He thought it best to corner Jesus at a time when He was not surrounded by a large crowd of people.

RECOMMENDED BIBLE READING

Mark 13:1–37 **Jesus Tells About Future Events**

Joel 2:1–11 **The Day of the Lord**

SECTION 3: JESUS' FAREWELL

Jesus Washes His Disciples' Feet—(Thursday Evening): (Matthew 26:17–19; Mark 14:12–16; Luke 22:7–13; John 13:1–20)

- In preparation for Passover, Jesus instructed two of His disciples to find a certain man in Jerusalem and tell him his upstairs room was needed for the Lord.

- As the two disciples entered the city, they found the man and made arrangements to prepare the Passover meal in his upstairs room.

- Later that evening, Jesus and all twelve of His disciples entered the room and sat down. Jesus then took off His robe and began washing the disciples' feet.

- When Jesus approached Peter, he did not want Jesus to wash his feet, thinking it was too lowly a job for Jesus to perform. Jesus said to Peter, *"Unless I wash you, you won't belong to me"* (John 13:8b). When Peter heard this, he wanted Jesus to wash his hands and head as well as his feet.

- Jesus told Peter and the other disciples that they were missing His point. He said to them, *"And since I, your Lord and Teacher, have washed your feet, you ought to wash each other's feet. I have given you an example to follow. Do as I have done to you"* (John 13:14–15).

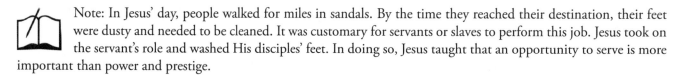 Note: In Jesus' day, people walked for miles in sandals. By the time they reached their destination, their feet were dusty and needed to be cleaned. It was customary for servants or slaves to perform this job. Jesus took on the servant's role and washed His disciples' feet. In doing so, Jesus taught that an opportunity to serve is more important than power and prestige.

Jesus Institutes the Lord's Supper—(Thursday Evening): (Matthew 26:20–30; Mark 14:17–26; Luke 22:14–30; John 13:21–30)

- Jesus then sat down at the table with His disciples. Holding the bread in His hands, Jesus thanked God for it. After breaking the bread into pieces, Jesus gave each of His disciples a piece and said, *"This is my body, which is given for you. Do this to remember me"* (Luke 22:19b).

- Jesus then held up a cup of wine and said, *"This cup is the new covenant between God and his people—an agreement confirmed with my blood, which is poured out as a sacrifice for you"* (Luke 22:20).

Note: "Covenant" is the term used to describe the various promises and agreements God entered into with mankind. Under the old covenant, Israel was in right standing with God if they obeyed His laws. The old covenant was sealed with animals' blood. Jesus established a new covenant and sealed it with His blood. In the new covenant, we are made righteous through faith in Jesus Christ. Jesus told His disciples to remember Him and the sacrifice He made for the remission of our sins. Today, Christ-followers remember Jesus' sacrifice in an observance called the Lord's Supper (also known as "The Last Supper," "Communion," and "Eucharist.")

- Visibly disturbed and deeply troubled, Jesus announced that one of His disciples would betray Him.

- The disciples were in shock. They had no idea to whom Jesus referred. One of the disciples leaned over and asked Jesus which of them would betray Him.

- Jesus answered saying, *"I will dip this piece of bread in the sauce and give it to the one I was talking about"* (John 13:26 CEV).

- Jesus then dipped His bread in the sauce and handed it to Judas Iscariot. Judas ate the bread and then left.

- Although Jesus knew why Judas left the room, the disciples had no idea what was going on. Since Judas was the treasurer, some thought He left to pay for the food or donate some money to the poor.

- Turning His attention to the eleven disciples, Jesus said, *"The time has come for the Son of Man to enter into his glory, and God will be glorified because of him . . . So now I am giving you a new commandment: Love each other. Just as I have loved you, you should love each other. Your love for one another will prove to the world that you are my disciples"* (John 13:31, 34–35).

- After the meal, the disciples started talking about the Kingdom of God. Before long, the discussion turned into another argument about which of them would be the greatest in God's Kingdom.

- Jesus interjected, *"In this world the kings and great men lord it over their people. . . . But among you it will be different. Those who are the greatest among you should take the lowest rank, and the leader should be like a servant. . . . For I am among you as one who serves"* (Luke 22:25–27).

Jesus Predicts Peter's Denial—(Thursday Evening) (Luke 22:31–38; John 13:31–38)

- Jesus knew His disciples would soon abandon Him. Turning to Peter, Jesus said, *"Simon, Simon, Satan has asked to sift each of you like wheat. But I have pleaded in prayer for you, Simon, that your faith should not fail. So when you have repented and turned to me again, strengthen your brothers"* (Luke 22:31–32).

- Peter insisted that he was ready to die for Jesus. In a prediction, Jesus said, *"Peter, I tell you that before a rooster crows tomorrow morning, you will say three times that you don't know me"* (Luke 22:34 CEV).

Jesus Comforts the Disciples—(Thursday Evening): (John 14:1–31)

- Although Jesus was in deep anguish, He tried to comfort His disciples, telling them He was leaving to prepare a place for them.

- Jesus then said, *"I am the way, the truth, and the life. No one can come to the Father except through me"* (John 14:6).

 As the Way, Truth, and Life, Jesus is our Guide to God the Father. He is the embodiment of God's character—His righteousness, justice, love, mercy, and grace. Jesus accompanies us through life, showing us the way to Truth and more abundant life. We can depend on Jesus to guide us successfully through life's difficult challenges.

- Confused about Jesus' relationship with God the Father, Philip asked Jesus to show them the Father. Jesus answered, *"Philip, I have been with you for a long time. Don't you know who I am? If you have seen me, you have seen the Father"* (John 14:9 CEV).

 Note: Jesus explained that He and God the Father are One. Jesus is God made human and is a mirror image of God the Father. (See John 1:1–3, 14; Colossians 1:9; Hebrews 1:3.) Jesus is the complete revelation of God's character and expresses God's will for all mankind.

- Jesus then said, *"I will ask the Father, and he will give you another Advocate, who will never leave you. He is the Holy Spirit, who leads into all truth. . . . When the Father sends the Advocate as my representative—that is, the Holy Spirit—he will teach you everything and will remind you of everything I have told you. I am leaving you with a gift—peace of mind and heart"* (John 14:16–17, 26–27).

Note: The Holy Spirit lives inside of every believer. He is a Counselor, Guide, Instructor, Comforter, Helper, Advocate, Teacher, and Friend. The Holy Spirit is the One who helps us recognize sin and points us toward the righteousness of God (John 14:16–17; 16:7–8).

Jesus' Farewell Message to His Disciples—(Thursday Evening): (John 15:1–17:26)

- Jesus encouraged the disciples to stay grounded in their faith and to stay focused on God. He told them to continue the good work He began.

- Jesus said, *"I am the true grapevine, and my Father is the gardener . . . Yes, I am the vine; you are the branches. Those who remain in me, and I in them, will produce much fruit. For apart from me you can do nothing"* (John 15:1, 5, 8).

 As the True Vine, Jesus is our Nurturer. God is the Gardener, the One who owns and oversees the garden. Jesus is the True Vine, the One who nourishes the branches, strengthening and helping them grow. The branches are the disciples, who are to produce fruit for the Gardener. The branches cannot bear fruit if they are separated from the vine. As disciples, we must stay connected to Jesus if we are to be productive members of God's Kingdom.

- Jesus wanted to share as much as possible with His disciples. He explained that they would be hated and persecuted saying, *"They will treat you this way because of my name, for they do not know the One who sent me . . . He who hates me hates my Father as well . . . But this is to fulfill what is written in their Law: 'They hated me without reason'"* (John 15:21, 23, 25 NIV).

- When Jesus shared that He would soon leave to join God the Father in heaven, the disciples were visibly saddened.

- Offering words of encouragement, Jesus said, *"But in fact, it is best for you that I go away, because if I don't, the Advocate (the Holy Spirit) won't come. If I do go away, then I will send him to you. And when he comes, he will convict the world of its sin, and of God's righteousness, and of the coming judgment. . . . When the Spirit of truth comes, he will guide you into all truth"* (John 16:7–8, 13).

- As Jesus finished His farewell speech, He prayed for Himself, the disciples, and all future believers.

 Note: After eating the Passover meal with His disciples, Jesus delivered a passionate farewell message. This message is documented in John 14:1–17:26 and is well worth reading.

Jesus Predicts the Disciples Would Desert Him—(Thursday Evening): (Matthew 26:31–35; Mark 14:27–31)

- After a closing prayer, Jesus and His disciples headed for the Mount of Olives.

- As they were walking, Jesus said to His disciples, *"All of you will desert me. For the Scriptures say, 'God will strike the Shepherd, and the sheep will be scattered'"* (Mark 14:27).

 The prophet Zechariah wrote, *"'Awake, O sword, against my shepherd, against the man who is close to me!' declares the LORD Almighty. 'Strike the shepherd, and the sheep will be scattered'"* (Zechariah 13:7 NIV). Quoting this scripture, Jesus predicted His disciples would lose courage and desert Him. After Jesus' arrest, John was the only one of Jesus' disciples who stayed and witnessed His crucifixion. All the other disciples fled, fulfilling Zechariah's prophecy.

Jesus Prays in the Garden of Gethsemane—(Late Thursday Evening): (Matthew 26:36–46; Mark 14:32–42; Luke 22:39–46)

- When Jesus and His disciples finally reached the Mount of Olives, they stopped in a garden grove called Gethsemane.

- Jesus told the disciples to stay there while He went off to pray. He asked Peter, James, and John to join Him in prayer.

- In great distress, Jesus cried out, *"Father, if it is possible, don't let this happen to me! Father, you can do anything. Don't make me suffer by having me drink from this cup. But do what you want, and not what I want"* (Mark 14:35–36 CEV).

- As Jesus was praying, Peter, James, and John fell asleep. An angel came and stood by Jesus to strengthen Him in His hour of grief.

- After awhile, Jesus woke the three disciples and said, *"Couldn't you watch with me even one hour? Keep watch and pray, so that you will not give in to temptation. For the spirit is willing, but the body is weak"* (Mark 14:37–38).

- Jesus then walked away and prayed again, more fervently and in great agony.

- After praying a while longer, Jesus walked over to the disciples and saw they had fallen asleep again. They were exhausted from the days' events and could not keep their eyes open. Jesus went back and prayed for a third time.

- When Jesus finished praying, He returned to find the disciples still sleep. He woke them saying, *"The time has come for the Son of Man to be handed over to sinners. Get up! Let's go. The one who will betray me is already here"* (Mark 14:41c–42 CEV).

- Judas suddenly appeared accompanied by a large number of Roman soldiers and Temple guards.

RECOMMENDED BIBLE READING

John 17:1–26 **Jesus' Prayers in the Upstairs Room**

1 Kings 8:22–30 **King Solomon's Prayer**

SECTION 4: JESUS' ARREST AND TRIAL

Jesus Is Betrayed and Arrested—(11:00 P.M.–1:00 A.M., Thursday Evening/Friday Morning): (Matthew 26:47–56; Mark 14:43–52; Luke 22:47–53; John 18:1–11)

- Judas led the soldiers directly to Jesus and then greeted Him with a kiss. Jesus said to him, *"Judas, would you betray the Son of Man with a kiss?"* (Luke 22:48).

- Turning to the soldiers, Jesus asked who they were looking for. The soldiers answered, saying they were looking for Jesus of Nazareth.

- As soon as Jesus identified Himself, the soldiers surrounded Him. Jesus did not resist. Instead, He asked the soldiers to take Him and let His disciples go.

- When the disciples realized what was happening, they rushed to Jesus' side. They asked Jesus if they should put up a fight. Peter grabbed a sword and cut off the right ear of a servant to the high priest.

- Jesus told Peter to put his sword away. Turning His attention to the servant of the high priest, Jesus touched the man's ear and miraculously healed it.

- Jesus then said to His disciples, *"Don't you realize that I could ask my Father for thousands of angels to protect us, and he would send them instantly? But if I did, how would the Scriptures be fulfilled that describe what must happen now?"* (Matthew 26:52c–54).

- The Roman soldiers and Temple guards arrested Jesus without a struggle. When this happened, the disciples ran away, fulfilling Jesus' prediction and Zechariah's prophecy—*"Strike the shepherd, and the sheep will be scattered."*

 The prophet Isaiah described the Messiah as a man condemned without cause. He wrote, *"Unjustly condemned, he was led away. No one cared that he died without descendants, that his life was cut short in midstream. But he was struck down for the rebellion of my people. He had done no wrong and had never deceived anyone"* (Isaiah 53:8–9a).

Annas Interrogates Jesus—(1:00 A.M.–6:00 A.M., Friday Morning): (John 18:12–24)

- After Jesus' arrest, the soldiers took Him to the residence of the high priest. Annas was the first to interrogate Jesus. He had been high priest before Caiaphas, the current high priest, was appointed to the position. Annas was Caiaphas' father-in-law.

- Peter and another disciple (most likely John) followed Jesus from a safe distance behind. After they arrived at the high priest's living quarters, a young woman saw Peter and asked if he was one of Jesus' disciples. Peter quickly said, "no."

- Inside the house, Annas was busy interrogating Jesus. When Annas asked Jesus what kind of message He had been teaching, Jesus answered, *"I have not spoken in secret. Why are you asking me this question? Ask those who heard me. They know what I said"* (John 18:20c–21).

- As soon as Jesus said this, one of the guards slapped Him and said His remark was disrespectful. Frustrated, Annas ordered the guards to take Jesus to Caiaphas, the high priest, for further interrogation.

Caiaphas Interrogates Jesus—(1:00 A.M.–6:00 A.M., Friday Morning): (Matthew 26:57–68; Mark 14:53–65)

- Caiaphas had already assembled members of the Sanhedrin—the Jewish high court—when the soldiers arrived with Jesus. He had also rounded up several people who had agreed to testify against Jesus.

- Caiaphas frantically tried to gather evidence against Jesus, but his so-called witnesses' stories were conflicting. Frustrated, Caiaphas finally asked Jesus directly if He was the Messiah, the Son of the Living God.

- Jesus replied, *"I AM. And you will see the Son of Man seated in the place of power at God's right hand and coming on the clouds of heaven"* (Mark 14:62).

- When Caiaphas heard Jesus' reply, he ripped his clothing in horror and declared Jesus guilty of blasphemy. Other members of the Sanhedrin agreed and said He must die.

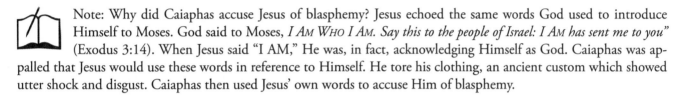

Note: Why did Caiaphas accuse Jesus of blasphemy? Jesus echoed the same words God used to introduce Himself to Moses. God said to Moses, *I AM WHO I AM. Say this to the people of Israel: I AM has sent me to you"* (Exodus 3:14). When Jesus said "I AM," He was, in fact, acknowledging Himself as God. Caiaphas was appalled that Jesus would use these words in reference to Himself. He tore his clothing, an ancient custom which showed utter shock and disgust. Caiaphas then used Jesus' own words to accuse Him of blasphemy.

Peter's Denial of Jesus—(1:00 A.M.–6:00 A.M., Friday Morning): (Matthew 26:69–75; Mark 14:66–72; Luke 22:54–65; John 18:25–27)

- Meanwhile, Peter was standing outside, trying to stay warm. When some people noticed Peter and said he was one of Jesus' disciples, he denied it.

- After hearing Peter's Galilean accent, one of the men confronted Peter, insisting he had to be one of Jesus' disciples because he was from Galilee.

- For the third time that night, Peter denied knowing Jesus. At that moment, a rooster began to crow.

- When Peter heard the rooster, he looked up in time to see the guards taking Jesus away. Peter immediately realized Jesus' words had come true. Walking away in utter shame, Peter cried bitter tears of deep sorrow.

Judas' Remorse—(Very Early Friday Morning): (Matthew 27:1–10)

- When Judas realized the religious leaders were planning to kill Jesus, he was full of remorse. He went to the Temple and told the priests Jesus was innocent.

- Judas tried to return the thirty pieces of silver he had received for betraying Jesus, but the priests refused to accept the money.

- When Judas realized there was nothing he could do or say to change their minds, he threw the coins on the floor and ran out of the Temple. Judas found a tree in a secluded area and hung himself.

- Meanwhile, the priests were trying to determine what they should do with the money. Their laws prohibited them from accepting money paid for murder.

- After discussing the situation, the priests decided to purchase a field owned by a potter and convert it into a cemetery for those unable to afford a proper burial.

With remarkable accuracy, the prophet Zechariah described what happened to the money paid for Jesus' betrayal. He wrote, *"'If you like, give me my wages, whatever I am worth; but only if you want to.' So they counted out for my wages thirty pieces of silver. And the LORD said to me, 'Throw it to the potter'—this magnificent sum at which they valued me! So I took the thirty coins and threw them to the potter in the Temple of the LORD"* (Zechariah 11:12–13).

Judas was paid thirty pieces of silver—a day's wages—for betraying Jesus. Judas threw the coins on the floor inside the Temple; and the priests picked up the coins and used them to pay a potter for his field.

Jesus' Trial Before Pilate—(6:00 A.M.–9:00 A.M., Friday Morning): (Matthew 27:11–14; Mark 15:2–5; Luke 23:1–5; John 18:28–38)

- Since the Sanhedrin council did not have the authority to issue a death sentence, they met to discuss plans for convincing Pilate to order Jesus' death. Very early Friday morning, the council was ready to present its case.

- As the soldiers led Jesus to Pilate's quarters, His accusers followed close behind. Along the way, the soldiers mocked Jesus and punched Him with their fists.

- When Jesus' accusers reached Pilate's quarters, they asked to meet with him outside. They did not want to go inside and become unclean, for it would have prevented them from participating in upcoming religious services.

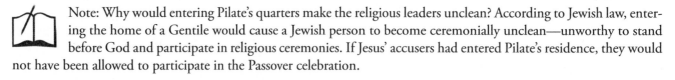 Note: Why would entering Pilate's quarters make the religious leaders unclean? According to Jewish law, entering the home of a Gentile would cause a Jewish person to become ceremonially unclean—unworthy to stand before God and participate in religious ceremonies. If Jesus' accusers had entered Pilate's residence, they would not have been allowed to participate in the Passover celebration.

- When Pilate came outside, He asked about the charges against Jesus. Jesus' accusers exclaimed, *"This man has been leading our people astray by telling them not to pay their taxes to the Roman government and by claiming he is the Messiah, a king"* (Luke 23:2).

- Turning to Jesus, Pilate asked, *"Are You the King of the Jews?"* Jesus simply answered, *"It is as you say"* (Luke 23:3 NASB). After hearing the accusations, Pilate said Jesus had not done anything wrong.

- Frantic, Jesus' accusers quickly huddled to come up with new allegations. Desperate for a conviction, they said Jesus' teachings had caused major disturbances throughout Galilee and Judea.

- When Jesus' accusers mentioned Galilee, Pilate asked if Jesus was a Galilean. They answered "yes." Pilate then ordered the guards to take Jesus to Herod Antipas. Herod had jurisdiction over Galilee and happened to be in Jerusalem for the Passover celebration.

Jesus' Trial Before Herod—(6:00 A.M.–9:00 A.M., Friday Morning): (Luke 23:6–12)

- Having heard about Jesus' miracles, Herod was excited to see Jesus. He was looking forward to watching Jesus perform a few miracles.

- Herod asked Jesus a series of questions, but Jesus did not answer. Herod and his soldiers then prodded and mocked Jesus, but He remained silent.

The prophet Isaiah described the Messiah as a silent lamb being led to the slaughter. Isaiah wrote, *"He was oppressed and treated harshly, yet he never said a word. He was led like a lamb to the slaughter. And as a sheep is silent before the shearers, he did not open his mouth"* (Isaiah 53:7). Jesus willingly gave up His life as a sacrifice for the sins of humanity. Jesus' silence was not an admission of guilt, but rather the humble submission to God's will.

- Herod soon became disinterested and ordered the guards to take Jesus back to Pilate.

Pilate Orders Jesus' Crucifixion—(6:00 A.M.–9:00 A.M., Friday Morning): (Matthew 27:15–31; Mark 15:6–20; Luke 23:13–25; John 18:39–19:16)

- After the guards returned with Jesus, Pilate informed Jesus' accusers that neither he nor Herod found the charges against Jesus serious enough for the death penalty.

- When Jesus' accusers heard Pilate's verdict, they incited the crowd to ask for Jesus' death. The people began shouting, "Crucify Him!"

Note: Jesus' trial was illegal according to both Jewish and Roman law for several reasons: 1.) The testimonies against Jesus were conflicting and unsubstantiated; 2.) He did not have access to legal counsel during the proceedings; 3.) Jesus was not allowed a defense; 4.) The trial was conducted very late at night in a special session of the Sanhedrin council; and 5.) Pilate himself said the charges against Jesus were insufficient for a death sentence.

- Pilate could not understand why Jesus' own people were so vehemently against Him. He turned to Jesus and asked what He had done.

- Jesus answered, *"My Kingdom is not an earthly kingdom"* (John 18:36). Hearing this, Pilate asked Jesus if He were a king.

- Jesus responded, *"You say I am a king. Actually, I was born and came into the world to testify to the truth. All who love the truth recognize that what I say is true"* (John 18:37).

- When Jesus said His mission was to bring the world God's Truth, Pilate sarcastically asked, *"What is truth?"* (John 18:38a).

- Turning to the crowd, Pilate again shouted out that Jesus was an innocent man. Pilate then received a note from his wife, which stated, *"Leave that innocent man alone. I suffered through a terrible nightmare about him last night"* (Matthew 27:19b).

- Addressing the crowd, Pilate reminded the Jews of their tradition to ask for one prisoner to be released during Passover. In keeping with this tradition, Pilate said he would have Jesus flogged and then released.

- Jesus' accusers were outraged. They stirred up the crowd, telling them to ask for Barabbas instead of Jesus.

Note: Who was Barabbas? He was a terrorist who had been arrested for leading an uprising against the Roman government. Barabbas advocated change through civil disorder and violence, while Jesus taught a message of peace. Barabbas had committed a criminal offense against the Roman government, while Pilate himself said Jesus was an innocent man.

- Pilate ordered Jesus' flogging. In mock fashion, the soldiers dressed Jesus in king's clothing and then hailed Him as King. In torturous humiliation, they beat, spit, kicked, and yelled obscenities.

Note: What is a flogging? In New Testament times, a flogging was a severe beating while in chains or shackles. Victims were whipped with a leather strap or metal spiked ball attached to an iron chain.

- After the flogging, Pilate brought Jesus back in front of the crowd so they could see He had been severely beaten. When the emotionally charged crowd saw Him, they cried out, "Crucify Him and release Barabbas!"

- Pilate announced that Jesus had been flogged and would now be released. Jesus' accusers protested saying, *"If you release this man, you are not a friend of Caesar"* (John 19:12b). They insisted Jesus was guilty because He called Himself a king and said Caesar was their only king.

- As the crowd grew louder, Pilate realized Jesus had been set up, but did not want such a minor situation to grow into an uncontrollable riot. He finally gave in to the people's demands.

 Note: As the Roman governor, Pilate's job was to maintain peace. According to the gospel writers, Pilate realized Jesus' accusers arrested Him out of envy. (See Matthew 27:18; Mark 15:10.) However, the situation was getting out of hand and Pilate did not want to lose control. A major uprising would have jeopardized his position or quite possibly his life.

- Pilate ordered his servants to bring him a bowl of water. In a symbolic gesture, Pilate washed his hands and said, *"I am innocent of this man's blood. The responsibility is yours!"* (Matthew 27:24b). Pilate then let Barabbas go free and ordered his soldiers to crucify Jesus.

 Note: In some manuscripts, Barabbas' full name is shown as Jesus Barabbas when it appears in Matthew 27:16–17. Barabbas' name means "son of the father." In an ironic twist, the crowd had a choice between Jesus Barabbas, the 'son of the father' of this world and Jesus of Nazareth, 'the Son of the Father' God, Creator of the Universe. The crowd chose Jesus Barabbas, telling Pilate they wanted Barabbas released and Jesus executed. Barabbas was literally the first person whose life was saved as a result of Jesus' death.

RECOMMENDED BIBLE READING

Matthew 27:11–31 **Jesus' Trial Before Pilate**

Isaiah 53:1–12 **Isaiah's Messianic Prophecy**

SECTION 5: THE CRUCIFIXION AND RESURRECTION

Jesus Nailed to the Cross—(9:00 A.M.–12:00 Noon, Friday Morning): (Matthew 27:32–44; Mark 15:21–32; Luke 23:26–43; John 19:17–27)

- The soldiers forced Jesus to carry a heavy wooden cross. As Jesus made the difficult journey to a place called the "Skull Hill"—translated *Calvary* in Latin and *Golgotha* in Hebrew—crowds followed close behind.

- Along the way, the soldiers stopped and forced Simon of Cyrene to carry Jesus' cross the rest of the way. Simon was from North Africa and happened to be in town for Passover.

- When the soldiers arrived at Skull Hill, they offered Jesus wine mixed with bitter gall—a pain-reducing drug—but He refused to drink it.

- Two criminals convicted of robbery were also being crucified that day. The criminals and Jesus were each nailed to a cross.

- Before lifting Jesus' cross in the air, the soldiers nailed a sign above His head. The sign read: *"Jesus of Nazareth, the King of the Jews"* (John 19:19). It was written in Hebrew, Latin, and Greek so that everyone could read it.

 Note: The official reason Pilate used for Jesus' execution was written on the sign above His head—Jesus of Nazareth claimed to be a king. Jesus claimed a position, which belonged to Caesar alone. On the other hand, the Jews called for Jesus' crucifixion because He claimed a title belonging only to God.

- At about 9:00 A.M. Friday morning, the soldiers nailed Jesus to a cross and hoisted it in the air. Jesus was in the center and the criminals were on each side.

- A large crowd watched as Jesus and the criminals suffered excruciating pain. In fulfillment of Scripture, the soldiers threw dice to determine which one of them would win Jesus' clothing (See Psalm 22:18).

- The crowd shouted insults and ridiculed Jesus. His accusers said if Jesus were the Son of God, He would come down from the cross.

Note: Why didn't Jesus come down from the cross? Jesus understood God's Plan of Redemption and Salvation for humanity could only be accomplished through His death on the cross. Jesus knew His purpose on earth was to execute God's Plan. If Jesus had come down from the cross, He would not have accomplished His mission—to save humanity from the power of sin. (See Hebrews 12:2.)

- From the cross, Jesus called out to God saying, *"Father, forgive them, for they don't know what they are doing"* (Luke 23:34a).

- One of the criminals turned to Jesus and sarcastically said, *"So you're the Messiah, are you? Prove it by saving yourself—and us, too, while you're at it!"* (Luke 23:39). The other criminal objected, saying the sarcastic remark showed a lack of reverence to God, for they deserved to die, but Jesus had done nothing wrong. He then asked Jesus to remember him in heaven. Jesus responded, *"I assure you, today you will be with me in paradise"* (Luke 23:43).

- Apostle John was standing nearby with Mary, Jesus' mother. Several of Jesus' faithful followers—all women—were also present.

- Looking down from the cross at John, Jesus instructed him to care for His mother. John accepted the responsibility and took care of Mary from that day forward.

Jesus' Death—(12:00 Noon–3:00 P.M., Friday): (Matthew 27:45–56; Mark 15:33–41; Luke 23:44–49; John 19:28–37)

- As the noon hour approached, darkness suddenly swept across the entire sky. There was no sunlight from noon until three o'clock.

- Jesus cried out in agony, *"Eloi, Eloi, lema sabachthani?"* which means *"My God, my God, why have you abandoned me?"* (Mark 15:34).

- Jesus knew the end was near. In fulfillment of Scripture, He said, *"I am thirsty"* (John 19:28). The soldiers soaked a sponge with wine and attached it to a stalk. Then they lifted the sponge next to Jesus' lips (See Psalm 69:21).

- As the soldiers wiped a wine-soaked sponge across Jesus' lips, he tasted it and then said, *"It is finished!"* (John 19:30a).

 Note: What did Jesus mean when He uttered the words, *"It is finished?"* Jesus used the Greek word *teleo*, meaning "paid in full." By His death, Jesus paid the penalty in full for our sins. No other sacrifice would ever be needed again. (See Hebrews 9:12.)

- By three o'clock, the sky was totally dark. In a loud voice, Jesus shouted, *"Father, I entrust my spirit into your hands!"* (Luke 23:46a).

- As Jesus hung His head and died, the curtain in the Temple separating the Holy Place from the Most Holy Place suddenly ripped apart.

Note: The curtain in the Temple was a thick piece of cloth, serving as a room-divider. It separated the Holy Place from the Most Holy Place. Only the High Priest was allowed behind the curtain and into the Most Holy Place. The High Priest entered only once a year on the Day of Atonement to offer a sacrifice for his and the people's sins. The Most Holy Place symbolically reminded the people that they were spiritually separated from God and in need of spiritual restoration. When Jesus died, the curtain ripped apart to symbolically show that access to God had been made possible through Jesus' death. We are no longer separated from God when we accept Jesus as our Lord and Savior. We can boldly enter into God's presence. (See Matthew 27:50–51; Hebrews 9:7–8; 10:19–22.)

- The earth trembled and shook violently, splitting rocks apart and opening tombs in the cemetery.

- Witnessing the earthquake and other supernatural events, the Roman soldiers exclaimed in awe, *"Truly this was God's Son!"* (Matthew 27:54b).

- Jesus and the two criminals were crucified on Friday. The religious leaders were anxious for all three victims to die before sundown, the beginning of the Sabbath.

Note: Why did the Jewish leaders want the victims to die before sundown? According to Jewish law, the religious leaders were prohibited from leaving dead bodies hanging on the cross overnight. However, they could not take them down after sundown because it was the beginning of the Sabbath. Taking the dead bodies down after sundown would be considered work, a violation of the Sabbath laws. (See Deuteronomy 21:22–23; Exodus 31:15; 34:21; Leviticus 23:3.)

- After discussing the situation, the religious leaders went to Pilate and asked him to speed up the deaths, so the bodies could be removed. Pilate agreed and ordered soldiers to break the three victims' legs to hasten their deaths.

- As the soldiers were carrying out their orders, they noticed Jesus was already dead, so they did not break His legs.

- One of the soldiers pierced Jesus' side with his sword as an extra precaution to ensure He was dead. When the soldier did this, Apostle John saw blood mingled with water flow from His side.

 Note: According to experts, the blood mixed with water indicated Jesus' death was the result of a ruptured heart. Based on this explanation, Jesus died from a physically and emotionally broken heart.

 In the Old Testament, the Passover lamb had to be perfect, without defects, and prepared with no bones broken. (See Exodus 12:5, 46; 1 Peter 1:18–19.) Jesus' death pictured Him as our Passover Lamb. He was perfect, without sin, and John's gospel carefully points out that Jesus' bones were not broken. (See John 19:33.) In a prophecy foreshadowing this event, King David wrote, *"For the LORD protects the bones of the righteous; not one of them is broken!"* (Psalm 34:20).

Zechariah prophesied that the Messiah would be pierced for the people's sins. Apostle John witnessed Scripture unfold as the soldiers pierced Jesus in His side. (See Zechariah 12:10; John 19:34.) John explains, *"These things happened in fulfillment of the Scriptures that say, 'Not one of his bones will be broken,' and 'They will look on the one they pierced'"* (John 19:36–37).

Jesus' Tomb—(3:00 P.M. Friday to Saturday morning): (Matthew 27:57–66; Mark 15:42–47; Luke 23:50–56; John 19:38–42)

- After Jesus' death, Joseph, a very wealthy man from Arimathea, asked Pilate's permission for Jesus' body.

- Pilate confirmed Jesus was, in fact, dead and then allowed Joseph and Nicodemus to take Jesus' body. Nicodemus was the same man Jesus had previously talked to about being "born again."

- Although Joseph and Nicodemus were members of the Sanhedrin council, they disagreed with the members who brought charges against Jesus. They believed in Jesus, but had remained silent until His death.

- Joseph and Nicodemus carried Jesus' body to an empty tomb located near Skull Hill. Joseph had previously purchased the tomb for himself. After the crucifixion, he used it to bury Jesus. Several women followed the men to see where they buried Jesus.

- After placing Jesus' body in the tomb, Joseph and Nicodemus rolled a large stone in front of the entrance.

 Old Testament Scripture prophesied about the Messiah's gravesite, *". . . But he was buried like a criminal; he was put in a rich man's grave"* (Isaiah 53:9b).

Scripture tells us that Joseph of Arimathea was a rich man, who had prepared a tomb for his own burial. Since there was not enough time to carve a new tomb for Jesus before the Sabbath, Joseph used the tomb he had prepared for himself to bury Jesus. In doing so, Isaiah's prophecy came to past, *". . . he was put in a rich man's grave."*

- The next day, Jesus' accusers remembered His statement about rising from the dead on the third day. They went to Pilate and asked him to place guards around the tomb so that Jesus' disciples could not steal His body and then claim He had risen from the dead.

- Saturday morning, guards were posted at the entrance of Jesus' tomb.

He is Risen—(Early Sunday morning): (Matthew 28:1–15; Mark 16:1–11; Luke 24:1–12; John 20:1–10)

- Early Sunday morning—before sunrise—Mary Magdalene and the other women went to the tomb to prepare Jesus' body for burial.

- When the women arrived, they were surprised to discover the stone in front of the entrance had been removed.

- Mary Magdalene ran back and told Peter and John, *"They have taken the Lord's body out of the tomb, and we don't know where they have put him!"* (John 20:2b).

- When Peter and John heard this, they jumped up and raced to the tomb. Looking inside, they noticed Jesus' head covering and linen strips were lying on the ground. The linen had been used to wrap Jesus' body. After verifying Mary's story, the two disciples left puzzled.

- Mary Magdalene later returned to the tomb with the other women. To their amazement, an angel was inside. The angel said, *"Don't be alarmed. You are looking for Jesus of Nazareth, who was crucified. He isn't here! He is risen from the dead!"* (Mark 16:6).

- Mary Magdalene stayed near the tomb while the other women ran back to tell the disciples about the angel.

- As Mary stood at the tomb confused and weeping, she noticed a shadowy figure. At first, Mary did not recognize the Person standing in front of her, but soon realized it was Jesus. He told Mary to tell the others He was alive and then left.

- While the other women were running back to find the disciples, they met Jesus along the way. He greeted them and said, *"Don't be afraid! Go tell my brothers to leave for Galilee, and they will see me there"* (Matthew 28:10).

- When the guards at the tomb realized what had happened, they left and told the religious leaders that Jesus was missing from the tomb. Shocked and embarrassed, the religious leaders bribed the guards, instructing them to tell Pilate Jesus' disciples stole His body while they were asleep.

- According to Matthew, *"The guards accepted the bribe and said what they were told to say. Their story spread widely among the Jews, and they still tell it today"* (Matthew 28:15).

Resurrection Appearances (Matthew 28:16–20; Mark 16:12–20; Luke 24:13–53; John 20:11–21:25)

- As two of Jesus' followers were walking to a village near Jerusalem, Jesus joined them and began explaining the Messianic prophecies in the Scriptures. The two men did not recognize Jesus.

- When the men reached their destination, they begged Jesus to come home with them. Jesus followed the men and joined them for a meal.

- As Jesus gave thanks for the bread, the men suddenly realized who He was. At that very moment, Jesus disappeared. The men got up and went into Jerusalem to find the disciples.

- The men found the disciples hiding in a room behind locked doors. While the two men were telling the disciples about their encounter, Jesus suddenly appeared in front of them.

- Jesus showed the disciples the nail wounds in His wrists and the wound in His side. After taking a deep inhale, Jesus gently blew His breath over them and said, *"Receive the Holy Spirit"* (John 20:22).

- Thomas was not in the room when Jesus appeared to the disciples. When the disciples later shared the news with Thomas, he refused to believe saying, *"I won't believe it unless I see the nail wounds in his hands, put my fingers into them, and place my hand into the wound in his side"* (John 20:25b).

- Eight days later, while the disciples were again meeting behind locked doors, Jesus suddenly reappeared. Thomas was present this time.

- Filled with compassion, Jesus walked over to Thomas and said, *"Put your finger here, and look at my hands. Put your hand into the wound in my side. Don't be faithless any longer. Believe!"* (John 20:27). In profound awe, Thomas declared Jesus as his Lord and God.

- The disciples later returned to Galilee. One day, seven of Jesus' disciples decided to go fishing. While fishing in their boats, the disciples spotted a Man standing on the distant shore.

- At first, the disciples did not recognize the Man. When they realized it was Jesus, they raced back to shore.

- Jesus prepared breakfast for the seven disciples. After breakfast, Jesus turned to Simon Peter and asked, *"Simon son of John, do you love me more than these?"* (John 21:15a).

- When Peter answered yes, Jesus told him to feed His sheep. Jesus asked Peter the same question two more times.

- Heartbroken that Jesus would doubt his love, Peter said, *"Lord, you know everything. You know that I love you."* Jesus said for a third time, *"Then feed my sheep"* (John 21:17c).

 Note: Peter had denied Jesus three times. In a demonstration of God's forgiving nature, Jesus did not ignore or withhold His love from Peter. Jesus confronted Peter, asking him three times if he loved Him. Jesus wanted Peter to commit and always remember he was responsible for feeding His sheep—the church of believers.

- Jesus later appeared to His disciples again in Galilee saying, *"I have been given all authority in heaven and on earth. Therefore, go and make disciples of all the nations, baptizing them in the name of the Father and the Son and the Holy Spirit. Teach these new disciples to obey all the commands I have given you. And be sure of this: I am with you always, even to the end of the age"* (Matthew 28:18–20).

 Note: Jesus commissioned His disciples and all future disciples to tell people the Good News. This is called the "Great Commission." Those who believe in Jesus are commanded to go and make disciples.

RECOMMENDED BIBLE READING

Matthew 27:57–28:20 **He is Risen!**

Psalm 16:7–11 **The Holy One Will Not Rot in the Grave**

Psalm 68:16–20 **Our God Saves!**

MEDITATION & PRAYER

Paul tells about Jesus' resurrection appearances:

"For what I received I passed on to you as of first importance: that Christ died for our sins according to the Scriptures, that he was buried, that he was raised on the third day according to the Scriptures, and that he appeared to Peter, and then to the Twelve. After that, he appeared to more than five hundred of the brothers at the same time, most of whom are still living, though some have fallen asleep. Then he appeared to James, then to all the apostles, and last of all he appeared to me also, as to one abnormally born."

(1 Corinthians 15:3–8 NIV)

Dear Heavenly Father,

I thank You so very much for Your Plan of Redemption and Salvation. Thank You for sending Your Son, Jesus Christ, to save the world. I am truly grateful Jesus, who was perfect in every way, never lost sight of His mission. He showed us the way to You by providing an example of how to live a life that pleases You. I thank You for loving us so much that You offered Your Son as a sacrifice to atone for our sins. In a great exchange, Jesus took my sins and washed them away with His blood. I thank You that You did not leave Jesus in the ground, but on the third day raised Him from the dead. I thank You for the host of witnesses who testified about Jesus' resurrection appearances. I thank You for showing us there is no fear in death, for as surely as Jesus rose from the dead, I too will live again!

Amen

Review Questions

1. Jesus pronounced God's judgment against seven sins the Pharisees commonly practiced. What were these seven sins? (See Matthew 23:13–30.)

_____

_____

_____

_____

2. Why were the Jews outraged that Jesus would use the words, "I AM" to describe Himself?

_____

_____

_____

_____

3. When Jesus predicted His death, the people said the Messiah was supposed to live forever. How did they know this?

_____

_____

_____

_____

4. What lesson did Jesus teach when He washed His disciples' feet?

_____

_____

_____

_____

5. When instituting the Lord's Supper, Jesus said *"This cup is the new covenant between God and his people—an agreement confirmed with my blood, which is poured out as a sacrifice for you"* (Luke 22:19). What is a covenant? What was God's old covenant with His people? How was it sealed or confirmed? What was God's new covenant? How was it sealed or confirmed? In what way is the new covenant better than the old covenant?

_____

_____

_____

_____

6. Jesus said, *"I am the Way, the Truth, and the Life."* What did Jesus mean by this?

_____

_____

_____

_____

7. What did the Jews find Jesus guilty of? What was Pilate's official reason for ordering Jesus' crucifixion?

_____

_____

_____

_____

8. Why didn't Jesus come down from the cross?

_____

_____

_____

_____

PERSONAL REFLECTIONS

9. Jesus said, *"I am the True Vine."* What lesson did Jesus want you to learn from this statement? What additional steps can you take to stay connected to Jesus, the True Vine?

_____

_____

_____

_____

_____

11. After Jesus' arrest, Peter denied knowing Jesus three times. What did you learn about human nature from Peter's denial? What did you learn about God?

_____

_____

_____

_____

_____

12. What was the difference between Judas and Peter's response to failure? How do you respond to failure?

_____

_____

_____

_____

_____

13. Review the Messianic prophecies listed in Appendix 7. Which of these prophecies used in this chapter are most meaningful to you? How do these prophecies affect your witness to others about Jesus?

_____

_____

_____

_____

_____

14. What does Jesus' crucifixion mean to you? His resurrection? In a prayer, thank God for what He did for you through Jesus' crucifixion and resurrection.

_____

_____

_____

_____

_____

CLOSING PRAYER

Job's declaration of a Redeemer:

"For I know that my Redeemer lives,
And He shall stand at last on the earth;

And after my skin is destroyed, this I know,
That in my flesh I shall see God,

Whom I shall see for myself,
And my eyes shall behold, and not another.
How my heart yearns within me."

(Job 19:25–27 NKJ)

Dear Lord,

I thank You for Jesus Christ, my Redeemer. He is alive and watching over me. I thank You for revealing Truth to me and giving me an opportunity to live with You forever. I am eternally grateful for Your offer of Redemption and Salvation through Jesus Christ. I am so happy You have a very forgiving nature. When I confess my sins, You blot them out and don't remember them anymore. Because of Jesus, my life has meaning and I have Your guaranteed promise of eternal life. All praise, glory, and honor belong to You forever!

Amen

CHAPTER 5

ESTABLISHING THE CHURCH

OPENING PRAYER

Heavenly Father,

Prepare my mind and heart to receive fresh new insights into Your Word. Speak to my heart as I read about how God used the disciples to establish the church and spread the Good News of redemption and salvation through Jesus Christ. Help me to see that the disciples were just ordinary men with extraordinary faith. Increase my faith, for I want to be ready when You call my name. Guide my steps to a more personal and intimate relationship with You.

Amen

CHAPTER SUMMARY

ESTABLISHING THE CHURCH

(Acts 1–12)

The book of Acts chronicles the history of the early church from 30 A.D. to about 62 A.D. Luke, a physician and companion of Apostle Paul, wrote the gospel of Luke and the book of Acts. Luke wrote his gospel to provide an accurate account of Jesus' life while on earth and to present the Good News of salvation through Jesus Christ. He penned Acts to tell how this Good News was embraced by believers in Jerusalem and then quickly spread to other parts of the world. While the gospel of Luke tells the story of Jesus—His words and actions—Acts records the words and actions of believers as they told the world about the Good News of Jesus Christ.

What is the Good News of Jesus Christ? Mankind was originally created to live in fellowship with God. However, fellowship with the Creator was severed when the first man and woman rebelled and disobeyed God. As a result of their disobedience, everyone is born with this same rebellious attitude. Rebellion against God is called sin. The penalty for sin is separation from God. All of us are born spiritually separated or out of fellowship with God because of sin (Romans 3:10–12; 23). Long ago, God promised through the Old Testament prophets to send a Messiah, a descendant of King David, who would free the world from the penalty of sin (Isaiah 53; Zechariah 3:8–9; 13:1). Jesus of Nazareth, born of a virgin into King David's family, was the promised Messiah. God became a man, in the person of Jesus, and lived on earth for a while, teaching and demonstrating the righteousness of God. After a three-and-a-half year ministry, Jesus exchanged His life for humanity's sins, suffering death by crucifixion. Jesus—the world's Passover Lamb—paid the price for humanity's sins, redeeming us with the shedding of His blood to restore our relationship with God. After three days in the grave, Jesus rose from the dead. Jesus' death and resurrection provided a way for mankind to live in fellowship with God now and throughout eternity (1 Corinthians 15:3–8; Romans 6:3–5). Our relationship with God is restored when we have faith in (believe and trust in) Jesus as our Lord and Savior. (John 3:16; Romans 10:9–10). (See Appendix 9: Accepting God's Free Gift of Redemption and Salvation.)

When the book of Acts opens, Luke explains that the disciples and other witnesses saw the resurrected Jesus from time to time over a period of forty days. During a resurrection appearance, Jesus told the disciples to stay in Jerusalem until God the Father sent the Holy Spirit as promised. Jesus then ascended in a cloud and returned to heaven.

After Jesus' ascension to heaven, the disciples and other devout followers stayed together, praying and waiting for God to send the Holy Spirit. Ten days later, they received the outpouring of the Holy Spirit. It happened fifty days after Passover on the day of Pentecost, a celebration in which Jews thanked God for their harvested crops. After the outpouring of the Holy Spirit, Jesus' disciples, called apostles, were endowed with tremendous power, gifts, and abilities just as Jesus promised. The apostles began boldly proclaiming Jesus as the Messiah, the Son of God. They testified about Jesus' death and resurrection; taught the Good News of redemption and salvation through Jesus Christ; performed numerous miracles; and established the early church of believers in Jerusalem.

When the apostles preached the Good News, some people believed in Jesus while others resented the gospel message. Jewish religious leaders were particularly outraged and tried to prevent the spreading of the Good News. A strict Pharisee named Saul led the movement to persecute believers and end the new religious sect called the Way—a first century name for Christianity. One day, while on his way to arrest believers in Damascus, Saul heard Jesus call out to him saying,

"Saul! Saul! Why are you persecuting me?" (Acts 9:4). After Saul's encounter with Jesus, he became an avid believer, boldly proclaiming the name of Jesus everywhere he went. Saul became the great Apostle Paul and powerfully spread the Good News he had once tried to extinguish.

Peter later had a vision about a sheet being lowered from heaven. The sheet was filled with all kinds of animals that Jews were prohibited from eating according to the law of Moses. Peter heard a voice say, *"Get up, Peter; kill and eat them"* (Acts 10:13). When Peter refused to eat, calling the animals unclean, the voice said, *"Do not call something unclean if God has made it clean"* (Acts 10:15). After this vision, the Holy Spirit helped Peter interpret its meaning. Before the vision, Peter thought the Good News of salvation through Jesus Christ was intended for Jews only. God pointed out through the vision that He is not partial and His offer of salvation is to all people—Jews and Gentiles.

The apostles and other believers were put in jail, beaten, and many suffered martyrdom for their faith. Although believers suffered great persecution, they continued to tell the Good News of Jesus Christ everywhere they went.

Key People in This Chapter

Believers of the Early Church in Jerusalem	The early church in Jerusalem started with 120 believers and then quickly grew each day as the Good News was preached. Believers included: Jesus' eleven disciples, Mary (Jesus' mother), Jesus' half-brothers, and others.	Acts 1:13–15, 26
Peter	An apostle and recognized leader of Jesus' twelve disciples. Although Peter denied knowing Jesus during His arrest and trial, he boldly proclaimed Jesus' name during and after Pentecost. He was instrumental in establishing the early church. He wrote 1st and 2nd Peter.	Acts 1:15–5:42; 8:14–25; 9:32–11:18; 12:1–19
John	An apostle, and along with Peter and James, one of three disciples closest to Jesus. John took care of Jesus' mother, Mary. He preached the Good News and was a founding father of the early church. He wrote the gospel of John; 1st, 2nd, and 3rd John; and Revelation.	Acts 3:1–4:31; Acts 8:14–25
Barnabas	A believer named Joseph, nicknamed Barnabas (which means Son of Encouragement). One of the first to sell property and donate the proceeds to the early church. One of the first to accept Paul as a true believer.	Acts 4:36–37; 9:27; 11:24–30; 12:25
Stephen	One of seven deacons responsible for distributing food to the needy in the early church at Jerusalem. He was stoned to death and became the first believer to die for his faith.	Acts 6:5–8:2
Philip	One of seven deacons responsible for distributing food to the needy in the early church at Jerusalem. He was also instrumental in spreading the gospel to people in Samaria. He preached the Good News to an Ethiopian eunuch.	Acts 6:5; 8:5–40; 21:8–9
Ethiopian Eunuch	Although the Bible does not record his specific contributions, he returned to Ethiopia as a believer and no doubt helped spread the Good News in that region of the world.	Acts 8:26–39
Saul (Paul)	A strict Pharisee and avid persecutor of Christians whom God powerfully transformed into an ambassador for Jesus Christ. After his conversion, Saul boldly proclaimed the Good News. Jesus commissioned Paul as an apostle to the Gentiles. He wrote thirteen New Testament letters.	Acts 7:58–8:3; 9:1–31; 11:25–30; 12:25
Cornelius	A Roman captain who believed in the One True God. He actively sought God. The Lord responded, using Peter to explain the Good News to Cornelius and his entire household. He was one of the first Gentile Christians.	Acts 10:1–11:18
John Mark	Author of the gospel of Mark. His mother's house was a meeting place for believers in Jerusalem.	Acts 12:25

	Approximate Timeline	Location	Biblical Scriptures	Author
The Outpouring of the Holy Spirit	30 A.D.	Jerusalem	Luke 24:50–53	Luke
			Acts 1:1–4:31	Luke
Good News in Jerusalem	30–35 A.D.	Jerusalem	Acts 4:32–7:60	Luke
Good News in Samaria and Judea	35–43 A.D.	Jerusalem, Samaria, Gaza, Azotus, Caesarea, Damascus, Judea	Acts 8:1–9:31; Galatians 1:17–18	Luke Paul
Good News to the Gentiles	43–44 A.D.	Lydda, Joppa, Caesarea, Antioch, Judea	Acts 9:3–11:30	Luke
The Apostles Face Persecution	44 A.D.	Judea	Acts 12:1–25	Luke

MAP OF KEY LOCATIONS

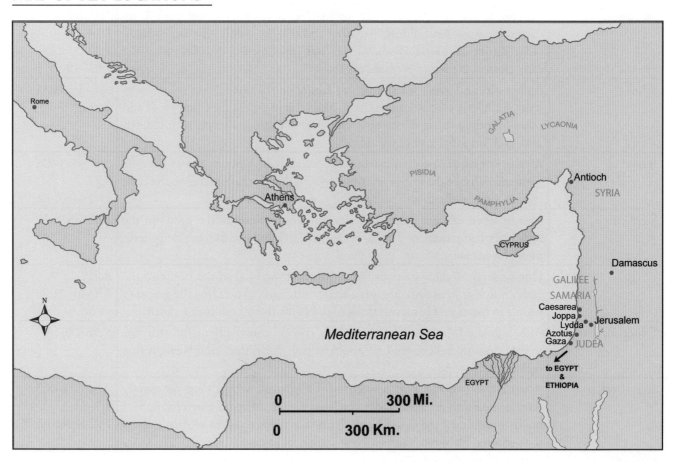

PHILIP BAPTIZES THE ETHIOPIAN EUNUCH

"As they went along the road they came to some water; and the eunuch said, 'Look! Water! What prevents me from being baptized?' And Philip said, 'If you believe with all your heart, you may.' And he answered and said, 'I believe that Jesus Christ is the Son of God.' And he ordered the chariot to stop; and they both went down into the water, Philip as well as the eunuch, and he baptized him." (Acts 8:36–38 NASB)

SECTION 1: THE OUTPOURING OF THE HOLY SPIRIT

Jesus Ascends to Heaven: (Luke 24:50–53; Acts 1:1–12)

- Three days after Jesus died on the cross, He rose from the dead. The disciples and others saw the resurrected Jesus at various times and places over a period of forty days.

- When Jesus appeared to His disciples, He held conversations with them, showed them His nail wounds, and ate meals with them—proving He had risen from the dead and was indeed alive!

 Note: After the resurrection, Jesus made numerous appearances to groups of people. These appearances cannot be easily explained as hallucinations. While one person might have been hallucinating, it is highly unlikely that multiple people would have been at the same location at the same time and experienced the same hallucination. (See John 20:19–29; 21:1–25; Acts 1:4–7.)

- During one of Jesus' resurrection appearances, He told His disciples to stay in Jerusalem and wait for God's gift of the Holy Spirit.

- The disciples were still under the impression that Jesus had come to free the Jews from Roman subjugation. They kept asking Him when He was going to restore Israel and establish His earthly kingdom.

- Jesus answered saying, *"The Father alone has the authority to set those dates and times, and they are not for you to know. But you will receive power when the Holy Spirit comes upon you. And you will be my witnesses, telling people about me everywhere—in Jerusalem, throughout Judea, in Samaria, and to the ends of the earth"* (Acts 1:7–8).

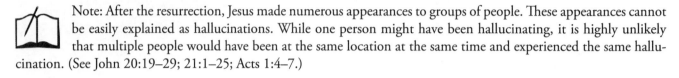 Note: The disciples thought the Kingdom of God would begin when Israel was restored to the glorious days of King David's reign. They did not realize the Kingdom of God was a spiritual rebirth of believers' hearts and a renewal of their minds.

- The disciples followed Jesus to the Mount of Olives near Bethany. Jesus prayed blessings over the disciples and then ascended in the air, disappearing in a cloud.

- As the disciples watched—intently gazing up at the sky—two men in white robes suddenly appeared in their midst.

- The men said, *"Why are you men from Galilee standing here and looking up into the sky? Jesus has been taken to heaven. But he will come back in the same way that you have seen him go"* (Acts 1:11 CEV).

- After witnessing Jesus' ascension, the disciples returned to Jerusalem, a distance of about a half mile.

Peter Addresses the Believers: (Acts 1:13–26)

- When they arrived in Jerusalem, the believers started a prayer vigil in the upstairs room where the disciples had been staying.

- Although Jesus' brothers initially lacked faith in Him, they had become believers. Jesus' brothers and His mother, Mary, were among 120 believers keeping a continuous prayer vigil.

- One day, Peter addressed the believers, saying Judas' betrayal and death were prophesied in Old Testament Scripture. Peter explained, *"This was written in the book of Psalms, where it says, 'Let his home become desolate, with no one living in it.' It also says, 'Let someone else take his position'"* (Acts 1:20).

Note: Peter said Judas' betrayal and death fulfilled Old Testament prophecy. For these prophecies, see Psalms 41:9; 69:25; and 109:8.

- Referring to Scripture, Peter said another disciple was needed to replace Judas as the twelfth apostle.

- Peter pointed out that the person chosen to replace Judas would become an apostle and join them as witnesses of Jesus' resurrection.

- Addressing the qualifications for apostleship, Peter said Judas' replacement must be someone who had been with them through Jesus' entire earthly ministry—from His baptism to His ascension.

- After nominating Joseph and Matthias—two of Jesus' followers—the disciples prayed and then chose Matthias to replace Judas.

The Outpouring of the Holy Spirit: (Acts 2:1–13)

- On the day of Pentecost, the believers were together in the upstairs room as usual, fervently praying with a single purpose in mind—God's promise of the Holy Spirit.

 Note: What was the Pentecost celebration? Pentecost was an annual festival celebrated by the Jews to thank God for their harvested crops. It was also called the Festival of Harvest or Weeks. (See Deuteronomy 16:16.) Jesus was crucified during Passover and the outpouring of the Holy Spirit occurred fifty days later on the day of Pentecost.

- All of a sudden, the believers heard from heaven a roaring sound like gale force winds rushing down from the sky.

- As the sound of a mighty windstorm permeated the room, flames—similar to tongues of fire—suddenly appeared above each of the believers' heads. Everyone in the room was filled with the Holy Spirit and began speaking in other tongues or foreign languages.

- When the people outside heard the commotion, they hurried to see what was going on. A large number of people from various countries were in Jerusalem for Pentecost. To the people's surprise, they heard the believers—many of whom were from Galilee—speaking in languages that were not their native tongue.

- Stunned and confused, some people wanted more details about what had happened, while others scoffed, saying the believers had to be drunk.

Peter Addresses the Crowd: (Acts 2:14–47)

- Peter boldly stepped forward and addressed the crowd saying, *"Listen carefully, all of you, fellow Jews and residents of Jerusalem! Make no mistake about this. These people are not drunk, as some of you are assuming. Nine o'clock in the morning is much too early for that. No, what you see was predicted long ago by the prophet Joel: 'In the last days,' God says, 'I will pour out my Spirit upon all people . . .'"* (Acts 2:14–17).

 After the resurrection, Jesus reminded the disciples about the promise of the Holy Spirit saying, *"And now I will send the Holy Spirit, just as my Father promised. But stay here in the city until the Holy Spirit comes and fills you with power from heaven"* (Luke 24:49).

On the day of Pentecost, God sent the Holy Spirit as promised. The Holy Spirit empowered the believers with boldness and the ability to speak in foreign languages. Peter explained the event as the fulfillment of Scripture. Quoting the prophet Joel, Peter said, *"'In the last days,' God says, 'I will pour out my Spirit upon all people . . .'"* (Acts 2:17). (See Joel 2:28–29 for cross-reference.)

- Peter spoke with eloquence and conviction as he explained the Good News. Peter reminded the people of God's promise to King David in which God said, *"I will establish your descendants as kings forever; they will sit on your throne from now until eternity"* (Psalm 89:4).

- Peter then announced that God's promise to David was fulfilled through Jesus Christ.

- Peter concluded his message saying, *"God raised Jesus from the dead, and we are all witnesses of this. Now he is exalted to the place of highest honor in heaven, at God's right hand. And the Father, as he had promised, gave him the Holy Spirit to pour out upon us, just as you see and hear today"* (Acts 2:32–33).

- When Peter finished, people in the crowd wanted to know what they must do to be saved. Peter answered, saying repent and then be baptized for the forgiveness of sins.

- Peter's message penetrated the hearts of about 3,000 people. They joined the group of 120 believers as fully devoted followers of Jesus Christ. This marked the beginning of the church in Jerusalem.

 Note: Before the outpouring of the Holy Spirit, Peter was an unstable and somewhat impulsive leader, who often spoke without thinking. After the outpouring of the Holy Spirit, Peter was transformed into a steadfast, committed leader of the early church. Empowered by the Holy Spirit, Peter became a dynamic speaker and witness for Jesus Christ.

- In the days that followed, many others accepted Jesus as their personal Savior and joined the church in Jerusalem.

- The believers met together each day for prayer services. They praised God and thanked Him for His goodness. In true fellowship, the believers shared everything they owned with each other out of their love for God and His people.

Note: God's gift of love—redemption and salvation through Jesus Christ—created an atmosphere of brotherly love and goodwill among the believers. The early church considered it a privilege to share their meals and earthly possessions with other believers. They gave willingly and joyously to their fellow brothers and sisters in Christ.

Peter Heals a Lame Beggar: (Acts 3:1–26)

- One day as Peter and John were on their way to the Temple, they saw a beggar lying down in front of one of the entrances. The beggar had been born lame.

- When the lame beggar asked Peter and John for a handout, Peter told the man he did not have any silver or gold, but would give him what he had.

- Looking directly into the beggar's eyes, Peter commanded him to get up and start walking in the name of Jesus Christ.

- As Peter reached down to help the man up, the lame man's ankles and legs suddenly became strong enough for him to stand on his own. The man began walking and then jumping, while praising God for his healing.

- The man created such a spectacle that a large number of people stopped to see what was going on. They were surprised to see the man, whom they knew had been lame from birth, jumping and leaping for joy.

- As the crowd gathered to watch, Peter saw an opportunity to minister to the people and began preaching the Good News of Jesus Christ.

Peter and John Arrested: (Acts 4:1–31)

- When some religious leaders heard Peter's message, they pushed through the crowd and ordered Temple guards to arrest Peter and John.

- Many of the people in the crowd were inspired by Peter's message and accepted Jesus as their Savior.

- The next day, Temple guards brought Peter and John before the Sanhedrin council for questioning. Moved by the Holy Spirit, Peter told the council that the man had been healed by the powerful name of Jesus, whom they crucified.

- Peter then said, *"He is the stone that you builders thought was worthless, and now he is the most important stone of all. Only Jesus has the power to save!"* (Acts 4:11–12a CEV).

> Quoting from Psalms, Peter said, *"The stone that the you builders rejected has now become the cornerstone"* (Acts 4:11). (See Psalm 118:22; Matthew 21:42.)
>
> Jesus was rejected and is now the cornerstone of the church. The cornerstone—the most important stone of a building—joins two sides of a building together. As our spiritual cornerstone, Jesus brings us together with God the Father.

- As members of the council listened, they were amazed that Peter spoke with such boldness and eloquence, for they knew he and John were mere fishermen with no special religious training.

- The council was furious because the apostles were teaching and healing in Jesus' name, but could not deny a miracle had taken place.

- After discussing the situation, the council decided to release Peter and John, but warned them to never speak in Jesus' name again.

- When Peter and John heard the terms of their release, they boldly addressed the council saying, *"Do you think God wants us to obey you rather than him? We cannot stop telling about everything we have seen and heard"* (Acts 4:19–20).

- The council did not know how to respond, for they heard the crowd outside praising God for the man's healing. Fearing the people would rise up against them, they decided to let Peter and John go free.

RECOMMENDED BIBLE READING

Acts 2:14–42 **Peter Explains the Outpouring of the Holy Spirit**

Joel 2:28–32 **God's Promise of the Holy Spirit**

SECTION 2: GOOD NEWS IN JERUSALEM

Believers Share Their Possessions: (Acts 4:32–5:11)

- The believers grew strong in their faith as the apostles preached the Good News and testified about Jesus' resurrection appearances.

- In a spirit of love, the believers generously shared their possessions so that everyone's needs were met. When extra money was needed, believers sold their property and donated the proceeds to the church.

- One such believer was a man named Joseph, who was called Barnabas (which means son of encouragement). Barnabas, a Levite from Cyprus, sold some of his land and gave the money to the apostles for the needy.

- One day, a man named Ananias and his wife, Sapphira, sold some property with plans of donating all the proceeds to the church.

- After talking it over, Ananias and Sapphira decided to cheat and keep some of the proceeds for themselves. When Ananias handed the apostles a portion of their proceeds, the Holy Spirit revealed the deception to Peter.

- Peter chastised Ananias saying, *"Why have you let Satan fill your heart? You lied to the Holy Spirit, and you kept some of the money for yourself. The property was yours to sell or not sell, as you wished. And after selling it, the money was also yours to give away. How could you do a thing like this? You weren't lying to us but to God!"* (Acts 5:3–4).

- After Peter's rebuke, Ananias immediately passed out on the floor and died. The believers were in utter shock. Some young men carried Ananias away and buried him.

- About three hours later, Ananias' wife—unaware of what had transpired—entered the room where the believers were gathered. Peter showed her the money he received from Ananias and asked if it was the price they had received for their land.

- When Sapphira said yes, Peter said to her, *"How could the two of you even think of conspiring to test the Spirit of the Lord like this? The young men who buried your husband are just outside the door, and they will carry you out, too"* (Acts 5:9).

- After Peter said this, Sapphira fell to the floor dead. The same young men carried Sapphira out of the room and buried her next to her husband.

- As news of this incident spread, the entire church community was gripped with fear.

Note: It was not wrong for Ananias and Sapphira to keep some of the money; however, it was wrong for them to lie about it. After selling their property, all the proceeds from the sale belonged to them to do whatever they pleased. They chose to lie and say they were donating the entire amount to the community of believers. Why did they do this? The Bible does not say. Regardless, they allowed Satan to deceive them. God, who sees everything we do in private, judged their sin. We cannot deceive God.

The Apostles Arrested: (Acts 5:12–42)

- The believers met each day at the Temple in an area known as Solomon's Colonnade while the apostles preached and performed healing miracles.

- Although most Jews had great respect for the apostles, many did not want to be seen with them in public for fear of what religious leaders would say or do.

- As a result of the apostles' miraculous healings, people began laying their sick family members and friends on mats in the streets in hopes that Peter's shadow would fall on their loved ones and heal them.

- After witnessing the apostles' miracles and hearing the gospel message, large numbers of people were accepting Jesus as their Savior.

- Envious of the apostles' large following, the high priest ordered Temple guards to arrest the apostles.

- Overnight, an angel freed the apostles from jail. The angel instructed the apostles to go back to the Temple and preach the Good News of new life in Christ.

- At daybreak, the apostles returned to the Temple and began preaching. Later that same morning, the Temple guards went to the jail to get the apostles and bring them before the Sanhedrin for trial. To their surprise, the apostles were not there.

- The guards hurried back and explained to the Sanhedrin that the jail was locked, but no one was inside.

- While the council was discussing the situation, someone entered and announced that the apostles were outside preaching in the Temple courtyard. When the Temple guards heard this, they ran out to the courtyard and brought the apostles back to the council chambers.

- The high priest chastised the apostles saying, *"We told you plainly not to teach in the name of Jesus. But look what you have done! You have been teaching all over Jerusalem, and you are trying to blame us for his death"* (Acts 5:28 CEV).

- Peter and the other apostles replied, *"We don't obey people. We obey God"* (Acts 5:29 CEV).

- Members of the Sanhedrin were furious. However, a man named Gamaliel, a highly respected Pharisee and religious teacher, advised the council to stop trying to fight the apostles.

- Gamaliel explained, *"If what they are planning is something of their own doing, it will fail. But if God is behind it, you cannot stop it anyway, unless you want to fight against God"* (Acts 5:38a–39 CEV).

- The council agreed with Gamaliel's advice. They had the apostles flogged and then ordered them never again to speak of Jesus or His death.

- After the flogging, the apostles rejoiced, happy to have suffered for the name of Jesus.

The Believers Complain: (Acts 6:1–7)

- Each day as the apostles proclaimed the Good News, more people accepted Jesus as their Savior.

- As the number of believers increased, so did the number of those in need of charity. Before long, the apostles found themselves spending much of their time overseeing food distributions to the needy.

- A disagreement eventually broke out among believers about how food was being distributed. Greek-speaking believers grumbled, saying Hebrew-speaking widows were receiving more food than Greek-speaking widows.

- When the apostles heard these complaints, all twelve agreed that their time would be best utilized preaching instead of handing out food.

- To resolve the issue, the apostles chose seven men to take over the job. All seven were well-respected for their wisdom and godly perspective.

- Stephen and Philip, men full of faith, were among the seven assigned as deacons responsible for distributing food to the poor.

 Note: The man named Philip who was made a deacon was not the same Philip who was one of Jesus' twelve apostles. All further references to Philip in Acts are about Deacon Philip and not Apostle Philip.

The Stoning of Stephen: (Acts 6:8–7:60)

- One day, Stephen got into a debate with some freed Jewish slaves. Stephen stated his position with such eloquence and Scriptural insight that the freed Jews finally walked away baffled. Outraged, the freed Jews conspired with others to accuse Stephen of blasphemy. When religious leaders heard the charge of blasphemy, they arrested Stephen.

- During the trial, a false witness testified against Stephen saying, *"This man is always speaking against the holy Temple and against the law of Moses. We have heard him say that this Jesus of Nazareth will destroy the Temple and change the customs Moses handed down to us"* (Acts 6:13–14).

- Stephen's face suddenly lit up and glowed as bright as an angel. As everyone gazed at Stephen's angelic appearance, the high priest asked Stephen if the accusations against him were true.

- In response, Stephen recounted the story of God's dealings with Israel. He spoke about the faith of Israel's patriarchs and mentioned Israel's failure to obey God and how they had rejected God's prophets.

- Stephen then suddenly shouted out, *"You stubborn people! You are heathen at heart and deaf to the truth. Must you forever resist the Holy Spirit? That's what your ancestors did, and so do you! Name one prophet your ancestors didn't persecute! They even killed the ones who predicted the coming of the Righteous One—the Messiah whom you betrayed and murdered. You deliberately disobeyed God's law, even though you received it from the hands of angels"* (Acts 7:51–53).

- The Sanhedrin and other Jews were furious. Looking up toward heaven, Stephen shouted, *"Look, I see the heavens opened and the Son of Man standing in the place of honor at God's right hand!"* (Acts 7:56).

- When Stephen said he saw the Son of Man, the religious leaders were even more outraged. Fuming, they dragged Stephen to the edge of the city and began throwing stones at him.

- Stephen's accusers took off their coats and laid them in front of a young man named Saul. As Stephen fell to his knees, he cried out, *"Lord, don't charge them with this sin!"* (Acts 7:60). After saying this, Stephen died.

 Note: Saul was an official witness at the stoning of Stephen. "Saul" is Aramaic for "Paul" in Greek. Saul would later become known as Apostle Paul.

RECOMMENDED BIBLE READING

Acts 7:1–60 **Stephen's Address**

Psalm 78:1–8 **Importance of Jewish History**

SECTION 3: GOOD NEWS IN SAMARIA AND JUDEA

The Believers Scatter: (Acts 8:1–25)

- After the stoning of Stephen, believers were sought out and persecuted. Saul led the movement, going into homes and arresting Christ-followers.

- With the exception of the apostles, most believers left Jerusalem and fled to Samaria and other cities in Judea to escape persecution. While en route, the believers spread the Good News in each city along the way.

Note: The Bible records the stoning of Stephen as the first Christian martyrdom. Stephen's death marked the beginning of a vast number of Christian persecutions in Jerusalem. Believers were forced out of their homes and arrested; many died because of their faith. As believers fled from Jerusalem to escape persecution, they carried the Good News with them. In this way, religious persecution helped the spreading of the gospel, fulfilling Jesus' words, *"And you will be my witnesses, telling people about me everywhere—in Jerusalem, throughout Judea, in Samaria, and to the ends of the earth"* (Acts 1:8b).

- Philip, one of the seven deacons responsible for distributing food to the needy, left Jerusalem and went to Samaria. While in Samaria, Philip preached and performed numerous healing miracles. As a result of Philip's teachings, a great number of Samaritans accepted Jesus as the Messiah and were baptized.

- When the apostles in Jerusalem heard about Philip's success, they sent Peter and John to Samaria to encourage the new believers.

- Peter and John stayed in Samaria for a while and then traveled back to Jerusalem. They made several stops along the way to preach the Good News.

Philip and the Ethiopian Eunuch: (Acts 8:26–40)

- Meanwhile, an angel appeared to Philip and instructed him to leave Samaria and travel southward on the road to Gaza.

- Philip obeyed the angel and soon ran into a man traveling in a carriage. The man was a eunuch in charge of the Queen of Ethiopia's treasury. He had gone to Jerusalem for worship and was on his way back home.

- Prompted by the Holy Spirit, Philip walked alongside the man's carriage and overheard him reading a passage from the book of Isaiah, which reads: *"He was led like a sheep to the slaughter. And as a lamb is silent before the shearers, he did not open his mouth. He was humiliated and received no justice. Who can speak of his descendants? For his life was taken from the earth"* (Acts 8:32b–33) (See Isaiah 53:7–8 for cross-reference).

- As the man sat in his carriage reading aloud, Philip asked him if he understood what he was reading. The man answered, saying he needed someone to explain it to him.

- Pointing to the passage of Scripture he had just read, the man asked Philip if the prophet Isaiah was talking about himself or someone else.

- Philip joined the man in his carriage and began teaching him as they rode along. Using the passage from Isaiah and many other Scriptures, Philip explained the Good News of salvation through Jesus Christ.

- As they were riding, the man saw some water and asked Philip to baptize him. They got out of the carriage and Philip baptized the man.

- When Philip and the man came up out of the water, the Holy Spirit suddenly carried Philip north to the city of Azotus.

Note: Scripture tells us in Acts 8:39 that the Holy Spirit suddenly took Philip away and he appeared in Azotus. Although it is not specifically stated, Philip appears to have been miraculously transported from Gaza to Azotus.

- The Ethiopian eunuch rejoiced and praised God for sending Philip to share the Good News of Jesus Christ.

Saul's Conversion: (Acts 9:1–19)

- In Jerusalem, Saul was determined to stomp out the new religious sect called the Way.

Note: Christianity was originally referred to as the Way. Perhaps it was called this because Jesus said, *"I am the way, the truth, and the life. No one can come to the Father except through me"* (John 14:6).

- Zealous to maintain Jewish tradition, Saul asked the high priest for permission to arrest all followers of the Way living in Damascus. The high priest honored Saul's request.

- With the high priest's approval, Saul headed for Damascus with plans of finding believers and bringing them back to Jerusalem in chains.

- When Saul reached the outskirts of Damascus, a bright beam of light suddenly flashed down from heaven and encircled him. As Saul fell to the ground, he heard a voice say, *"Saul! Saul! Why are you persecuting me?"* (Acts 9:4).

- Terrified, Saul asked who had called him. The voice replied, *"I am Jesus, the one you are persecuting! Now get up and go into the city, and you will be told what you must do"* (Acts 9:5–6).

- Saul's traveling companions were in shock. They heard the voice, but did not see anyone. When Saul got up, he could not see.

- Blinded by the light, Saul continued the trip to Damascus with his traveling companions guiding him by the hand. After Saul arrived in Damascus, he fasted in prayer for the next three days.

- Meanwhile, the Lord appeared in a vision to a believer in Damascus named Ananias. The Lord said to Ananias, *"Go over to Straight Street, to the house of Judas. When you get there, ask for a man from Tarsus named Saul. He is praying to me right now. I have shown him a vision of a man named Ananias coming in and laying hands on him so he can see again"* (Acts 9:11–12).

- Ananias responded to the Lord, saying Saul was the one responsible for persecuting believers in Jerusalem and planned to arrest believers in Damascus.

- The Lord replied, *"Go, for Saul is my chosen instrument to take my message to the Gentiles and to kings, as well as to the people of Israel. And I will show him how much he must suffer for my name's sake"* (Acts 9:15–16).

- Ananias then got up and found Saul. Placing his hands on Saul, Ananias said, *"Brother Saul, the Lord Jesus, who appeared to you on the road, has sent me so that you might regain your sight and be filled with the Holy Spirit"* (Acts 9:17b).

- As soon as Ananias said this, something resembling scales immediately fell from Saul's eyes and he was able to see again. Ananias then baptized Saul.

Saul's Early Ministry: (Acts 9:20–31; Galatians 1:17–18)

- A few days later, Saul began preaching the Good News and proclaiming Jesus as the Son of God. As Saul preached in nearby synagogues, all who heard him were astonished.

- People could not believe Saul, who had so aggressively persecuted believers in Jerusalem, had become a follower of the Way.

Note: According to Galatians 1:17–18, Paul (Saul) left Damascus and went to Arabia shortly after his conversion. Paul tells us he stayed in Arabia for three years. While in Arabia, Paul says he did not consult with anyone, but received his gospel message directly from God. We can therefore assume Paul studied Scripture during these three years in Arabia and was taught by the Holy Spirit. Paul later returned to Damascus.

- As Saul studied the Scriptures, his faith increased. The Holy Spirit gave Saul tremendous insight, showing him how Jesus of Nazareth fulfilled Messianic prophecies.

- Saul soon began debating non believers in Damascus, using Scripture to prove Jesus Christ was the Messiah. Many devout Jews rejected Saul's message. As Saul continued preaching, some dissenters eventually decided to kill him.

- Those plotting against Saul posted men at the city gates to prevent his escape. When believers heard about the plot, they waited until nightfall and then lowered Saul in a basket over a section of the city wall.

- After escaping, Saul traveled to Jerusalem. He tried to meet with the disciples there, but everyone was afraid of him. They thought Saul was only pretending to be a follower so that he could identify true believers and arrest them.

- Barnabas believed Saul and arranged a meeting with the disciples. After Barnabas shared the details of Saul's conversion and his ministry in Damascus, the disciples accepted Saul. He immediately began preaching the name of Jesus in Jerusalem.

- One day, Saul got into a religious debate with some Greek Jews. Saul so outraged them that they tried to kill him.

- When believers heard about the attempt on Saul's life, they escorted him safely out of Jerusalem. Saul headed for Tarsus, his hometown.

RECOMMENDED BIBLE READING

Acts 8:26–40 **The Ethiopian Eunuch**

Isaiah 56:1–5 **Eunuchs and All of God's People Will Be Blessed**

SECTION 4: GOOD NEWS TO THE GENTILES

Peter's Ministry: (Acts 9:32–42)

- Peter decided to travel outside of Jerusalem preaching the Good News. While visiting Lydda, a town northeast of Jerusalem, Peter met a man named Aeneas.

- Aeneas had been paralyzed for eight years. Calling on the name of Jesus, Peter healed Aeneas. When people saw Aeneas walking on his own, they were amazed and readily accepted Peter's message of salvation.

- Shortly afterward, two men from Joppa found Peter and asked him to return with them at once. They explained, saying a very devout woman had become ill and died. Her name was *Tabitha* in Aramaic, which is translated *Dorcas* in Greek.

- Peter followed the men back to Joppa. When they arrived, the mourners took Peter to the room where Dorcas' body had been laid in preparation for her burial.

- As the mourners showed Peter the beautiful handmade clothes Dorcas had sewn, they told him wonderful stories about how kind and generous she had been.

- Peter asked everyone to leave the room and then kneeled down in prayer. He called the dead woman by name and commanded her to get up.

- Dorcas opened her eyes and sat up. Peter then called the people back into the room and presented Dorcas to them alive.

- As news spread of this miracle, people in Joppa began accepting Jesus as their Savior. Peter decided to stay for a while and minister to the new believers.

Peter's Vision: (Acts 10:1–48)

- One day in the city of Caesarea, a Roman officer named Cornelius was praying to the One True God.

- Cornelius and his entire household were non-Jews, who had converted to Judaism, but had not heard the Good News of salvation through Jesus Christ.

- While Cornelius was praying, an angel appeared to him and told him to send some men to Joppa for a man named Peter.

- Cornelius immediately sent two of his servants and a trusted soldier to Joppa to find Peter and bring him back to Caesarea.

- As the men neared Joppa, Peter was praying on the rooftop of the house where he was staying. When Peter finished praying, he fell asleep and into a trance.

- Peter saw a large sheet being lowered from heaven. All kinds of animals, reptiles, and birds were inside the sheet.

- Peter suddenly heard a voice call out, *"Peter, get up! Kill these and eat them"* (Acts 10:13 CEV). While still in a trance, Peter answered, *"Lord, I can't do that! I've never eaten anything that is unclean and not fit to eat"* (Acts 10:14 CEV).

Note: According to Jewish law, certain animals were unclean and therefore not fit to eat. When the Israelites were in the desert on their way to Canaan, God gave the people instructions through the prophet Moses about what kinds of meat they could eat and what was strictly forbidden. (See Leviticus 11:1–47.) During Old Testament times, these dietary laws were needed to help God's people maintain good health. The animals forbidden by God often carried germs. God's laws prevented the people from acquiring diseases from infected animals. Peter had faithfully kept the dietary laws God gave Moses.

- The voice called out again to Peter saying, *"When God says that something can be used for food, don't say it isn't fit to eat"* (Acts 10:15 CEV). This same vision happened three times and then the sheet was pulled up into heaven.

- Peter came out of the trance and immediately wondered what the vision meant. As Peter sat pondering the vision's meaning, Cornelius' men were outside looking for him.

- The Holy Spirit spoke to Peter saying, *"Three men are here looking for you. Hurry down and go with them. Don't worry, I sent them"* (Acts 10:19–20 CEV).

- Following the Holy Spirit's prompting, Peter got up and went downstairs. He found Cornelius' men and asked them what they needed. The men answered saying an angel instructed Cornelius, a righteous man of God, to send for a man named Peter who would explain the Good News to him. Peter then invited the men to stay overnight.

- The next day, Peter and a few believers from Joppa traveled with Cornelius' men to Caesarea. When Peter arrived, Cornelius fell to his knees in worship. Peter raised him up and explained that he was not God, but a mere man.

- As Peter entered the house, he saw Cornelius' family and friends had gathered to meet him. Peter addressed the group saying, *"You know that we Jews are not allowed to have anything to do with other people. But God has shown me that he doesn't think anyone is unclean or unfit. I agreed to come here, but I want to know why you sent for me"* (Acts 10:19–20 CEV).

Note: Gentiles did not practice Jewish dietary laws. (See Leviticus 11.) As a result, Jews would not eat meals with Gentiles for fear of eating foods forbidden by Jewish law. Over time, Jews began to view Gentiles as unclean and would not associate with them. God showed Peter in a vision that he must erase this prejudicial view. Before the vision, Peter thought the Good News of Jesus Christ was for the Jews only. God pointed out through Peter's vision that His offer of salvation is to all people—Jews and Gentiles.

- Cornelius explained to the apostle that an angel had instructed him to send for a man named Peter.

- Peter responded saying, *"Now I am certain that God treats all people alike. God is pleased with everyone who worships him and does right, no matter what nation they come from. This is the same message that God gave to the people of Israel, when he sent Jesus Christ, the Lord of all, to offer peace to them"* (Acts 10:34–36 CEV).

- Peter then explained the Good News. He declared Jesus as the Messiah and said God forgives all who believe in Jesus' name.

- As Peter was speaking, the Holy Spirit suddenly descended on Cornelius and his household. They began speaking in other languages the same way the apostles and other Jewish believers did on Pentecost.

- The Jewish believers who came with Peter from Joppa were surprised, for they thought the outpouring of the Holy Spirit was for the Jews only.

- Peter turned to the believers from Joppa and said, *"These Gentiles have been given the Holy Spirit, just as we have! I am certain that no one would dare stop us from baptizing them"* (Acts 10:47 CEV).

- Hearing no objections, Peter arranged for Cornelius and those in his household to be baptized in Jesus' name.

Peter Explains About the Gentiles: (Acts 11:1–18)

- When Peter returned to Jerusalem, the apostles and other believers criticized him for entering Cornelius' house and eating with Gentiles.

- Defending his actions, Peter gave a sequential account of everything God had revealed to him. Peter shared his vision and then described how the Holy Spirit descended on Cornelius and his entire household.

- Peter then said, *"And since God gave these Gentiles the same gift he gave us when we believed in the Lord Jesus Christ, who was I to stand in God's way?"* (Acts 11:17).

- When the apostles and other believers heard Peter's explanation, they stopped complaining and praised God for extending His offer of salvation to the Gentiles.

The Church in Antioch: (Acts 11:19–30)

- After the stoning of Stephen, some believers moved to Antioch in Syria and began spreading the Good News to the Gentiles. As a result, a number of Gentiles in Antioch were accepting Jesus as their Savior.

- When the church in Jerusalem heard about Gentile believers in Antioch, they sent Barnabas to verify the reports. Barnabas was overjoyed to discover the reports were true.

- Barnabas later went to Tarsus and returned to Antioch with Saul. Together they preached in Antioch for a full year. The believers in Antioch were the first to refer to Christ-followers as Christians.

- Meanwhile, a famine soon spread throughout Judea. When believers in Antioch heard about the food shortage, they collected a generous offering to help Christians in Jerusalem. They gave the offering to Barnabas and Saul, who traveled to Jerusalem to deliver it to the apostles.

RECOMMENDED BIBLE READING

Acts 10:1–48 **Peter's Vision**

Leviticus 11:1–23 **Clean and Unclean Animals**

SECTION 5: THE APOSTLES FACE PERSECUTION

Herod Kills James: (Acts 12:1–5)

- King Herod Agrippa I—grandson of Herod the Great and nephew of Herod Antipas—started persecuting believers in Jerusalem. Herod ordered the execution of Apostle James, John's brother.

 Note: James was the first of the apostles to suffer martyrdom. James was put to death by the sword in 44 A.D. for proclaiming Jesus as the long-awaited Messiah.

- Herod gained considerable favor among Jewish religious leaders for ordering James' death. When Herod saw how much this pleased religious leaders, he ordered Peter's arrest with plans of having him put to death as well.

- Peter was arrested and put in a heavily guarded prison. As soon as believers heard about Peter's imprisonment, they started praying for his release.

Peter's Miraculous Escape: (Acts 12:6–19)

- The night before Peter's trial, an angel came to his prison cell. Peter was asleep, chained in between two guards with more guards posted at the entrance.

- When the angel nudged Peter to wake him, his chains miraculously fell off his wrist. The angel then instructed Peter to follow him.

- Half asleep, Peter thought he was experiencing a vision. He and the angel passed by the guarded stations without being seen. As they exited the prison and walked into the streets, the angel disappeared.

- Peter suddenly realized he was not dreaming. Grateful for his miraculous escape, Peter began praising the Lord. He then quickly ran to the house of Mary, John Mark's mother, where believers were gathered, praying for his release.

- When Peter arrived at Mary's house, he knocked on the door and a young girl named Rhoda came to open it. Rhoda recognized Peter and was overjoyed.

- In her excitement, Rhoda left Peter standing at the door. She ran to the believers and joyfully announced that Peter was standing at the door.

- Knowing there was no way humanly possible for Peter to escape, the believers thought Rhoda was out of her mind. When Rhoda insisted, the believers thought she must have seen Peter's angel. Meanwhile, Peter was still outside knocking on the door.

- When the believers finally went to the door, they were surprised to see Peter standing there. Peter signaled for them to be quiet and then explained what had happened.

- After telling the believers about the miracle, Peter told them to share the news with James and the others. Peter then left to find a more secure hiding place.

 Note: When Peter told the believers to share the news with James, he was referring to Jesus' half-brother named James, who headed the church in Jerusalem.

- Very early the next morning, the entire prison was in chaos as the guards frantically searched for Peter. When Herod discovered Peter had indeed escaped, he ordered the guards' execution.

Note: Under Roman law, a guard assumed total responsibility for a prisoner. When an escape occurred, those responsible for guarding the prisoner received the same penalty as the escaped prisoner. Since Herod planned to have Peter put to death, the guards on duty during his escape were executed.

Herod's Death: (Acts 12:20–25)

- A disagreement later broke out between Herod and the people of Tyre and Sidon. Since the people in these cities were dependent on Herod for their food supplies, they desperately wanted to make peace with him.

- The people of Tyre and Sidon sent representatives to Judea to negotiate a peace settlement with Herod. After befriending one of Herod's assistants, the representatives were granted a meeting with the king.

- When Herod appeared before his royal throne, everyone cheered and shouted out, *"It's the voice of a god, not of a man!"* (Acts 12:22).

- Full of pride, Herod allowed the people to worship him as a god instead of redirecting their praises to the One True God. As the people praised Herod, he suddenly became very sick and later died.

 Note: Luke described Herod's death saying, *"Instantly, an angel of the Lord struck Herod with a sickness, because he accepted the people's worship instead of giving the glory to God. So he was consumed with worms and died"* (Acts 12:23).

- After Herod's death, the Good News continued to spread and new believers joined the church daily.

- Meanwhile, Barnabas and Saul arrived in Jerusalem with the gifts and offerings from believers in Antioch. After completing their goodwill mission, Barnabas and Saul returned to Antioch with John Mark.

RECOMMENDED BIBLE READING

Acts 12:6–19 **Peter's Miraculous Escape**

Daniel 3:19–30 **Three Hebrews' Miraculous Escape**

MEDITATION & PRAYER

Apostle Paul explains the Good News:

"For I am not ashamed of this Good News about Christ. It is the power of God at work, saving everyone who believes—the Jew first and also the Gentile. This Good News tells us how God makes us right in his sight. This is accomplished from start to finish by faith. As the Scriptures say, 'It is through faith that a righteous person has life.'"

(Romans 1:16–17)

Dear Heavenly Father,

I thank You for the Good News of Jesus Christ, for it is Your power at work, saving those who believe. I thank You for providing a way for mankind to be made right in Your sight. I thank You for showing me that it is faith and not deeds that makes me right in Your sight. Strengthen me through the Holy Spirit and teach me to better articulate my faith. Help me to show others Your love through my words and actions. I want others to see Your power at work in my life!

Amen

REVIEW QUESTIONS

1. How did Jesus prove to the disciples He had risen from the dead and was indeed alive?

    _____

    _____

    _____

    _____

2. On the day of Pentecost, God sent the Holy Spirit as promised. What role does the Holy Spirit play in the life of believers?

    _____

    _____

    _____

    _____

3. Describe Peter's character before the outpouring of the Holy Spirit. What specific changes occurred in Peter's character and actions after the outpouring of the Holy Spirit?

    _____

    _____

    _____

    _____

4. What is the Good News of Jesus Christ?

    _____

    _____

    _____

    _____

5. Describe the atmosphere among believers during the formative years of the early church? What specific actions demonstrated their love for God and His people?

_____

_____

_____

_____

6. How did Stephen's death help spread the Good News?

_____

_____

_____

_____

7. Who was Philip? How did Philip help spread the Good News?

_____

_____

_____

_____

8. Describe Saul's character and actions before he believed in Jesus?

_____

_____

_____

_____

9. What happened that caused Saul to believe in Jesus? What specific changes occurred in Saul's character and actions after his conversion experience?

_____

_____

_____

_____

10. God showed Peter a vision about a sheet being lowered from heaven with all kinds of unclean animals inside it. What was the significance of this vision?

_____

_____

_____

_____

PERSONAL REFLECTIONS

11. What lesson did you learn from the story of Ananias and Sapphira? What is your position toward supporting the church and other charitable organizations with your time, talent, and money? How has the charitable giving of your time, talent, and money benefited you personally?

_____

_____

_____

_____

_____

12. The early church understood the need for Christian fellowship. In your opinion, what is the importance of Christian fellowship? What are you doing to strengthen your fellowship with other Christians? What additional steps can you take to strengthen your Christian fellowship?

_____

_____

_____

_____

_____

13. What are you doing to reach out to non believers? How do you show them the love of Jesus Christ? What additional steps can you take to reach out to non believers?

_____

_____

_____

_____

_____

CLOSING PRAYER

The prophet Joel foretells of the outpouring of the Holy Spirit:

"Then, after doing all those things,
I will pour out my Spirit upon all people.
Your sons and daughters will prophesy.
Your old men will dream dreams,
and your young men will see visions.
In those days I will pour out my Spirit
even on servants—men and women alike.
And I will cause wonders in the heavens and on the earth—
blood and fire and columns of smoke.
The sun will become dark,
and the moon will turn blood red
before that great and terrible day of the LORD arrives.
But everyone who calls on the name of the LORD
will be saved . . ."

(Joel 2:28–32a)

Dear Lord,

You search my heart and know my thoughts. You are the One who gives me faith to believe. Because of Your amazing grace, I can call out to You and You will answer. It is so wonderful to know that everyone who acknowledges Jesus Christ as their personal Savior will be saved. You seal all believers with Your gift of the Holy Spirit. Your Spirit is always there to correct when needed. The Holy Spirit is my Advocate, Helper, Encourager, Counselor, Guide, Instructor, Comforter, Teacher, and Friend. He leads me toward righteousness and helps me glorify You. I thank You for sending the Holy Spirit, Your seal that says I belong to You.

Amen

CHAPTER 6

SPREADING THE GOOD NEWS

OPENING PRAYER

Dear God,

I thank You for the Good News of Jesus Christ. As I come before You, I ask You to strengthen me in the faith. Give me spiritual insight to better understand the challenges the apostles faced while spreading the Good News. Give me spiritual boldness to have the same kind of commitment to the faith as the apostles demonstrated. Give me spiritual wisdom to know when You are calling me to action and the faith to respond in accordance with Your will. Help me to become a fully devoted follower, well-grounded in the faith. I want to know You better and live a life that is well-pleasing to You.

Amen

CHAPTER SUMMARY

SPREADING THE GOOD NEWS

(Acts 13–28, Galatians, James, 1st and 2nd Thessalonians, 1st and 2nd Corinthians, Romans, Ephesians, Colossians, Philemon, Philippians, 1st Timothy, Titus, 1st Peter, 2nd Timothy, 2nd Peter, Jude, Hebrews, 1st, 2nd, and 3rd John, and Revelation)

 Note: The letters to the early churches are presented in this study based on the approximate date they were written and not the order they appear in the Bible.

While Barnabas and Saul (Paul) were in Antioch, the Holy Spirit inspired the elders of the church to commission them to perform special missionary work. Responding to God's call, Paul and Barnabas set out on their first missionary journey in about 46 A.D.

During this first missionary journey, Paul and Barnabas visited the island of Cyprus, Antioch of Pisidia, and the cities of Iconium, Lystra, and Derbe in southern Galatia (present day Turkey). When Paul and Barnabas arrived in each city, they went to the local synagogue and began explaining how Jesus Christ fulfilled Old Testament prophecies about the Messiah. While some Jews believed their message, many devout followers of Judaism rejected the Good News and turned people against Paul and Barnabas. When this happened, Paul and Barnabas reached out to Gentiles with the gospel message. Although Paul and Barnabas experienced numerous hardships and setbacks, they continued preaching the Good News and established several churches in Galatia. They returned to Antioch of Syria in about 48 A.D.

After Paul and Barnabas returned, a major dispute erupted in the church at Antioch of Syria. Jewish believers insisted that Gentile converts must be circumcised and observe Old Testament laws to be saved. Paul and Barnabas argued that the only requirement for salvation was faith in Jesus Christ. To resolve this issue, church elders in Antioch sent Paul and Barnabas to meet with church leaders in Jerusalem for guidance. The Jerusalem Council met and issued a resolution, which agreed with Paul and Barnabas' position. Gentile believers were overjoyed when they heard circumcision and observance to most Jewish laws were not required for salvation.

Shortly after the Jerusalem Council's resolution, the church in Antioch of Syria commissioned Paul and Barnabas for a second missionary journey. While preparing for the journey, Paul and Barnabas had a disagreement and decided to separate. Barnabas traveled with John Mark to Cyprus and Silas, another dedicated minister of the gospel, joined Paul on his second missionary journey. Paul and Silas left Antioch of Syria in about 50 A.D. They visited the churches in Galatia established during Paul's first missionary journey and encouraged believers in the faith. Inspired by the Holy Spirit, Paul and his traveling companions went to Macedonia (present day northern Greece). While in Macedonia, Paul ministered in Philippi, Thessalonica, and Berea. He then traveled to Athens and Corinth, preaching the Good News. After spending one-and-a-half years in Corinth, Paul returned to Antioch of Syria in 52 A.D.

Paul began his third missionary journey in about 53 A.D. He returned to the churches he helped establish in Galatia. After spiritually strengthening believers in Galatia, Paul traveled to Ephesus, where he ministered for about three years. He then went to Macedonia and Greece, preaching the Good News. After about three-and-a-half years, Paul headed for Jerusalem. The Holy Spirit revealed to several believers the danger Paul would face in Jerusalem. However, Paul was determined to go to Jerusalem, saying he was ready to die for the gospel.

Paul arrived in Jerusalem in about 57 A.D. While Paul was attending a religious ceremony in the Temple, some Jews from Asia who had previously opposed Paul recognized him and incited the people against him. They attacked Paul inside the Temple. Roman soldiers rescued Paul from the angry mob and then arrested him. When the commander of the Roman regiment discovered Paul was a Roman citizen, he protected Paul to ensure a fair trial, a legal right of Roman citizenship. The commander ordered soldiers to escort Paul safely to Caesarea and deliver him to the Roman governor. After Paul arrived in Caesarea, the Roman governor held a hearing, but did not make a decision in the case. The governor left Paul in prison.

After Paul had been in custody for two years, Rome replaced the governor. The new governor immediately held another hearing for Paul. In an attempt to gain favor with religious leaders, the new governor asked Paul if he would stand trial before the Sanhedrin council in Jerusalem. Paul refused and appealed to Caesar. As a result of Paul's appeal, the Roman governor sent Paul to Rome. On the way to Rome, Paul and the crew traveling with him encountered a terrible storm. They were shipwrecked, but everyone swam safely to shore. Paul and the other crew members eventually boarded another ship headed for Italy.

When Paul arrived in Rome, he was allowed to rent a house for two years with a Roman soldier guarding him at all times. This type of imprisonment is called house arrest. While under house arrest, Paul shared the gospel with everyone who would listen, including the Roman soldiers guarding him. Luke's historical account of the spreading of the gospel ended with Paul under house arrest in Rome. According to tradition, Paul never appeared before Caesar. He was released after spending two years under house arrest.

Meanwhile, several major problems threatened the early church's existence. In 64 A.D., Emperor Nero blamed Christians for a fire, which burned significant sections of Rome. After the fire, Nero began persecuting Christians in Rome. Many historians believe Emperor Nero set the fire himself to speed up his plans for urban renewal. As opposition to Christianity increased in and outside of Rome, believers were forced to flee from their homes. False teachers infiltrated the church with doctrines contradictory to the Truth of God. Many of these false teachings condoned immorality, minimized Jesus' role in securing believers' salvation, and mixed other pagan religions or Judaism with Christianity. With the influx of problems for the early church, the apostles wrote letters to encourage believers to stay grounded in their faith. These letters helped establish doctrinal truths for the early church and believers everywhere for all times.

Key People in This Chapter

Paul (Saul)	An apostle and minister of the gospel. He traveled on three missionary journeys, spreading the Good News. Although he suffered numerous trials and hardships, he continued preaching and defending the faith.	Acts 13:1–28:31
Barnabas	Partnered with Paul and traveled with him on his first missionary journey.	Acts 13:1–15:39
John Mark	Author of the gospel of Mark. A valuable companion of Peter, Barnabas, and Paul. He was Barnabas' cousin.	Acts 13:5–15:39; Colossians 4:10
Peter	Apostle instrumental in establishing the early church and spreading the gospel.	Acts 15:6–21
James	Jesus' half-brother. He was leader of the church in Jerusalem and the Jerusalem Council. He later wrote a letter called James.	Acts 15:13–21
Silas	One of the elders of the church in Jerusalem. He partnered with Paul and traveled with him on his second missionary journey.	Acts 15:22–18:5
Timothy	A young believer whom Paul met during his second missionary journey. He became Paul's traveling companion and assisted in Paul's ministry. Paul addressed two pastoral letters to Timothy.	Acts 16:1–5; 17:14–15; 18:5; 19:22; 20:4
Lydia	A business woman Paul met in Philippi during his second missionary journey. After hearing the Good News, Lydia became a believer. She invited Paul and his companions to stay at her house as guests while they were in Philippi.	Acts 16:14–15, 40

Priscilla and Aquila	A married couple whom Paul met and stayed with while in Corinth. Aquila and Priscilla, his wife, were tentmakers. They ministered together as a team, effectively teaching and spreading the Good News.	Acts 18:2–3, 18, 26
Apollos	A dynamic speaker and believer whom Priscilla and Aquila met in Ephesus. After Priscilla and Aquila shared the gospel with him, he studied the Scriptures and became an effective communicator of the Good News.	Acts 18:24–19:1
Titus	A young Greek believer, who assisted in Paul's ministry. He was one of Paul's faithful companions. Paul addressed a pastoral letter to Titus.	See Titus
Jude	Jesus' half-brother. He wrote a letter called Jude.	See Jude
John	Apostle instrumental in establishing the early church and spreading the gospel.	See 1st, 2nd, and 3rd John; and Revelation

	Approximate Timeline	**Location**	**Biblical Scriptures**	**Author**
Paul's First Missionary Journey	46–48 A.D.	Antioch of Syria, Cyprus, Galatia, Jerusalem	Acts 13:1–15:41 Galatians James	Luke Paul James
Paul's Second Missionary Journey	50–52 A.D.	Antioch of Syria, Galatia, Philippi, Thessalonica, Berea, Athens, Corinth, Ephesus, Caesarea, Jerusalem	Acts 16:1–18:22 1 Thessalonians 2 Thessalonians	Luke Paul Paul
Paul's Third Missionary Journey	53–57 A.D.	Galatia, Ephesus, Macedonia, Corinth, Troas, Miletus, Tyre, Caesarea	Acts 18:23–21:14 1st Corinthians 2nd Corinthians Romans	Luke Paul Paul Paul
Paul's Arrest	57–59 A.D.	Jerusalem, Caesarea, Crete, Malta, Rome	Acts 21:1–28:30	Luke
Building the Faith	60–95 A.D.	Rome, Roman provinces	Ephesians Colossians Philemon Philippians 1st Timothy Titus 1st Peter 2nd Timothy 2nd Peter Jude Hebrews 1st, 2nd, and 3rd John Revelation	Paul Paul Paul Paul Paul Paul Peter Paul Peter Jude Unknown John John

MAP OF KEY LOCATIONS

PAUL'S FIRST MISSIONARY JOURNEY

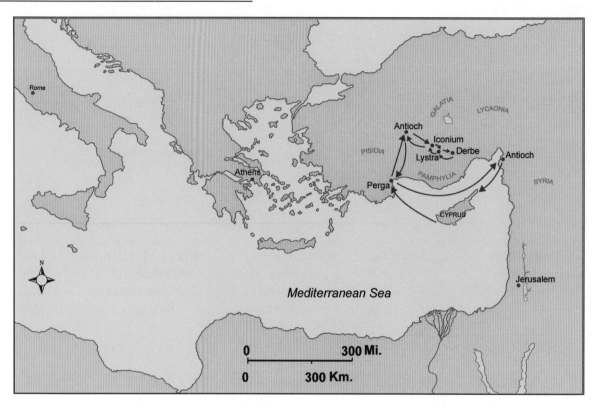

PAUL'S SECOND MISSIONARY JOURNEY

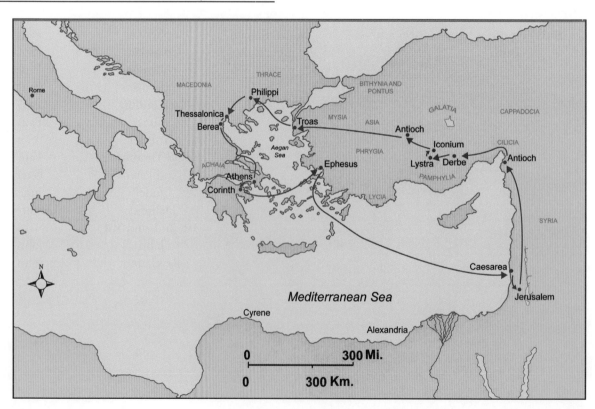

PAUL'S THIRD MISSIONARY JOURNEY

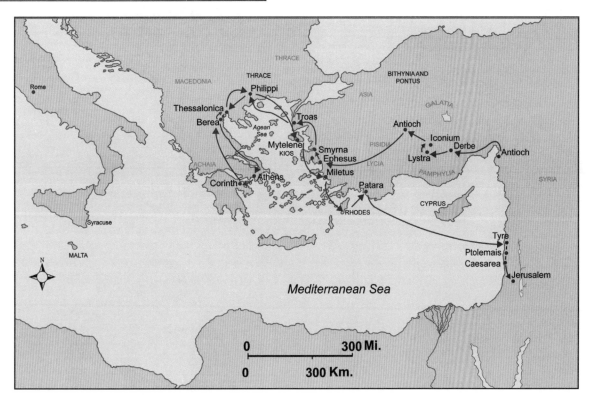

PAUL'S JOURNEY TO ROME

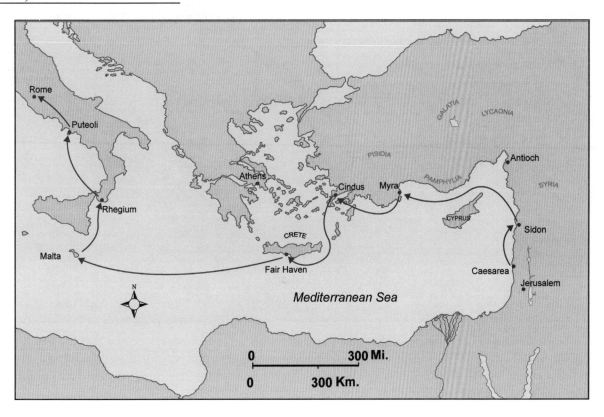

PAUL IN ATHENS

"Paul then stood up in the meeting of the Areopagus and said: 'People of Athens! I see that in every way you are very religious. For as I walked around and looked carefully at your objects of worship, I even found an altar with this inscription: TO AN UNKNOWN GOD. So you are ignorant of the very thing you worship—and this is what I am going to proclaim to you.'" (Acts 17:22–23) TNIV

SECTION 1: PAUL'S FIRST MISSIONARY JOURNEY

Barnabas and Saul's Commissioning: (Acts 13:1–4)

- One day, leaders of the church at Antioch of Syria were gathered together in worship. While they were praising God, the Holy Spirit spoke to them saying, *"Dedicate Barnabas and Saul for the special work to which I have called them"* (Acts 13:2).

- When the church leaders finished their praises, they commissioned Barnabas and Saul as missionaries dedicated to God's special work. After receiving their commissioning, Barnabas and Saul set out for the island of Cyprus. John Mark went along with them as their assistant.

Barnabas and Saul in Cyprus: (Acts 13:5–12)

- When Barnabas and Saul reached the island of Cyprus, they initially preached in a local synagogue. They later began traveling from town to town on the island spreading the Good News.

 Note: Luke introduces Apostle Paul in Acts 7:58 as Saul, Aramaic for Paul. Luke refers to him by this name until Acts 13:13 when he transitions to Paul, the Greek equivalent of Saul.

Paul and Barnabas in Antioch of Pisidia: (Acts 13:13–52)

- Paul and Barnabas left the island of Cyprus and traveled by ship to the port town of Perga. When they arrived in Perga, John Mark decided to return to Jerusalem.

- Paul and Barnabas continued their journey, traveling inward until they reached the town of Antioch of Pisidia. They found the local synagogue and attended a Sabbath service. After the Scriptural readings, those in charge of the service offered them an opportunity to speak.

- Paul stood up and announced the Good News of salvation through faith in Jesus Christ. Quoting Old Testament Scriptures, Paul explained how Jesus of Nazareth fulfilled prophecies about the Messiah.

- When Paul finished speaking, the people were eager to hear more. They begged him to come back and speak again.

- The next Sabbath, almost everyone in Antioch of Pisidia came to hear Paul and Barnabas' message at the synagogue.

- When some devout Jews saw the large gathering, they became envious and started arguing in opposition to Paul's message. They abusively attacked Paul's reputation in their attempts to discredit him.

- Paul and Barnabas soon realized they would not be allowed to preach. As they prepared to leave, they announced to the crowd, *"It was necessary that we first preach the word of God to you Jews. But since you have rejected it and judged yourselves unworthy of eternal life, we will offer it to the Gentiles"* (Acts 13:46).

- When the Gentiles heard this news, they were overjoyed and began thanking God. Paul and Barnabas stayed in Antioch of Pisidia for a while longer preaching to the Gentiles.

- Some Jews later stirred up a few of the town's influential people and turned them against Paul and Barnabas. Before long, they drove Paul and Barnabas out of town.

Paul and Barnabas in Iconium: (Acts 14:1–6)

- Paul and Barnabas left Antioch of Pisidia and traveled to Iconium. As usual, they found the local synagogue and delivered a powerful message. As a result, a great number of people believed the Good News.

- Some of the people refused to accept Paul's message. They were so enraged that they decided to kill Paul and Barnabas. When Paul and Barnabas heard about the threat against their lives, they fled to the towns of Lystra and Derbe.

Paul and Barnabas in Lystra and Derbe: (Acts 14:7–21)

- While preaching in Lystra, Paul and Barnabas met a man who had been born lame. As the man sat listening to the two missionaries, Paul sensed the man had faith and commanded him to stand up. The man obediently jumped to his feet and began walking.

- When people saw the man had been healed, they thought Paul and Barnabas were Greek gods. Following their pagan beliefs, the people began preparations for offering sacrifices to Paul and Barnabas.

- When Paul and Barnabas realized what was happening, they were appalled and rushed out to stop the people.

- In the midst of the confusion, some Jews from Antioch and Iconium arrived on the scene. They discredited Paul and Barnabas and turned the people of Lystra against them. Although the people had earlier praised Paul and Barnabas as gods, they were now ready to kill them.

- The people were so stirred up, they began stoning Paul. When they thought Paul was dead, they dragged him to the outskirts of the city and left him there.

- A few believers found Paul and gathered around him. Sometime later, Paul revived and went back into the city. He and Barnabas left Lystra the next day and headed for Derbe.

- When Paul and Barnabas arrived in Derbe, they immediately began preaching the Good News. A large number of people believed their message and became Christ-followers.

Paul and Barnabas Return to Antioch in Syria: (Acts 14:21–28)

- After Paul and Barnabas finished preaching in Derbe, they went back to the cities of Lystra, Iconium, and Antioch of Pisidia to strengthen and encourage their new converts. Paul and Barnabas appointed leaders, whom they called elders, for each of the new churches they helped establish in southern Galatia.

 Note: Paul and Barnabas returned to the cities where their lives had been in danger. They recognized the importance of spiritually strengthening the new believers and establishing church leadership. Paul and Barnabas risked their lives to help ground them in the faith.

- After praying for the elders, Paul and Barnabas returned to Antioch of Syria. They called the church members together and provided a full report of everything that happened during their first missionary journey.

- Paul and Barnabas explained how God opened the door for Gentiles to receive the Good News.

Note: After Paul's first missionary journey, he wrote a letter called Galatians. There are two theories about when Galatians was written. Some scholars believe it was written in about 49 A.D. to churches in southern Galatia (Iconium, Lystra, and Derbe). Paul helped establish these churches during his first missionary journey. Others believe Galatians was written in about 56 A.D. to churches in northern Galatia. While Luke informs us in Acts that Paul later traveled through northern Galatia, there is no record of his ministry in this area. For this reason, Galatians was most probably written in about 49 A.D. to the churches Paul ministered to during his first missionary journey in southern Galatia.

Galatians: The churches in Galatia had allowed some Jews, who professed Jesus, to teach a false doctrine of salvation based on works (strict adherence to the law of Moses) instead of faith alone. These Jews taught that in addition to faith in Jesus Christ, Gentile believers must obey Old Testament laws to be saved. When Paul learned believers in Galatia seemed content with this false teaching, he penned a letter attacking the doctrine of works and defending the gospel of faith.

In Galatians, Jesus is the One who makes us right with God, freeing us from the law. (See Galatians 2:16; 3:13; 5:1.)

Paul explains that salvation comes by faith alone. The purpose of the law is to show people how unrighteous they are before God. Jesus fulfilled the requirements of the law through His sacrificial death on the cross. Those who believe in Jesus as Lord and Savior have been freed from the law. Paul advises believers to live in freedom and be guided by the Holy Spirit. God's Spirit leads us from an old life of unrighteousness into a new life of love, joy, peace, patience, kindness, goodness, faithfulness, gentleness, and self-control. These are known as the "Fruit of the Spirit." (See Galatians 5:22–23.)

The Jerusalem Council's Decision: (Acts 15:1–35)

- After Paul and Barnabas had been in Antioch of Syria for a while, some Jews from Judea came to the church insisting that Gentile believers must obey Jewish laws and customs.

- These Jews taught that circumcision and adherence to the law of Moses were required for salvation. Paul and Barnabas vehemently opposed this doctrine and a heated argument erupted.

- To resolve the issue, the church in Antioch of Syria sent Paul and Barnabas, along with a few other believers, to consult with the apostles and elders in Jerusalem.

- Paul and Barnabas met with the church in Jerusalem and reported everything God had accomplished through them. When they mentioned Gentile converts, some Jewish believers interrupted and said Gentile believers must adhere to Jewish laws and be circumcised. An intense debate ensued.

- The apostles and elders realized the issue needed to be resolved, so they dismissed the congregation and held a separate meeting.

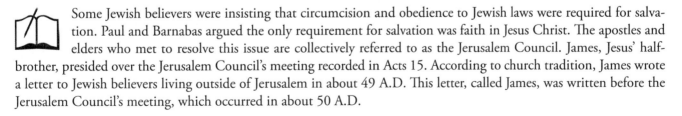

Some Jewish believers were insisting that circumcision and obedience to Jewish laws were required for salvation. Paul and Barnabas argued the only requirement for salvation was faith in Jesus Christ. The apostles and elders who met to resolve this issue are collectively referred to as the Jerusalem Council. James, Jesus' half-brother, presided over the Jerusalem Council's meeting recorded in Acts 15. According to church tradition, James wrote a letter to Jewish believers living outside of Jerusalem in about 49 A.D. This letter, called James, was written before the Jerusalem Council's meeting, which occurred in about 50 A.D.

James: A great number of believers fled religious persecution and were living outside of Jerusalem. James apparently heard about believers scattered abroad whose actions were not aligned with the faith. Believers were professing Christ, but not living according to God's Word. James wrote a letter to confront this hypocrisy and explain that true faith in Christ produces a changed life for Christ.

In James, Jesus is the Judge standing at the door. (See James 5:7–9.)

James encourages believers to endure the test of faith, ask God for wisdom, and demonstrate their faith by obeying God's Word. James writes, *"But don't just listen to God's word. You must do what it says"* (James 1:22). Good deeds and righteous living are by-products of faith in Christ. James warns against prejudice, uncontrolled tongues, and judging others. Believers are instructed to live righteously, act wisely, draw close to God, resist the devil, pray in faith, and confess sins.

- After a lengthy debate, James stood up and addressed the council. James agreed with Paul and Barnabas. He decided the council should not make Christianity burdensome for Gentile believers by requiring them to keep Jewish laws and be circumcised.

- James then pointed out a few exceptions. The council documented their decision in a resolution which stated, *"For it seemed good to the Holy Spirit and to us to lay no greater burden on you than these few requirements: You must abstain from eating food offered to idols, from consuming blood or the meat of strangled animals, and from sexual immorality. If you do this, you will do well"* (Acts 15:28–29).

- The apostles and elders then chose representatives to travel with Paul and Barnabas to deliver the resolution to the church in Antioch. A man named Silas was one of the men chosen to represent the council. When the church in Antioch heard the resolution, they were overjoyed.

Paul and Barnabas Disagree: (Acts 15:36–41)

- Paul later suggested he and Barnabas return to the cities they visited during their first missionary journey to see how the churches were progressing. Barnabas agreed and said they should take John Mark with them. Paul strongly objected, saying John Mark abandoned them for no apparent reason during their previous journey.

- Paul was so opposed to taking John Mark that he and Barnabas decided to go their separate ways. Barnabas traveled with John Mark to Cyprus, while Paul partnered with Silas and headed for Derbe in Galatia.

Note: Paul and Barnabas were in such disagreement about taking John Mark that they chose to separate. As a result, two missionary teams were formed. Paul's issue with Mark was apparently reconciled as indicated by several letters Paul wrote after this disagreement. In a letter to the church in Colosse, Paul writes, *"And as you were instructed before, make Mark welcome if he comes your way"* (Colossians 4:10b). Another letter informs us that Mark later became important to Paul's ministry. Paul writes, *"Only Luke is with me. Bring Mark with you when you come, for he will be helpful to me"* (2 Timothy 4:11).

RECOMMENDED BIBLE READING

Acts 13:13–48 **Paul, Apostle to the Gentiles**

Isaiah 49:1–7 **A Light to the Gentiles**

SECTION 2: PAUL'S SECOND MISSIONARY JOURNEY

Paul Meets Timothy: (Acts 16:1–10)

- During Paul's second missionary journey, he and Silas first visited believers in Derbe and then moved on to Lystra. While in Lystra, they met a young man named Timothy.

- Paul was impressed with Timothy and asked him to join their missionary team. Timothy agreed and became Paul and Silas' assistant.

- One night, Paul had a vision of a man begging him to come and help the people in Macedonia (northern Greece). After the vision, Paul and those with him headed for Macedonia.

 Note: In Acts 16:10, Luke transitions from third person to first person, describing events with the pronoun "we." This seems to indicate that Luke joined Paul and Silas on their journey.

Paul and Silas in Philippi: (Acts 16:11–40)

- When Paul and his team arrived in Philippi, a major city in Macedonia, they went to the riverbank where they heard Jews regularly met for prayer.

- At the riverbank, they met a business woman named Lydia, who sold expensive purple cloth. Lydia worshiped the One True God.

- Paul began explaining the Good News to Lydia. She listened intently and then accepted Jesus as her personal Savior. After Lydia and her household were baptized, she invited Paul and his missionary team into her home as guests. They accepted Lydia's offer and stayed with her while they were in Philippi.

- One day, as Paul and the others were on their way to the riverbank for prayer services, a demon-possessed slave girl began following them. She earned large sums of money for her masters as a fortune teller.

- As the demon-possessed girl walked behind Paul and his team, she shouted out for all to hear saying, *"These men are servants of the Most High God! They are telling you how to be saved"* (Acts 16:17 CEV).

- When this continued for several days, Paul became annoyed. Turning to the girl, Paul commanded the demons to leave in the name of Jesus. Hearing the name of Jesus, the demons immediately left.

- After Paul freed the girl of her demons, she was no longer able to see into the future and make money for her masters as a fortune teller.

- When the girl's masters realized the source of their income had vanished, they blamed Paul. They dragged Paul and Silas to city officials. A large crowd followed close behind them. The girl's masters accused Paul and Silas of teaching against Roman customs. As the crowd listened, they turned against the two missionaries and began attacking them.

- The city officials ordered Paul and Silas' arrest. After suffering a severe beating, the missionaries were thrown in jail. As midnight approached, Paul and Silas were praying and singing in worship to God while the other prisoners were listening to them in silence. Suddenly, a massive earthquake shook the entire prison.

- The prison's foundation began swaying violently back and forth. The jail doors suddenly flew open from the force of the earthquake and the prisoners' chains became loose.

- When the jailer saw the open doors, he thought his prisoners had escaped. As the jailer drew his sword to kill himself, Paul shouted out, *"Don't harm yourself! No one has escaped"* (Acts 16:28 CEV).

 Note: The jailer was about to kill himself because he would be severely punished or perhaps killed for allowing prisoners to escape during his watch.

- Trembling and in awe, the jailer asked Paul and Silas what he must do to be saved. They told him to believe in Jesus Christ, and he and his household would be saved.

- That night, as Paul and Silas shared the gospel, the jailer and his entire household believed. The two missionaries then baptized them.

- The next morning, the city officials ordered the missionaries' release. When the jailer told them they were free to go, Paul was outraged.

- Paul said to the jailer, *"They have publicly beaten us without a trial and put us in prison—and we are Roman citizens. So now they want us to leave secretly? Certainly not! Let them come themselves to release us!"* (Acts 16:37).

- When the city officials heard Paul and Silas were Roman citizens, they were panic-stricken. The city officials immediately apologized to the missionaries and politely asked them to leave Philippi.

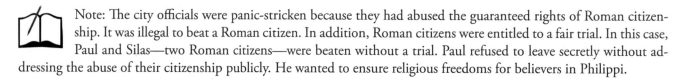 Note: The city officials were panic-stricken because they had abused the guaranteed rights of Roman citizenship. It was illegal to beat a Roman citizen. In addition, Roman citizens were entitled to a fair trial. In this case, Paul and Silas—two Roman citizens—were beaten without a trial. Paul refused to leave secretly without addressing the abuse of their citizenship publicly. He wanted to ensure religious freedoms for believers in Philippi.

- After their release, Paul and Silas returned to Lydia's house and encouraged the believers before leaving town.

Paul and Silas in Thessalonica: (Acts 17:1–10)

- Paul and Silas left Philippi and went to Thessalonica. When they arrived, they attended Sabbath services in the local synagogue for three weeks in a row.

- Each week, Paul stood up and explained how Jesus of Nazareth fulfilled prophecies about the Messiah. Some people listened and believed the Good News, while others rejected it.

- Those who rejected the Good News were determined to prevent Paul and Silas from preaching in Thessalonica. They met with local officials and filed charges against them.

- When believers in Thessalonica heard about the heightened opposition, they advised Paul and Silas to leave at once and go to Berea.

Paul and Silas in Berea: (Acts 17:11–15)

- When Paul and Silas arrived in Berea, they visited the local synagogue. The people in Berea were more receptive than those in Thessalonica. They attentively listened and then researched the Scriptures to determine if Paul and Silas were teaching the Truth of God.

- After thoroughly scrutinizing Paul's message, a large number of Bereans—Jews and Gentiles—believed the Good News.

- When some Jews in Thessalonica heard Paul was preaching in Berea, they went there and started rallying people against Paul.

- After hearing about the danger to Paul's life, the believers sent him to Athens. Silas and Timothy stayed in Berea a while longer.

Paul in Athens: (Acts 17:16–34)

- When Paul arrived in Athens, he was deeply troubled by the statues honoring idol gods erected all over the city. Paul began debating anyone who would listen, speaking in the local synagogue and the marketplace.

- One day, Paul tried to reason with some Greek philosophers. The philosophers decided to allow Paul to speak at the Areopagus, Athens' high council of philosophers.

- Paul stood up and addressed the council saying, *"Men of Athens, I notice that you are very religious in every way, for as I was walking along I saw your many shrines. And one of your altars had this inscription on it: 'To an Unknown God.' This God, whom you worship without knowing, is the one I'm telling you about. He is the God who made the world and everything in it"* (Acts 17:22–24a).

- Paul explained that God designed mankind with an innate desire to know Him. God is our Creator and as such, His creations should not think of Him as a man-made object. God has patiently endured such misunderstandings in the past, but is now calling people everywhere to turn away from sin and to His righteousness.

- Paul continued his speech, saying a day is coming when the world will be judged by the One whom God powerfully raised from the dead.

- When council members heard Paul mention God raising the dead, some scoffed while others wanted to hear more. They interrupted Paul's speech and began debating their various views on life after death.

- Having lost the council's attention, Paul left. A few people believed Paul's message that day and became followers of Jesus.

Paul in Corinth: (Acts 18:1–11)

- Paul left Athens and traveled to Corinth. There he met a man named Aquila and his wife Priscilla, who made tents for a living. Paul stayed with them. Since Paul was a tentmaker, he worked alongside them in their business. Paul stayed in Corinth for a year-and-a-half preaching the Good News.

1st Thessalonians: Most scholars believe Paul wrote two letters to the church in Thessalonica while he was in Corinth. About two or three years earlier, Paul helped establish the church in Thessalonica. Believers in Thessalonica embraced Christianity and were looking forward to Jesus' second coming. As time passed, they began to question what happens to believers who die before Jesus' return. When Paul heard about their concerns, he wrote a letter to encourage believers and explain the events that will occur when Jesus returns. 1st Thessalonians was written in about 51 A.D.

In 1st Thessalonians, Jesus is the Resurrection and Life. (See 1 Thessalonians 4:14; 5:10.)

Paul explains that the Day of the Lord's return is known only to God and will happen unexpectedly. Jesus will suddenly appear in the sky. Believers who have already died will rise from their graves. Believers who are still alive will join resurrected believers to meet the Lord Jesus in the air. All believers in Christ will then live in God's presence forever.

2ⁿᵈ Thessalonians: After Paul's first letter, he heard about more confusion in Thessalonica. The issue this time was about the timing of the Lord's return. As believers experienced persecution and hardships for their faith, word soon spread that the Day of the Lord had already started. As a result, some believers stopped working and had become idle while they waited for the Lord's return. Paul penned a second letter to the Thessalonians in about 51 or 52 A.D. to clear up this misconception.

In 2ⁿᵈ Thessalonians, Jesus is the One who will judge the world. (See 2 Thessalonians 1:7b–8.)

Paul outlined the events that will take place before Jesus' second coming. He encouraged believers to stand firm in the faith, and admonished those who had become idle to return to work and earn a living.

Paul's Return Trip to Antioch of Syria: (Acts 18:18–22)

- When Paul finished ministering in Corinth, he began the journey back to Antioch of Syria, his ministry's home base.

- Paul left Corinth and sailed to Ephesus with Priscilla and Aquila. When Paul departed for Jerusalem, Priscilla and Aquila stayed in Ephesus.

- Paul fellowshipped with the church in Jerusalem and then traveled back to Antioch of Syria, his ministry's home base.

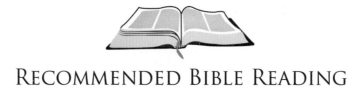

RECOMMENDED BIBLE READING

Acts 17:16–34 **Idolatry in Athens**
Psalm 96:1–13 **Praise God, the Creator**

SECTION 3: PAUL'S THIRD MISSIONARY JOURNEY

Priscilla and Aquila Meet Apollos: (Acts 18:23–28)

- After Paul had been in Antioch of Syria for a while, he decided to set out on a third missionary journey.

- Meanwhile in Ephesus, Priscilla and Aquila met a man named Apollos, a devout follower of John the Baptist's message. Apollos was a dynamic speaker, but had not heard the Good News of Jesus Christ.

- When Priscilla and Aquila heard Apollos preaching in the synagogue, they immediately realized he needed to hear about Jesus. After the service, Priscilla and Aquila met privately with Apollos and explained the complete gospel message.

- When Apollos heard about Jesus, he began studying the Scriptures and soon embraced the Good News. He started preaching in Ephesus, powerfully explaining how Jesus of Nazareth fulfilled prophecies about the Messiah. Apollos later set out on a missionary journey of his own to Achaia (present day Greece).

Paul in Ephesus: (Acts 19:1–41)

- Paul left Galatia and traveled to Ephesus where he preached in the local synagogue for three months until some Jews began opposing him. He then left the synagogue and preached to Jews and Gentiles at a lecture hall in Ephesus for the next two years.

1st Corinthians: While Paul was in Ephesus, he wrote a letter to the church in Corinth, established during his second missionary journey. Disagreements and incorrect teachings had created disharmony in the church. Believers were quarrelling with each other and some had become arrogant, claiming their spiritual gifts were better than others. Paul wrote 1st Corinthians in about 55 A.D. to identify and correct problems, which had caused believers to lose sight of what it means to live for Jesus Christ.

In 1st Corinthians, Jesus is the Wisdom of God. Jesus brings unity, righteousness, spiritual purity, and redemption. (See 1 Corinthians 1:30.)

Paul instructed believers to focus on God and spiritual growth. Paul then addressed several issues on Christian lifestyle and faith. He condemned sexual immorality, spiritual pride, and disharmony among believers. Paul had previously received a list of questions from believers in Corinth. He answered their questions on marriage, eating food sacrificed to idols, and other Christian freedoms. Paul provided instructions for observing the Lord's Supper in a manner that honors Christ, using spiritual gifts in a way that creates harmony and unity among believers, and conducting orderly worship. He also wrote about the importance of love—God's greatest gift—and the significance of the resurrection.

- Sometime later, a man named Demetrius, a local silversmith who made idols for a living, became highly upset with Paul. Demetrius was losing customers as a result of Paul's teachings against idol worship.

- When Demetrius' customers converted to Christianity, they stopped buying his idols. Outraged, Demetrius held a meeting with silversmiths, craftsmen, and others whose businesses had been affected by Paul's teachings.

- As Demetrius spoke out against Paul's teachings, the group became enraged. They began shouting praises to the Greek goddess Artemis in support of their pagan beliefs.

- Other people in Ephesus came to see what was happening. They joined in the commotion. People started pushing each other and creating all kinds of confusion. Before long, a riot erupted.

- A city official soon arrived on the scene. After quieting the angry mob, he reminded them that the Roman government would charge them with disturbing the peace.

- The city official urged the people to file charges and settle their disputes in court. He then dismissed the crowd and everyone left.

 Note: Ephesus was a province of the Roman Empire. The city official reminded the crowd that Rome would take away their civic freedoms if they continued to riot.

Paul in Macedonia and Greece: (Acts 20:1–6)

- After the riot, Paul left and headed for Macedonia, stopping in several towns along the way to spiritually strengthen believers.

 2ⁿᵈ Corinthians: While Paul was in Macedonia, he wrote another letter to the church in Corinth. Paul had written three previous letters to the Corinthians, two of which are lost. Scholars believe 1ˢᵗ Corinthians was Paul's second letter and 2ⁿᵈ Corinthians was Paul's fourth letter to the Corinthians. False teachers in Corinth were questioning Paul's authority and his character. Paul wrote 2ⁿᵈ Corinthians sometime between 55 and 57 A.D. to defend his ministry and authority as an apostle.

In 2ⁿᵈ Corinthians, Jesus is the One who reconciles us with God. (See 2 Corinthians 5:17–19.)

Paul responds to attacks against his ministry, saying his authority as an apostle came directly from God. He points out that he had suffered many trials and personal hardships as an apostle. Paul says his commitment to endure comes from his faith in the resurrection, the glory God receives when others accept Jesus, and the spiritual growth that comes from his dependence on God. Paul encourages the Corinthians, reminding them of their hope of eternal life. He instructs them to assist fellow believers experiencing hardships in Jerusalem. He admonishes them not to be deceived by false apostles and challenges them to examine their faith.

- After visiting Macedonia, Paul traveled to Greece. He stayed in Corinth for three months, teaching and preaching the Word of God.

 Romans: While in Corinth, Paul wrote a letter to believers in Rome. He had heard many good reports about the church in Rome, but had never been there. Paul was planning to visit Rome after his return to Jerusalem. He wrote to believers in Rome to introduce himself and explain the foundational truths of the gospel message. Paul's letter to believers in Rome was written in about 57 A.D.

In Romans, Jesus is God's Plan of Redemption and Salvation. (See Romans 1:16–17; 3:24–25.)

Paul systematically outlines what Jesus' death and resurrection means for believers. He defines sin as rebellion against God and explains a day is coming when God will judge sin and unrighteousness. God entrusted the Jews with the law to show mankind how sinful humanity is compared to His standard of righteousness. God through His grace provided a way for mankind to be made righteous in His sight. God presented His Son, Jesus Christ, as a sacrificial offering for the sins of the world. Jesus fulfilled the requirements of the law for righteousness. He took mankind's sins upon Himself and substituted His life for ours. In this great exchange, Jesus paid the price of redemption with His blood, freed us from the penalty of sin, made us righteous before God, and reconciled our relationship with God the Father.

Paul explains that God's free gift of salvation is available to anyone who believes in Jesus Christ as Lord and Savior. Paul exhorts believers to live for God, grow spiritually, and use spiritual gifts to glorify God.

- While preparing for his return trip, Paul heard about a plot to kill him.

- After hearing this, Paul changed his return route. Instead of sailing from Greece, he traveled inland back to Macedonia and then sailed from Philippi to Troas.

Paul in Troas: (Acts 20:7–12)

- When Paul arrived in Troas, he stayed for a week. During his last night in Troas, Paul met with believers and began preaching.

- As midnight approached, Paul was still preaching. A young man, who was listening while seated on the window-sill, became very drowsy. He eventually dozed off and fell from the third story window to his death.

- Paul hurried downstairs and bent over the young man. He grabbed the young man and held him in a tight embrace. Paul then announced that the man was alive.

- Paul returned upstairs and continued preaching until dawn. The young man was alive and doing well. As friends escorted the young man home, they thanked God for the miracle.

Paul Meets With Elders from Ephesus in Miletus: (Acts 20:13–37)

- After leaving Troas, Paul traveled to Miletus. He asked the elders in Ephesus to come to Miletus and meet with him. Paul did not want to spend additional time traveling to Ephesus because he was trying to get back to Jerusalem in time for Pentecost.

- After the elders from Ephesus arrived in Miletus, Paul delivered a farewell message. Paul informed the elders they would not see him again. He encouraged the elders to continue ministering to those God placed under their leadership and then prayed for them.

- When Paul finished praying, the elders were visibly saddened by his news. After saying their farewells, Paul set sail for Tyre.

Paul Stays with Philip in Caesarea: (Acts 21:1–14)

- When Paul arrived in Tyre, some local believers told him they had received divine insight from the Holy Spirit and he should not go to Jerusalem.

- After fellowshipping with believers in Tyre for about a week, Paul traveled to Caesarea. In Caesarea, Paul and his companions stayed with Philip, one of the seven deacons who distributed food in the church at Jerusalem.

- One day, a believer came to visit Paul. He took Paul's belt and strapped it around his own feet and wrists. The believer prophesied saying, *"The Holy Spirit declares, 'So shall the owner of this belt be bound by the Jewish leaders in Jerusalem and turned over to the Gentiles'"* (Acts 21:11b).

- When Paul's traveling companions and others heard the prophecy, they were greatly alarmed. They pleaded with Paul to reconsider and not travel to Jerusalem.

- Paul responded, *"Why all this weeping? You are breaking my heart! I am ready not only to be jailed at Jerusalem but even to die for the sake of the Lord Jesus"* (Acts 21:13).

- When believers saw how determined Paul was to go to Jerusalem, they gave up and prayed for his safety.

RECOMMENDED BIBLE READING

Acts 19:21–41   **Idolatry in Ephesus**

Isaiah 44:6–20   **The Foolishness of Idolatry**

SECTION 4: PAUL'S ARREST

Paul Arrives in Jerusalem: (Acts 21:15–40)

- After arriving in Jerusalem, Paul met with the apostles and elders in Jerusalem and provided a detailed report on his third missionary journey.

- When Paul finished his report, the council informed him of a false rumor, which was circulating about his ministry. People were saying that Paul was teaching Gentiles against the law of Moses.

- To correct the people's misconception, the council advised Paul to participate in an upcoming Jewish ceremony. They said Paul's participation should demonstrate the falsehood of these rumors.

- The apostles and elders then confirmed their support for Paul's ministry. Paul agreed with the council's suggestion and participated in the Jewish ceremony.

- While Paul was in the Temple for the ceremony, some Jews from Asia who were opposed to his ministry recognized him. They stirred up the people against him.

- When the crowd heard the accusations against Paul, they attacked him. They dragged Paul out of the Temple with plans of killing him.

- The commander of the Roman regiment and his soldiers rushed to the scene. He ordered his soldiers to arrest Paul. Turning to the boisterous crowd, the commander asked what crime had Paul committed. Although several people shouted accusations, they were not in agreement.

- Since the allegations against Paul were inconsistent, the commander ordered his soldiers to escort Paul back to the military barracks. As the soldiers carried Paul away, the crowd followed close behind. They became disorderly and began attacking Paul again.

- The soldiers picked Paul up and lifted him over their shoulders to shield him from the angry mob. As they reached the barracks, Paul asked the commander for permission to speak to the crowd and he agreed.

Paul Addressed the Angry Crowd: (Acts 22:1–30)

- Addressing the crowd, Paul explained how he used to avidly seek out and persecute believers. He then described his conversion experience.

- Paul told the crowd he became a believer and Jesus later spoke to him saying, *"Hurry! Leave Jerusalem, for the people here won't accept your testimony about me . . . Go, for I will send you far away to the Gentiles!"* (Acts 22:17, 21).

- As soon as Paul mentioned the Gentiles, the crowd became riled up again and shouted abusive remarks against Paul. Eager to find out what Paul had done to infuriate the crowd, the commander ordered his soldiers to whip Paul and force him to explain.

- As the soldiers were strapping Paul down, he asked, *"Is it legal for you to whip a Roman citizen who hasn't even been tried?"* (Acts 22:25). The officer overseeing Paul's punishment abruptly halted the whipping and told the commander what Paul said.

- When the commander found out Paul was a Roman citizen, he was exceedingly troubled, for he had ordered the whipping. He then requested a meeting with the Sanhedrin council in hopes of finding out the specifics of Paul's crime. The next day, the commander brought Paul before a special session of the Sanhedrin.

Paul Addresses the Sanhedrin Council: (Acts 23:1–11)

- When Paul addressed the Sanhedrin council, he created such confusion among council members that they started pushing and yanking him violently back and forth. Concerned for Paul's safety, the commander ordered his soldiers to take Paul back to the military barracks.

- During the night, the Lord appeared next to Paul saying, *"Be encouraged, Paul. Just as you have been a witness to me here in Jerusalem, you must preach the Good News in Rome as well"* (Acts 23:11).

The Plot to Kill Paul: (Acts 23:12–35)

- The next morning, forty Jewish men got together and vowed to kill Paul. Paul's nephew heard about the assassination plot and reported it to the commander. After hearing the details of the plot, the commander wrote a letter to Governor Felix and ordered soldiers to escort Paul safely to Caesarea, where the governor resided.

- When Paul arrived in Caesarea, Governor Felix read the commander's letter. He told Paul he would hear his case as soon as his accusers arrived from Jerusalem.

Paul's Hearing With Governor Felix: (Acts 24:1–27)

- Five days later, the high priest and several religious leaders arrived in Caesarea from Jerusalem. After listening to both sides of Paul's case, Felix postponed his decision and kept Paul in custody. While in prison, Paul was allowed visitors and other special privileges.

- Two years later, a man named Festus succeeded Felix as governor of Judea. When Festus arrived, Paul was still in prison.

Paul Meets With Governor Festus: (Acts 25:1–27)

- Governor Festus immediately arranged to hear Paul's case. Jewish leaders from Jerusalem came to Caesarea and presented their accusations against Paul. However, none of their allegations were verifiable.

- In an attempt to win favor with Jewish leaders, Festus asked Paul if he would be willing to stand trial in Jerusalem before the Sanhedrin council. Paul immediately answered "no." He then asked for a trial before Caesar, a right entitled to him as a Roman citizen. Festus responded, *"Very well! You have appealed to Caesar, and to Caesar you will go!"* (Acts 25:12).

- Sometime later, King Agrippa and his sister Bernice visited Festus. When they arrived, Festus arranged for Paul to present his case to Agrippa. After hearing Paul's case, King Agrippa said to Festus, *"He (Paul) could have been set free if he hadn't appealed to Caesar"* (Acts 26:32). Festus later ordered his officers to make arrangements for Paul's trip to Rome, courtesy of the Roman government.

Paul Sails to Rome: (Acts 27:1–28:10)

- When it was time to depart, a Roman officer assumed custody of Paul and several other prisoners. The next day, they boarded a cargo ship and set sail.

- The ship traveled north from Caesarea and made several stops along the way. During one of the stops, the Roman officer transferred Paul and the other prisoners to an Egyptian ship bound for Italy.

- The Egyptian ship soon ran into rough sailing due to bad weather. The crew had a difficult time steering the ship. After struggling along the coast, the ship finally reached the island of Crete.

- Paul then warned of a possible shipwreck if they continued. However, the ship's captain and crew ignored Paul's warning and continued the journey. The bad weather intensified and a terrible storm soon arose.

- The raging storm persisted for days, tossing the ship violently back and forth. With no end in sight, the crew lost all hope of survival.

- Paul then called the crew together and announced, *"Last night an angel of the God to whom I belong and whom I serve stood beside me, and he said, 'Don't be afraid, Paul, for you will surely stand trial before Caesar! What's more, God in his goodness has granted safety to everyone sailing with you.' So take courage! For I believe God. It will be just as he said. But we will be shipwrecked on an island"* (Acts 27:23–26).

- Peering through the raging storm, the crew finally spotted dry land. As they headed for shore, the ship began to break apart from the force of the waves. Everyone jumped overboard and made it safely to shore.

- After reaching shore, Paul and the others discovered they were on the island of Malta. They received a warm greeting from the local people.

- While on Malta, Paul healed a local official's father. When people heard this news, others came for healing. Many were healed through Paul's prayers.

- After three months, Paul and the rest of the shipwrecked crew boarded another ship bound for Italy.

Paul Arrives in Rome: (Acts 28:11–30)

- When Paul finally arrived in Rome, he was placed under house arrest. Paul was allowed to live in his own house with a soldier guarding him at all times.

- A few days later, Paul called together local Jewish leaders and explained the circumstances of his arrest. The Jewish leaders told Paul they had not heard anything about the charges against him and then expressed interest in hearing Paul's message.

- Paul invited a large number of Jews to his home and began explaining how Jesus Christ fulfilled prophecies about the Messiah. After hearing Paul's teaching, some Jews believed while others rejected the gospel message.

- Paul remained under house arrest for the next two years, teaching and boldly proclaiming the name of Jesus to everyone who visited him.

RECOMMENDED BIBLE READING

Acts 26:1–32 **Paul's Defense Before King Agrippa**

Lamentations 3:17–27 **Great Is God's Faithfulness**

SECTION 5: BUILDING THE FAITH

 Note: The book of Acts comes to an end with Paul proclaiming the Good News to his visitors while under house arrest in Rome. According to tradition, Paul never appeared before Caesar in a trial. He was released after spending two years under house arrest. Although the Biblical account of the spreading of the gospel ends in the book of Acts, the apostles wrote letters, which provide insight into this period of early church history. During the two years Paul spent under house arrest, he wrote letters to the churches in Ephesus, Colosse, and Philippi. Paul also wrote a personal letter to a Christian friend named Philemon. These letters are often called Paul's "prison letters."

 Ephesians: Paul wrote a letter to the church in Ephesus in about 60 A.D. During Paul's third missionary journey, he stayed in Ephesus for about three years teaching and sharing the Good News. Paul's letter to the Ephesians did not address a specific problem. Paul wrote to make believers aware of the many spiritual blessings available through Christ and to exhort believers to use these spiritual blessings to grow in Christ.

In Ephesians, Jesus is the One who provides spiritual blessings for the benefit of the church. (See Ephesians 1:22–23.)

Paul explains God's spiritual blessings for those who are in Christ. Believers are adopted into God's family, redeemed through Jesus' blood, forgiven of sins, given an inheritance, identified as belonging to God through the gift of the Holy Spirit, saved by grace to new life in Christ, united in peace, and more. Paul encourages believers to stay focused on Christ and grounded in the faith. He instructs them to use their spiritual gifts to equip believers for God's work and to build up the church. Paul exhorts believers to live guided by the Holy Spirit and to put on the full armor of God. (See Ephesians 6:10–18.)

 Colossians: Paul's letter to the church in Colosse was written about the same time as his letter to the Ephesians in 60 A.D. Paul had never been to Colosse. He heard the church in Colosse had become infiltrated with false teachings. These teachings combined paganism and Judaism with Christianity, which diminished Christ's role as Redeemer and Savior. Paul wrote the Colossians to refute false teachings, correct misconceptions, and establish a proper view of Christ.

In Colossians, Jesus is Supreme Head of the church. (See Colossians 1:15, 18–20.)

Paul firmly establishes Jesus Christ as Redeemer and Savior. He explains that Jesus completely provides everything believers need to be reconciled with God and enter into His presence. Paul tells believers not be misguided by false teachings. He exhorts them to stay grounded in the faith and focused on Christ. Paul provides instructions for living a new life in Christ and encourages believers to stay prayerful.

Philemon: Paul wrote a brief letter to a Christian friend named Philemon in about 60 A.D. This letter was written about the same time as his letters to the Ephesians and Colossians. Philemon owned a slave named Onesimus, who had stolen from him and run away to Rome. While Onesimus was in Rome, he met Paul and accepted Jesus as his Lord and Savior. After Onesimus' conversion, Paul sent him back to Philemon with a letter. In Paul's letter, he asks Philemon to forgive his runaway slave and accept him as a brother in Christ.

In Philemon, Jesus is an Advocate. Paul intercedes for Onesimus as his advocate in the same way Jesus intercedes with God the Father and advocates on behalf of all believers. (See Philemon 1:16–18.)

Philippians: Paul helped to establish the church in Philippi during his second missionary journey. While Paul was under house arrest in Rome, the church in Philippi sent Paul a gift. Paul wrote a letter to the Philippians in about 61 A.D. to express his gratitude for their support and to encourage them to grow in Christ in spite of adversities. Paul explains that Jesus is the One who gives true joy.

In Philippians, Jesus is the Source of believer's joy and power over circumstances. (See Philippians 4:4, 13.)

Paul encourages believers to live as citizens of heaven and work together in humility with the same attitude as Christ. Paul warns against false teachings. He exhorts believers to rejoice in the Lord and pray instead of worrying. Paul tells believers to allow God's peace to guard their hearts and minds by staying focused on *"things that are excellent and worthy of praise"* (Philippians 4:8b).

Note: Most scholars believe Paul was released from house arrest in about 62 A.D. After his release, Paul wrote letters to Timothy and Titus, two faithful companions in his ministry. These letters are often called Paul's "pastoral letters" because they focus on church oversight and pastoral care.

1st Timothy: Paul wrote his first letter to Timothy, a close friend and traveling companion, in about 64 A.D. Paul left Timothy in Ephesus to correct false teachings and oversee the church in his absence. Paul wrote to encourage his young assistant and provide guidance for establishing church leadership in Ephesus and teaching the truths of the faith.

In 1st Timothy, Jesus is Mediator between God and man. (See 1 Timothy 2:5–6.)

Paul advises Timothy on his responsibilities as a minister overseeing the church in Ephesus. He provides guidance for conducting worship, appointing church leadership, and caring for church membership. He then warns Timothy about false teachings and instructs him to teach doctrinal truths.

Titus: Paul wrote a letter to Titus, a young Greek believer assisting in his ministry. Paul's letter to Titus was much like his first letter to Timothy and was written about the same time in 64 A.D. Paul had been teaching doctrinal truths on the island of Crete. He left Titus in Crete with instructions to finish the work he had started and appoint elders in each town. Paul wrote to encourage Titus and provide guidance on organizing and overseeing the church in Crete.

In Titus, Jesus is our Savior. (See Titus 2:12–14.)

Paul outlines the qualifications for church elders. He instructs Titus to teach the truths of the faith and correct false teachings. Paul tells Titus to encourage believers to live upright and obey societal laws. He exhorts Titus to set a godly example and deal strongly with people to correct unrighteous behavior.

Note: In 64 A.D., Emperor Nero blamed Christians for a fire, which burned significant sections of Rome. After the fire, Nero began persecuting Christians in Rome. Many historians believe Emperor Nero set the fire himself to speed up his plans for urban renewal. While Nero was making life extremely difficult for believers in Rome, opposition to Christianity intensified world-wide. Believers everywhere faced danger and personal hardships. Apostle Peter wrote a letter to encourage Jewish believers who had fled from religious persecution and were scattered throughout Asia Minor.

1ˢᵗ Peter: During a time of great suffering and religious persecution, Peter wrote a letter to Jewish believers living in several Roman provinces to encourage, comfort, and offer hope. Peter's first letter was written between 62 and 64 A.D.

In 1ˢᵗ Peter, Jesus is the One who provided believers a priceless inheritance. (See 1 Peter 1:3–5.)

Peter encourages believers to stay spiritually strong in the midst of their trials. He comforts believers, reminding them of their hope of eternal life. Peter explains that salvation is a gift from God as a reward for faith in Jesus Christ. Those who suffer for Christ become partners with Christ and will receive the joy of salvation. Peter encourages believers to continue living holy, get rid of unrighteous behavior, respect authority, follow Christ's example of endurance and suffering for righteousness sake, love each other, and use spiritual gifts to help each other. Peter instructs church elders to love and care for those under their leadership. He urges believers to serve with humility, turn their worries over to God, and stand firm against the devil's attacks.

Note: After a few years of freedom, Paul was apparently arrested and put in prison again. This is indicated in Paul's second letter to Timothy, written while he was in prison and facing death. (See 2 Timothy 2:9.) Christians suffered persecution under Emperor Nero in Rome from 64 to 67 A.D. According to church tradition, Paul was executed under Emperor Nero in about 67 A.D. About this same time, Peter wrote a second letter to encourage and strengthen believers. Church tradition states that Peter suffered martyrdom shortly after Paul's death.

2ⁿᵈ Timothy: While in prison and facing execution, Paul wrote a second letter to Timothy in about 66 or 67 A.D. Shortly after writing this letter, Paul was executed for his faith in Jesus Christ. Paul wrote to give Timothy some final words of wisdom and to encourage him to stay strong in the faith.

In 2ⁿᵈ Timothy, Jesus is the Way to Life and Immortality. (See 2 Timothy 1:10; 2:11–12.)

Paul reminds Timothy of his responsibilities as a minister and pastor. He encourages Timothy to faithfully use the spiritual gifts God gave him to teach, correct, rebuke, and encourage others. He warns about a time when evil and false teachings will abound. Paul exhorts Timothy to stay true to the faith through good and bad times.

2ⁿᵈ Peter: Anticipating his own death, Peter wrote some final words of wisdom to believers. He exhorted believers to grow spiritually in the knowledge of Jesus Christ and warned against false teachings. Peter wrote his second letter in about 67 A.D. According to church tradition, Peter suffered martyrdom shortly after writing this letter.

In 2ⁿᵈ Peter, Jesus is the Source of knowledge and spiritual growth. (See 2 Peter 1:5–8.)

Peter encourages spiritual growth and exhorts believers to study the Scriptures so they will not be deceived by false teachings. He declares the Day of the Lord is surely coming when the world will be judged. On that day, believers will experience a new heaven and new earth, while non believers will face God's righteous judgment against sin.

Note: The church was only about thirty years old. In the midst of religious persecution, another pressing problem threatened the church's survival. False teachers were increasingly working their way into the church, attempting to destroy the message of the gospel. Jude, another one of Jesus' half-brothers, had planned to write a letter to believers on salvation. When Jude heard the magnitude of the problem with false teachers, he changed the subject of his letter. Jude wrote a stern letter to oppose false teachers, warn about the dangers of false doctrines, and encourage believers to remain true to the faith.

Jude: False teachers were condoning immorality. They claimed it was alright to live immoral lifestyles because God in His grace forgives sin. When Jude heard about this, he wrote a letter to condemn these teachings and urge believers to defend the truths of the faith. Jude was most probably written between 65 and 70 A.D.

In Jude, Jesus is the One who keeps us safe in His care. (See Jude 1:24–25.)

Jude warns against false teachers and their lenient views on immorality. Pointing to Israel's past, Jude reminds believers that God condemns immorality and will ultimately judge sin. Jude describes false teachers as godless, self indulgent, complainers, braggarts, scoffers, and deceivers. He urges believers to build their faith through prayer, staying focused on Christ, and showing mercy to others.

Note: The message of salvation through faith in Jesus Christ was difficult for Jews to accept. They were well versed in the practice of Judaism. Some Jews rejected the message of the gospel, while others who accepted Jesus as the Messiah often struggled with their new faith. A letter, entitled Hebrews, was written to Jewish Christians to establish the superiority of the gospel message over Judaism and other religions. The author of Hebrews is unknown. However, Paul and others who assisted in Paul's ministry have often been suggested as possible authors.

Hebrews: Hebrews was written to Jewish believers to establish the superiority of Christianity over Judaism and all other religions. Jesus Christ was the perfect one-time sacrifice for our sins and no other sacrifices are needed. Hebrews was most probably written before the destruction of Jerusalem in 70 A.D.

In Hebrews, Jesus is our Great High Priest, ruling over God's house. (See Hebrews 10:19–22.)

The author of Hebrews explains that Jesus is both divine and human. Jesus is God's Son and is the exact representation of God. Jesus became human to fulfill God's Plan of Redemption and Salvation for mankind. Jesus is the Messiah, God's promise of hope. Jesus is superior to angels, the patriarchs, the priesthood and the old covenant laws. Christianity is superior because Jesus' one-time sacrifice guarantees salvation for all.

Believers are encouraged to stop wavering and grow in faith, fully trusting in Jesus. The author then defines faith. (See Hebrews 11:1.) He gives examples of Old Testament patriarchs, who demonstrated faith. Believers are exhorted to endure the test of their faith by staying focused on Jesus.

Note: Jews in Jerusalem revolted against Roman domination in 66 A.D. The Roman government dispatched troops led by General Titus, the Roman emperor's son, to squelch the uprising. After holding the city under siege for several years, the Romans finally broke through Jerusalem's walls in 70 A.D. They set Jerusalem on fire, destroying everything. Apostle John lived well past the destruction of Jerusalem. According to church tradition, John ministered in Ephesus for a while. He wrote three letters after Jerusalem's destruction. These letters are called 1st, 2nd, and 3rd John. The Roman government later exiled John to Patmos, a desolate rocky island where the Romans banished criminals and terrorists. While exiled on the island of Patmos, John received a prophetic vision. John's vision is described in his final letter, called Revelation.

1ˢᵗ John: During a time of great religious persecution, John wrote a letter to all believers to encourage them in their faith. John promoted Christian fellowship and love. He opposed false prophets, who taught against the truth of Jesus Christ. This letter was written between 85 and 90 A.D.

In 1ˢᵗ John, Jesus is our Advocate and the Giver of Eternal Life. (See 1 John 2:1–2; 5:11–12.)

John proclaims that he is an eyewitness of Jesus' ministry. He encourages believers to grow in faith so they can fully share in the joy of knowing Christ. John admonishes believers to love one another and says their actions should demonstrate their love. Anyone who does not demonstrate Christian love does not know God, for God is love. He calls believers to righteous living and warns against false prophets. John reminds believers that the Holy Spirit helps them overcome the battles of this world. He expresses the hope of eternal life through faith in Jesus Christ.

2ⁿᵈ John: John addressed a second letter to "the chosen lady and to her children." (See 2 John 1:1.) Some scholars believe John was writing to a specific woman and her children while others believe the letter was addressed to a local church and its members. Regardless, John wrote to encourage believers to stay grounded in the faith, living in the love of God. He warned against false teachers. John's second letter was written about the same time as his first letter, between 85 and 90 A.D.

In 2ⁿᵈ John, Jesus is the Source of our relationship with God. (See 2 John 1:9.)

John praises believers for living in the Truth of God and encourages them to love one another. John advises believers not to associate with teachers who distort the true message of Jesus Christ.

3ʳᵈ John: John addressed a third letter to a believer named Gaius, calling him a dear friend. In a demonstration of true Christian love, Gaius had been welcoming traveling ministers with warm hospitality. John wrote to commend Gaius for assisting God's messengers of the gospel. John's third letter was written about the same time as his other two letters, between 85 and 90 A.D.

In 3ʳᵈ John, Jesus is the Source of Truth. (See 3 John 1:6–8.)

John praises Gaius for his faithfulness. He commends Gaius for the hospitality he has shown traveling ministers and encourages him to continue supporting those who are spreading the gospel. John then rebukes another leader in the church named Diotrephes whose behavior is directly opposite of Gaius' righteous example. John uses Diotrephes' ungodly behavior as an opportunity to encourage Gaius in the faith.

Revelation: The Roman government banished John to the small rocky island of Patmos for preaching the gospel message. While John was on the island, he received a revelation of future events in a prophetic vision. John recorded everything he saw for seven churches in Asia and all present and future believers. John promises a blessing to everyone who reads and obeys the prophecy and issues a stern warning to all who add or detract from it. (See Revelation 1:3; 22:18–19.) John wrote Revelation, which means "unveiling" or "disclosure," between 90 and 95 A.D.

In Revelation, Jesus is the Eternal One, who will judge the world. (See Revelation 1:17–18.)

John's vision begins with Jesus giving him seven messages for seven churches in Asia that were in existence during John's time. The messages address specific areas in each church: commending strengths, rebuking spiritual weaknesses, and commanding faith in action. John's vision suddenly shifts from the churches to scenes of worship in heaven. John watches as God the Father is worshiped and Jesus, the Lamb of God, is declared worthy to judge the earth. God gives the worthy Lamb a scroll with seven seals. As the worthy Lamb opens each seal, a new vision appears. Each vision unveils a series of God's judgments poured out on the earth along with increasing evil throughout the world. The vision culminates with the return of Christ. Jesus imprisons Satan in an abyss and then reigns over earth for 1,000 years in undisturbed peace. After the 1,000 year period, Jesus issues final judgment of Satan and all unbelievers. Jesus then establishes a kingdom for all believers, who will live with Him eternally. John's vision concludes with Jesus promising, *"Yes, I am coming soon!"* (Revelation 22:20).

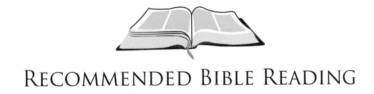

RECOMMENDED BIBLE READING

Ephesians 6:10–20 **The Whole Armor of God**

Isaiah 59:14–21 **The Redeemer Cometh**

MEDITATION & PRAYER

Apostle Peter encourages us to grow in our knowledge of God and Jesus our Lord:

"Grace and peace be yours in abundance through the knowledge of God and of Jesus our Lord. His divine power has given us everything we need for a godly life through our knowledge of him who called us by his own glory and goodness . . . For this very reason, make every effort to add to your faith goodness; and to goodness, knowledge; and to knowledge, self-control; and to self-control, perseverance; and to perseverance, godliness; and to godliness, mutual affection; and to mutual affection, love. For if you possess these qualities in increasing measure, they will keep you from being ineffective and unproductive in your knowledge of our Lord Jesus Christ."

(2 Peter 1:2–3; 5–8 TNIV)

Dear God,

All praise, glory, and honor are Yours always. I thank You for the grace and peace that comes with knowing Jesus Christ as my Lord and Savior. Strengthen me through Jesus' divine power and keep me grounded in Your Truths. I know Jesus has everything I need to live a life that pleases You. So, here I am . . . ready and eager to know more about Your will and Your ways. Increase my faith and help me show others the goodness of Your mercy and grace. Increase my knowledge and self-control so that I am able to persevere. Help me to grow in godliness, showing others affection and love. Teach me how to become a more effective witness for Jesus Christ as it is my desire to be a productive citizen of Your Kingdom.

Amen

REVIEW QUESTIONS

1. What prompted Paul and Barnabas to set out on their first missionary journey?

    _____

    _____

    _____

    _____

2. As Paul traveled to each city, he sought out the local synagogue and preached the Good News. Most devout Jews in the local synagogues rejected His message. Why?

    _____

    _____

    _____

    _____

3. What did Paul do when local synagogues rejected his message?

    _____

    _____

    _____

    _____

4. Why did Paul return to cities where his life had been threatened?

    _____

    _____

    _____

    _____

5. Paul and Barnabas met with apostles and elders in Jerusalem for guidance on an issue that threatened to divide the early church. What was this issue? How was it resolved?

_____

_____

_____

_____

6. Why were city officials in Philippi panic-stricken when they found out Paul and Silas were Roman citizens? What was the significance of Roman citizenship?

_____

_____

_____

_____

7. How did Paul's Roman citizenship help him accomplish God's work—the spreading of the gospel?

_____

_____

_____

_____

8. What major problems threatened the early church's existence, causing the apostles to write letters?

_____

_____

_____

_____

PERSONAL REFLECTIONS

9. How would you respond if God called you to perform a special work for Him? What steps would you take to ensure the call was from God?

_____

_____

_____

_____

_____

10. What did you learn from Paul about handling rejection and personal hardships? What Scriptures strengthen you in times of trouble and personal hardships?

_____

_____

_____

_____

_____

11. What did you learn from Paul about leadership?

_____

_____

_____

_____

_____

12. What reasons do non-believers give for rejecting the Good News? How would you defend your faith against these objections?

_____

_____

_____

_____

_____

13. What are your spiritual gifts? What do you do well that can be used to build God's Kingdom or show others His love? You might want to ask this question to someone who knows you well.

_____

_____

_____

_____

_____

14. Write a prayer asking God to identify the special work He is calling you to do.

_____

_____

_____

_____

CLOSING PRAYER

God commissioned Isaiah for a special work:

"In the year that King Uzziah died, I saw the Lord seated on a throne, high and exalted, and the train of his robe filled the temple. Above him were seraphs, each with six wings: With two wings they covered their faces, with two they covered their feet, and with two they were flying. And they were calling to one another: 'Holy, holy, holy is the LORD Almighty; the whole earth is full of his glory.' . . . Then one of the seraphs flew to me with a live coal in his hand, which he had taken with tongs from the altar. With it he touched my mouth and said, 'See, this has touched your lips; your guilt is taken away and your sin atoned for.' Then I heard the voice of the Lord saying, 'Whom shall I send? And who will go for us?' And I said, 'Here am I. Send me!'"

(Isaiah 6:1–3; 6–8 NIV)

Dear Lord God,

You are seated on the throne, high and exalted. Holy, holy, holy is the Lord Almighty. The whole earth is full of Your glory. I am a sinner in need of Your grace and mercy. I thank You for sending Your Son, Jesus Christ to redeem and save the world from sin. I repent of my sins and profess Jesus Christ as my Lord and Savior. Remove the stains of my guilt and cleanse me with Jesus' blood. The blood Jesus shed on the cross makes me righteous in your sight. I thank You for the free gift of salvation and look forward to Your call for a special work. Strengthen me so that I, like Isaiah, will say, "Here am I. Send me!"

Amen

REVIEW ANSWERS

Chapter 1

1. When Jesus was born, Roman soldiers were occupying Israel. Although the Romans made Herod the Great the local king, it was clear real power belonged to Rome. The Roman soldiers' primary responsibility was to keep the Jews under control. The Jews despised the Romans and longed to be free from foreign rule. They were eagerly awaiting the prophesied Messiah, whom they thought would free them from Roman subjugation.

2. The four gospel writers were Matthew, Mark, Luke, and John. Matthew was a tax collector and one of Jesus' twelve disciples. Matthew wrote for a Jewish audience and presents Jesus as "King of Israel." Mark was a companion of Peter. Mark's gospel targeted a Roman audience and presents Jesus as the "Servant." Luke was a close friend and traveling companion of Apostle Paul. Luke describes Jesus as "the Son of Man," identifying Him with humanity. John was a fisherman and one of the twelve disciples. John wrote for all mankind, emphatically declaring Jesus as the "Son of God."

3. Jesus' genealogy was important because it verified His claim. Centuries earlier, God revealed through the prophets that the Messiah would be a descendant of King David. (See Isaiah 9:6–7; Jeremiah 23:5–6; Ezekiel 34:23–24.)

4. The angel Gabriel announced to Mary she would soon have a Son who would be called the Son of the Most High God. An angel appeared to Joseph in a dream and told him Mary's Child had been conceived by the Holy Spirit. Shepherds were in fields caring for their flocks. God's glory filled the night sky and an angel appeared, announcing the Savior's birth. The wise men followed a star, which led them to the Messiah (Matthew 1:18–22, 2:1–2; Luke 1:26–38, 2:8–14).

5. During the final month of Mary's pregnancy, Caesar Augustus ordered a census. Everyone was required to register in the town of their family's origin. Since Joseph was a descendant of King David, he and Mary had to register in Bethlehem, David's hometown. This was important because it fulfilled prophecy about the Messiah's birthplace (Micah 5:2; Luke 2:1–5).

6. John the Baptist was the forerunner of Jesus Christ. He was also Jesus' cousin. (See Luke 1:36.) God ordained John from birth as the prophet who would prepare the people for the coming of the Messiah. John delivered a message of repentance for the remission of sins. John baptized those who acknowledged their sins and asked God for forgiveness. John used water baptism as a symbolic representation of one's sins being washed away (Matthew 3:1–3; Luke 3:3–9).

7. John received a revelation from God that at the time of the Messiah's baptism, the Holy Spirit would descend upon His Anointed One. When John baptized Jesus, he saw the Holy Spirit descending on Jesus in the form of a dove. Having witnessed this, John knew Jesus was indeed the Messiah (John 1:29–34).

8. The Samaritan woman was shocked because Jews despised Samaritans and refused to speak to them. Jesus offered the woman living water, which quenches spiritual thirst, cleanses sins, and leads to eternal life. By talking to the Samaritan woman, Jesus offered the woman salvation and taught a valuable lesson about God. Men and women are equal in God's sight (John 4:9).

Chapter 2

1. During the Sermon on the Mount, some of Jesus' major themes were: to serve God wholeheartedly; let others see God's character in you and give God the glory; put God first and make Him a priority in your life; keep a godly perspective while going about your daily routine; love your neighbors and pray for your enemies; do not retaliate or judge others; and choose God's way, for it leads to eternal life (Matthew 5:1–7:29).

2. Jesus performed very few miracles in Nazareth because the people lacked faith. They knew His family and refused to accept Him as the Messiah. Miracles require faith in God (Matthew 13:53–58; Mark 6:1–6).

3. Jews despised tax collectors because they collected taxes on behalf of the Roman government. Tax collectors often overtaxed their own people and kept the overage for themselves. Jesus answered accusations saying, *"Healthy people don't need a doctor—sick people do. . . . For I have come to call not those who think they are righteous, but those who know they are sinners"* (Matthew 9:12–13).

4. Jesus supported His claim by pointing to His witnesses. He said John the Baptist had testified about Him; His miracles proved He had been sent by God; Scripture foretold of His coming; and Moses wrote about Him (John 5:31–47).

5. The Pharisees objected because, in their sight, Jesus was breaking God's law of the Sabbath. Jesus addressed their accusations by pointing out that the Sabbath was made for man. The purpose of the Sabbath was to prevent people from overworking, creating physical and emotional stress in their lives, and losing sight of God (Exodus 20:8–10; Mark 2:27–28).

6. Jesus called the Pharisees hypocrites because they claimed to love God, but were more concerned about keeping their traditions than obeying God (Matthew 6:2–16; 15:1–9).

7. As the Bread of Life, Jesus is our spiritual sustenance. Jesus sustains us spiritually in the same way bread sustains us physically. He satisfies our spiritual hunger and leads us to righteousness (John 6:35; 47–51).

8. A parable is a short story with an underlying spiritual meaning. Jesus used parables because He knew believers would be able to discern the underlying message of His parables, while non believers would not be able to understand their true meaning. By using parables, Jesus could teach His disciples in public without getting into lengthy debates with religious leaders (Luke 8:9–10).

Chapter 3

1. The three major complaints the Pharisees had against Jesus were that He associated with sinners; performed healings and other kinds of work on the Sabbath; and claimed to be God (blasphemed).

2. Jesus changed His focus from teaching crowds to mentoring His disciples. He encouraged them to stay focused on God. He told them repeatedly that He would be killed in Jerusalem and would rise on the third day. He allowed Peter, James, and John to witness the Transfiguration. He also told them about His Second Coming (Matthew 17:1–5; Mark 8:31; 9:31; 10:33; Luke 17:20–37).

3. There was great controversy about the blind man's healing because: 1.) The healing occurred on the Sabbath; and 2.) The man had been blind from birth. People would have understood a healing in which the man had simply regained his sight; however, this man had been born blind. The blind man's parents were afraid to say Jesus had healed their son because the Pharisees had threatened to excommunicate anyone who said they believed in Jesus (John 9:13–34).

4. As the Gate (Door), Jesus is our Intercessor. He intercedes for us as our entryway to God, the Father. He opens the gate, which separates us from God and allows us to enter into God's presence (John 10:1–10).

5. As the Good Shepherd, Jesus is our Caregiver. He feeds us, calms us, leads us, renews us, guides us, accompanies us, protects us, comforts us, befriends us, invites us, welcomes us, and so much more (John 10:11–21).

6. Jesus told His followers this parable to explain that God expects us to use our talents and gifts to glorify Him. He wants us to live as productive citizens of His Kingdom. Jesus told the parable before entering Jerusalem to help the people understand He was going away, but would return at a future date (Luke 19:11–27).

7. When Jesus raised Lazarus from the dead, the Pharisees and other religious leaders were upset because the miracle caused more people to believe Jesus was the Messiah. They were concerned about losing their religious authority and social status. This miracle was a turning point because the religious leaders decided Jesus must die (John 11:45–50).

Chapter 4

1. The seven sins that Jesus condemned were: keeping people in the dark with false teachings; leading people away from God; making people follow their rules instead of God's Word; seeking prestige; ignoring justice and mercy; pretending to be righteous; and covering up their secret sins (Matthew 23:13–30).

2. The Jews recognized these words as the name God used to identify Himself to Moses. God told Moses His name was *Yahweh*, which is translated, *"I am who I am"* (Exodus 3:14). When Jesus used the name "I AM" in reference to Himself, it was clear to everyone He was claiming to be God, which was blasphemy (Mark 14:62–64).

3. The people knew the Messiah was supposed to live forever because of Old Testament prophecies. Having learned Scripture from childhood, they were very much aware of Old Testament prophecies about the Messiah living forever. (See Isaiah 9:7; Ezekiel 37:25, and Daniel 7:13–14.)

4. When Jesus washed His disciples' feet, He taught a valuable lesson about servanthood. In the Kingdom of God, an opportunity to serve humanity is more important than power and prestige (John 13:12–15).

5. Covenant is the term used to describe the various promises and agreements God entered into with mankind. Under the old covenant, Israel was in right standing with God if they obeyed His laws. The old covenant was sealed with animals' blood. Jesus established a new covenant and sealed it with His blood. In the new covenant, we are made righteous through faith in Jesus. The new covenant is better because Jesus died as a perfect sacrifice for all of our past, present, and future sins. Under the old covenant, a sacrificial offering was needed with each occurrence of sin, making it an ongoing process. With the new covenant, Jesus' blood washes away sin once and for all when we accept Him as Lord of our lives. No other sacrifice is ever needed again (Matthew 26:28; Luke 22:20; Hebrews 9:13–15, 22).

6. As the Way, Truth, and Life, Jesus is our Guide. Jesus is the embodiment of God's character—His righteousness, justice, love, mercy and grace. He accompanies us through life, showing us the way to Truth and more abundant life (John 14:6–7).

7. The Jews accused Jesus of blasphemy because He made Himself equal with God. Pilate's official reason was that He claimed to be a king, a position belonging to Caesar alone (John 19:7, 19).

8. Jesus did not come down from the cross because He knew His death was God's Plan of Redemption and Salvation. In obedience to God the Father, Jesus completed His mission—to give His life as a sacrifice for our sins (Matthew 26:52–54).

Chapter 5

1. After the resurrection, Jesus appeared to the disciples and others on numerous occasions over a forty day period. Jesus held conversations with the disciples, showed them His nail wounds and ate meals with them. Jesus appeared to groups of people all of whom witnessed the same events at the same time (John 20:19–29; 21:1–25; Acts 1:3–4).

2. On the day of Pentecost, God sent the Holy Spirit as a gift to all believers. The Holy Spirit empowers believers. He helps believers recognize sin and points us to the righteousness of God. He is our Advocate, Helper, Encourager, Counselor, Guide, Instructor, Comforter, Teacher, and Friend (John 14:16–17; 16:7–8).

3. Before the outpouring of the Holy Spirit, Peter was an unstable and somewhat impulsive leader, who often spoke without thinking. Peter denied knowing Jesus during His arrest and trial. After the outpouring of the Holy Spirit, Peter was transformed into a committed leader of the early church. He boldly and confidently proclaimed the Good News during and after Pentecost (John 18:17, 25–27; Acts 1:14–41).

4. God became a man, in the person of Jesus, and lived on earth for a while, teaching and demonstrating the righteousness of God. After a three-and-a-half year ministry, Jesus exchanged His life for humanity's sins, suffering death by crucifixion. Jesus—the world's Passover Lamb—paid the price for humanity's sins, redeeming us with the shedding of His blood to restore our relationship with God. After three days in the grave, Jesus rose from the dead. Jesus' death and resurrection provided a way for mankind to live in fellowship with God now and throughout eternity (1 Corinthians 15:3–8; Romans 6:3–5). Our relationship with God is restored when we have faith in (believe and trust in) Jesus as our Lord and Savior, the One who paid the penalty for our sins through His death on the cross (John 3:16; Romans 10:9–10).

5. There was an atmosphere of brotherly love and goodwill in the early church. They gave willingly and joyously to their fellow brothers and sisters. Believers met together each day for prayer services. In true fellowship, they shared everything they owned with each other. When extra money was needed, believers sold their property and donated the proceeds to the church (Acts 4:32–37).

6. Stephen's death marked the beginning of a vast number of Christian persecutions which triggered the spreading of the Good News to areas outside Jerusalem. As believers fled from Jerusalem to escape persecution, they spread the Good News with others everywhere they went (Acts 8:1–4).

7. Philip was one of the seven deacons responsible for distributing food to the needy in the early church at Jerusalem. Philip was instrumental in spreading the Good News in Samaria. He explained the Good News to an Ethiopian eunuch traveling on the road to Gaza (Acts 8:5–40).

8. Saul was a strict Pharisee and avid persecutor of Christians. (See Philippians 3:5–6.) He was an official witness at the stoning of Stephen (Acts 8:1).

9. Saul had a conversion experience while on his way to persecute Christians in Damascus. A bright beam of light flashed down from heaven, blinding Saul. A voice said, *"Saul! Saul! Why are you persecuting me?"* When Saul asked who had called him, the voice replied, *"I am Jesus, the one you are persecuting!"* After this, Saul became a powerful ambassador for Jesus Christ. Although Paul experienced numerous hardships and threats against his life, he boldly proclaimed the Good News everywhere he went (Acts 9:3–6).

10. God showed Peter in a vision that he must erase his prejudicial view about Gentiles. Before the vision, Peter thought the Good News of Jesus Christ was for the Jews only. God pointed out in Peter's vision that He is not partial and His offer of salvation is to all people—Jews and Gentiles (Acts 10:11–16).

Chapter 6

1. Paul and Barnabas launched their first missionary journey in obedience to the Holy Spirit's divine inspiration. The Holy Spirit spoke to elders in the church at Antioch saying, *"Dedicate Barnabas and Saul for the special work to which I have called them"* (Acts 13:2).

2. Many Jews were opposed to Paul's message because they believed right standing with God was achieved through obeying Jewish laws and traditions. Paul taught salvation through faith in Jesus Christ. He disagreed with Jews who wanted Gentile converts to adhere to Jewish laws and be circumcised. Paul's message contradicted their traditional beliefs (Acts 15:1–2, 4–5).

3. When the local synagogues rejected Paul's message, he shared the Good News with Gentiles (Acts 13:46).

4. Paul returned to these cities because he recognized the importance of spiritually strengthening new believers and establishing church leadership. Paul risked his life to help ground new believers in the faith (Acts 14:21–28).

5. The issue in need of resolution was about the requirements for salvation. Some Jewish believers insisted that Gentile believers must be circumcised and obey Jewish laws to be saved. Paul argued that the only requirement for salvation was faith in Jesus Christ. The Jerusalem Council met and issued a resolution, which agreed with Paul's position (Acts 15:8–29).

6. City officials in Philippi were panic-stricken because they had abused the guaranteed rights of Roman citizenship. Paul and Barnabas were both Roman citizens and had been beaten without a trial. It was illegal to beat a Roman citizen. In addition, Roman citizens were entitled to a fair trial (Acts 16:35–39).

7. Paul's Roman citizenship helped him get to Rome and accomplish God's plan for spreading the gospel in Rome. After a two year imprisonment in Caesarea, Paul appealed to Caesar for a trial. As a result, Paul received a government paid trip to Rome. While under house arrest in Rome, Paul shared the Good News with everyone who visited him (Acts 25:8–12).

8. Among the problems threatening the early church's existence were religious persecution; opposition to Christianity; false teachings contradictory to the Truth of God; disagreements between Jewish and Gentile believers over requirements for salvation; division among believers over teaching ministries and spiritual gifts; and ungodly behavior; i.e. immorality, hypocrisy, etc.

HOW WE GOT THE NEW TESTAMENT

The books that make up our New Testament were originally written in Greek as letters to first-century believers. Apostle Paul wrote most of these letters. The rest were written by other apostles or close companions of the apostles, as in the case of Mark and Luke. The apostles wrote to explain the Good News of Jesus Christ and to address issues in various churches. All of our New Testament letters were written between approximately 49 and 95 A.D.

For the most part, the apostles' letters were originally addressed to specific churches and read aloud. The churches soon realized the letters provided good sound doctrine and began sharing them. As the letters were copied and circulated, they were eventually accepted as basic teachings of the Christian faith.

During the 2nd century A.D., questionable New Testament books came into circulation. These books are called Apocryphal Books or Gnostic Gospels. After much debate about their authenticity, the early church rejected these books as the inspired Word of God. The primary reason for this is their inconsistency with Jesus' message as compared to those known to be the apostles' writings. In 397 A.D., a council met in Carthage and formally established twenty-seven books as New Testament canon. They were the same letters accepted by the early church and are the twenty-seven books of today's New Testament.

Note: The word *canon* literally means "cane" or "measuring rod" and is the measure used to authenticate a book of the Bible. The tests for canonicity of the New Testament books are as follows: 1.) Was it written by an apostle or close companion of an apostle? 2.) Are quotations from the Hebrew Bible (Old Testament) accurate? 3.) Is the book consistent with Jesus' message? 4.) Was the book accepted by the early church fathers?

Copies of the original letters were passed down from generation to generation. These copies are called manuscripts. While none of the original letters have yet been discovered, thousands of manuscripts have been preserved. Over 14,000 manuscripts are in Greek or Latin and many more exist in other languages. About 4,000 are dated between 2nd and 15th century A.D. The three oldest and most important New Testament manuscripts are the Vatican, Sinaitic, and Alexandrian. While scholars have found variation in specific details among manuscripts, none of these details involve differences in the basic teachings of the Christian faith.

During the 3rd century, most manuscripts were only available in Latin. John Wycliffe was the first to translate the Bible into English using the Latin Vulgate manuscript in 1382. The Roman Catholic Church condemned Wycliffe's translation, declaring that the interpretation of God's Word was the sole responsibility of the church. Wycliffe was excommunicated and most copies of his Bible were burned.

William Tyndale provided a more accurate English translation of the New Testament based on original Greek and Hebrew manuscripts in 1525. Tyndale was burned at the stake in 1536 for translating the Bible into English for the common people. After much turbulence over Bible translations, King James of England appointed men to translate a version that would satisfy all religious factions. Much of Tyndale's earlier New Testament translation was used to create this version, known as the Authorized King James Version. It was initially published in 1611.

Over the years, the English language began to change. This created the need for a translation people could more easily read and comprehend. As a result, numerous translations are in existence today. (See Appendix 2 for selecting a Bible and Appendix 3 for comparisons of Bible translations.)

SELECTING A BIBLE

The Bible was written in Hebrew, Greek, and some Aramaic. If we were able to read Hebrew, Greek, and Aramaic, there would be no need for the various Bible versions or translations. Since most of us are not able to read the Bible in its original languages, Bible scholars have taken it upon themselves to translate it for us. The various Bible versions are actually different translations of our Bible. There is only one Protestant Bible and it has been translated in various ways.

Find a good Bible that you can read and understand. Bibles that include comments and author's notes are called Study Bibles. While this type of Bible might help in understanding scripture, it interjects its author's point of view. Nevertheless, a Study Bible can be very useful in illuminating scripture and providing fresh new insights into the Word.

When selecting a Bible, it is important to understand the different translation methods. Let's take a look at them.

Word for Word Translations

"Word for Word" translations are also known as literal or formal equivalent translations. The goal of these translations is to capture each word of the original Bible text. While no true "word for word" translation exists, there are some that come very close to achieving this objective. In today's times, we have several "word for word" translations to choose from. A few of them are:

- ✓ English Standard Version (ESV)

- ✓ King James Version and New King James (KJV, NKJ)

- ✓ New American Standard Bible (NASB)

Thought for Thought Translations

The second type of translations are called "Thought for Thought" also called dynamic equivalent translations. The objective of these translations is to capture the thought of the sentence or paragraph of the original text. In these two translations, ensuring each word of text is represented in the translation becomes less important and achieving a translation that maintains the overall thought of the original text becomes the primary goal. Examples of these are:

- • Capture the Sentence

    - ✓ The Amplified Bible (AMP)

    - ✓ Contemporary English Version (CEV)

    - ✓ New International Version (NIV)

    - ✓ New Living Translation (NLT)

- • Capture the Paragraph

    - ✓ The Message (MSG)

    - ✓ The Living Bible (LB)

COMPARISON OF BIBLE TRANSLATIONS

Greek Transliteration	KJV	NKJ	NASB	NIV	NLT	MSG
Romans 8:37–39						
All en toútois pásin hupernikoómen diá toú agapeésantos heemás Pépeismai gár hóti oúte thánatos oúte zooeé oúte ángeloi oúte archaí oúte enestoóta oúte méllonta oúte dunámeis oúte húpsooma oúte báthos oúte tis ktísis hetéra choorísai heemás apó teés agápees toú Theoú leesoú toó Kuríoo heemoón	Nay, in all these things we are more than conquerors through him that loved us. For I am persuaded, that neither death, nor life, nor angels, nor principalities, nor powers, nor things present, nor things to come, Nor height, nor depth, nor any other creature, shall be able to separate us from the love of God, which is in Christ Jesus our Lord.	Yet in all these things we are more than conquerors through Him who loved us. For I am persuaded that neither death nor life, nor angels nor principalities nor powers, nor things present nor things to come, nor height nor depth, nor any other created thing, shall be able to separate us from the love of God which is in Christ Jesus our Lord.	But in all these things we overwhelmingly conquer through Him who loved us. For I am convinced that neither death, nor life, nor angels, nor principalities, nor things present, nor things to come, nor powers, nor height, nor depth, nor any other created thing, will be able to separate us from the love of God, which is in Christ Jesus our Lord.	No, in all these things we are more than conquerors through him who loved us. For I am convinced that neither death nor life, neither angels nor demons, neither the present nor the future, nor any powers, neither height nor depth, nor anything else in all creation, will be able to separate us from the love of God that is in Christ Jesus our Lord.	No, despite all these things, overwhelming victory is ours through Christ, who loved us. And I am convinced that nothing can ever separate us from God's love. Neither death nor life, neither angels nor demons, neither our fears for today nor our worries about tomorrow—not even the powers of hell can separate us from God's love. No power in the sky above or in the earth below—indeed, nothing in all creation will ever be able to separate us from the love of God that is revealed in Christ Jesus our Lord.	None of this fazes us because Jesus loves us. I'm absolutely convinced that nothing—nothing living or dead, angelic or demonic, today or tomorrow, high or low, thinkable or unthinkable—absolutely nothing can get between us and God's love because of the way that Jesus our Master has embraced us.
John 3:16						
Hoútoos gár eegápeesen ho Theós tón kósmon hoóste tón Huión tón monogeneé édooken hína pás ho pisteúoon eis autón meé apóleetai all échee zooeén aioónion	For God so loved the world, that he gave his only begotten Son, that whosoever believeth in him should not perish, but have everlasting life.	For God so loved the world that He gave His only begotten Son, that whoever believes in Him should not perish but have everlasting life.	For God so loved the world, that He gave His only begotten Son, that whoever believes in Him shall not perish, but have eternal life.	For God so loved the world that he gave his one and only Son, that whoever believes in him shall not perish but have eternal life.	For God loved the world so much that he gave his one and only Son, so that everyone who believes in him will not perish but have eternal life.	This is how much God loved the world: He gave his Son, his one and only Son. And this is why: so that no one need be destroyed; by believing in him, anyone can have a whole and lasting life.

ORGANIZATION OF THE NEW TESTAMENT

New Testament

The New Testament tells the Good News of the new covenant God entered into with humanity and how this Good News was spread throughout the world. Its primary focus is on how God fulfilled His promise of a Messiah through Jesus Christ, providing a way for all mankind, Jews and non-Jews alike, to commune with Him on earth and throughout eternity. God became a man in the person of Jesus Christ and lived on earth for a while. After a three-and-a-half year ministry, Jesus voluntarily gave up His life to save and redeem mankind. Through Jesus' death and resurrection, God entered into a new covenant with humanity. In the new covenant, mankind's relationship with God is restored through faith in Jesus Christ. There are twenty-seven New Testament books in our English or Protestant Bible. These books are arranged according to types of writings. There are three major types of writings. They are as follows:

Historical (5 books)

The initial four books of the New Testament are called the gospels or the Good News. These four books describe Jesus' life story—His rescue mission while on earth. The gospels provide four different perspectives of Jesus' teachings and miracles, His sacrificial death on the cross, and His resurrection from the dead. The fifth book of history is called Acts. After Jesus' resurrection, He commissioned His disciples to spread the Good News of salvation throughout the world. The book of Acts provides an account of the apostles' work in establishing the early church and the spreading of the Good News. The five books of history are:

- ✓ Matthew
- ✓ Mark
- ✓ Luke
- ✓ John
- ✓ Acts

Letters (Epistles) (21 books)

There are twenty-one letters or epistles in the New Testament. They were written to encourage and strengthen believers in the faith, and to address issues in the early church. These twenty-one letters provide basic doctrinal truths of the Christian faith for living as a fully devoted follower of Jesus Christ. The first thirteen were written by Apostle Paul. After Paul's letters, the next is Hebrews, whose author is unknown. Paul and others who assisted in Paul's ministry have often been suggested as possible authors of Hebrews. After Hebrews, the next letter was written by James, Jesus' half-brother, followed by two letters written by Apostle Peter. After Peter's letters, the next three letters were written by Apostle John and the last letter was written by Jude, another one of Jesus' half-brothers.

Paul's Letters (13)

- ✓ Romans
- ✓ 1 Corinthians

- ✓ 2 Corinthians

- ✓ Galatians

- ✓ Ephesians

- ✓ Philippians

- ✓ Colossians

- ✓ 1 Thessalonians

- ✓ 2 Thessalonians

- ✓ 1 Timothy

- ✓ 2 Timothy

- ✓ Titus

- ✓ Philemon

Other Letters (8)

- ✓ Hebrews

- ✓ James

- ✓ 1 Peter

- ✓ 2 Peter

- ✓ 1 John

- ✓ 2 John

- ✓ 3 John

- ✓ Jude

Prophecy (1)

There is only one book of prophecy in the New Testament. It is the book of Revelation, which was written by Apostle John. The word revelation means "unveiling" or "disclosure." The book of Revelation is an unveiling of the future events leading up to Jesus' second coming; His final victory; and His final judgment—eternal life with God for believers and eternal separation from God for non believers.

- ✓ Revelation

NEW TESTAMENT SUMMARY OF MAJOR EVENTS

Biblical Event	Approximate Date B.C.
Rome Took Control of Palestine	63
Herod the Great Begins His Reign	37
Augustus Caesar Becomes Emperor of Rome	27
Augustus Caesar Orders a Census / Jesus is Born	6/5
The Escape to Egypt	5/4
Herod the Great Dies / Herod Antipas is King of Galilee	4
Called Out of Egypt / Return to Galilee	4/3 (?)
	Approximate Date A.D.
Jesus Visits the Temple	6/7
Tiberius Caesar Becomes Emperor of Rome	14
John the Baptist's Ministry Begins	26
Jesus' Ministry Begins	26/27
Jesus' Crucifixion, Resurrection, and Ascension	30
Founding of Church in Jerusalem / Outpouring of the Holy Spirit	30
Stephen Stoned to Death / Paul's Conversion	35
Apostle James Martyred / Peter Imprisoned	44
Paul's 1st Missionary Journey	46–48
The Jerusalem Council's Decision	50
Paul's 2nd Missionary Journey	50–52
Paul's 3rd Missionary Journey	53–57
Paul is Imprisoned and Appears before Felix	57–59
Paul Appears before Festus and Agrippa. Paul Appeals to Caesar	59
Paul's Journey to Rome	59
Paul Under House Arrest in Rome	60–62
Nero burns Rome, Christians Blamed and Persecuted	64
Great Jewish Revolt Begins	66
Paul Martyred / Peter Martyred	67–70 (?)
Jerusalem Destroyed by Rome under Titus' Command	70

NEW TESTAMENT RULERS

Roman Emperors	Biblical Reference	Approx. Date
Augustus Caesar	Luke 2:1	27 B.C.–14 A.D.
Tiberius Caesar	Luke 3:1	14–37 A.D.
Gaius (Caligula) Caesar		37–41 A.D.
Claudius Caesar	Acts 11:28; 18:2	41–54 A.D.
Nero Caesar		54–68 A.D.
Vespasian		69–79 A.D.
The Herods		
Herod the Great	Matthew 2:1–22; Luke 1:5	37 B.C.–4 B.C.
Kingdom Split into Territories Ruled by Herod's Sons		4 B.C.
Archelaus (Judea)	Matthew 2:22	4 B.C.–6 A.D.
Herod Antipas (Galilee)	Matthew 14:1–11; Mark 6:14–29; Luke 3:1, 19–20; 13:31; 23:7–12	4 B.C.–39 A.D.
Herod Philip (Iturea and Traconitis)	Luke 3:1	4 B.C.–34 A.D.
		A.D.
Herod Agrippa I (Judea)	Acts 12:1–24	41–44
Herod II (Chalcis)		41–48
Herod Agrippa II (Chalcis and northern territory)	Acts 25:13–26:32	50–93
Roman Governors		
Coponius		6–10
M. Ambivius		10–13
Annius Rufus		13–15
Valerius Gratus		15–26
Pontius Pilate	Matthew 27:2–65; Mark 15:1–15; Luke 13:1, 23:1–52; John 18:29–19:38; Acts 3:13; 4:27; 13:28	27–36
Marcellus		36–38
Maryllus		38–44
Cuspius Fadus		44–46
Tiberius Alexander		46–48
Ventidius Cumanus		48–52
M. Antonius Felix	Acts 23:24–25:14	52–58
Porcius Festus	Acts 24:27–26:32	59–61
Albinus		61–65
Gessius Florus		65–70

MESSIANIC PROPHECIES FULFILLED BY JESUS OF NAZARETH

Prophecy	Old Testament Scriptures	New Testament Fulfillment
Offspring of a Woman	*"And I will cause hostility between you and the woman, and between your offspring and her offspring. He will strike your head, and you will strike his heel"* (Genesis 3:15).	Galatians 4:4
Descendant of the Patriarchs, Abraham, Isaac, and Jacob	*"And through your descendants all the nations of the earth will be blessed—all because you have obeyed me"* (Genesis 22:18). (See also Genesis 12:3; 17:6; 26:4; 28:14; Numbers 24:17.)	Matthew 1:1–2
Descendant of the Tribe of Judah	*"The scepter will not depart from Judah, nor the ruler's staff from his descendants, until the coming of the one to whom it belongs, the one whom all nations will honor"* (Genesis 49:10).	Luke 3:23, 34
Prophet	*"I will raise up a prophet like you from among their fellow Israelites. I will put my words in his mouth, and he will tell the people everything I command him"* (Deuteronomy 18:18).	Matthew 21:11; Acts 3:20, 22
Descendant of King David to Reign Forever	*"The Lord said, 'I have made a covenant with David, my chosen servant. I have sworn this oath to him: "I will establish your descendants as kings forever; they will sit on your throne from now until eternity"'"* (Psalm 89:3–4).	Luke 3:23, 31; Matthew 28:20
Descendant of King David to Rule With Justice and Righteousness	*"He will reign on David's throne and over his kingdom, establishing and upholding it with justice and righteousness from that time on and forever"* (Isaiah 9:7b NIV).	Luke 3:23, 31; John 5:28–30
Descendant of King David to Rule with Wisdom	*"For the time is coming," says the Lord, "when I will raise up a righteous descendant from King David's line. He will be a King who rules with wisdom. He will do what is just and right throughout the land"* (Jeremiah 23:5).	Luke 3:23, 31; Matthew 13:54
Descendant of King David to Shepherd God's People	*"And I will set over them one shepherd, my servant David. He will feed them and be a shepherd to them. And I, the Lord, will be their God, and my servant David will be a prince among my people. I, the LORD, have spoken!"* (Ezekiel 34:23–24).	Luke 3:23, 31; John 10:11, 14
Messiah's Forerunner to Shout in the Wilderness	*"Listen! It's the voice of someone shouting, 'Clear the way through the wilderness for the Lord! Make a straight highway through the wasteland for our God!'"* (Isaiah 40:3).	John 1:23
Messiah's Forerunner to Prepare the Way	*"'Look! I am sending my messenger, and he will prepare the way before me. Then the Lord you are seeking will suddenly come to his Temple. The messenger of the covenant, whom you look for so eagerly, is surely coming,' says the Lord of Heaven's Armies"* (Malachi 3:1).	Mark 1:3

Cont'd . . .

Prophecy	Old Testament Scriptures	New Testament Fulfillment
Became Human	*"For to us a child is born, to us a son is given, and the government will be on his shoulders. And he will be called Wonderful Counselor, Mighty God, Everlasting Father, Prince of Peace"* (Isaiah 9:6).	John 1:1–3, 14
Born to a Virgin	*"The Lord himself will give you the sign. Look! The virgin will conceive a child! She will give birth to a son and will call him Immanuel (which means 'God is with us')"* (Isaiah 7:14).	Matthew 1:18
Born in Bethlehem	*"But you, O Bethlehem Ephrathah, are only a small village among all the people of Judah. Yet a ruler of Israel will come from you, one whose origins are from the distant past"* (Micah 5:2).	Matthew 2:1
Called Out of Egypt	*"When Israel was a child, I loved him, and I called my son out of Egypt"* (Hosea 11:1).	Matthew 2:14–15, 19–20
A Light in Galilee	*"Nevertheless, that time of darkness and despair will not go on forever . . . but there will be a time in the future when Galilee of the Gentiles, which lies along the road that runs between the Jordan and the sea, will be filled with glory. The people who walk in darkness will see a great light. For those who live in a land of deep darkness, a light will shine"* (Isaiah 9:1–2).	Matthew 4:12–15; John 8:12; 9:5
A Fountain to Cleanse Sins	*"On that day a fountain will be opened for the dynasty of David and for the people of Jerusalem, a fountain to cleanse them from all their sins and impurity"* (Zechariah 13:1).	John 4:10; 7:38
The Spirit of the Lord Will Rest on Him	*"And the Spirit of the Lord will rest on him—the Spirit of wisdom and understanding, the Spirit of counsel and might, the Spirit of knowledge and the fear of the Lord. He will delight in obeying the LORD. He will not judge by appearance nor make a decision based on hearsay"* (Isaiah 11:2–3).	Matthew 3:16–17
Perform Healing Miracles	*"Say to those with fearful hearts, 'Be strong, and do not fear, for your God is coming to destroy your enemies. He is coming to save you.' And when he comes, he will open the eyes of the blind and unplug the ears of the deaf. The lame will leap like a deer, and those who cannot speak will sing for joy!"* (Isaiah 35:4–6).	Matthew 8:16; 8:35; John 5:36
Anointed to Bring Good News to the Poor	*"The Spirit of the Sovereign Lord is upon me, for the Lord has anointed me to bring good news to the poor. He has sent me to comfort the brokenhearted and to proclaim that captives will be released and prisoners will be freed. He has sent me to tell those who mourn that the time of the LORD's favor has come . . ."* (Isaiah 61:1–2).	Luke 4:16–21
Speak in Parables	*"For I will speak to you in a parable. I will teach you hidden lessons from our past"* (Psalm 78:2).	Matthew 13:34
Rejected Stone	*"The stone that the builders rejected has now become the cornerstone"* (Psalm 118:22).	Luke 9:22; 20:17
Despised and Rejected	*"He was despised and rejected—a man of sorrows, acquainted with deepest grief. We turned our backs on him and looked the other way. He was despised, and we did not care"* (Isaiah 53:3).	John 1:11; 7:5, 48; John 11:47–50; Luke 19:41–44
King Riding on a Donkey	*"Rejoice, O people of Zion! Shout in triumph, O people of Jerusalem! Look, your king is coming to you. He is righteous and victorious, yet he is humble, riding on a donkey—riding on a donkey's colt"* (Zechariah 9:9).	Matthew 21:1–7

Cont'd . . .

Prophecy	Old Testament Scriptures	New Testament Fulfillment
Hated for No Reason	"They have set an ambush for me. Fierce enemies are out there waiting, LORD, though I have not sinned or offended them. I have done nothing wrong, yet they prepare to attack me. . . . Those who hate me without cause outnumber the hairs on my head. Many enemies try to destroy me with lies" (Psalms 59:3–4; 69:4).	Luke 23:13–21; John 15:24–25
Betrayed by a Friend	"Even my close friend, whom I trusted, he who shared my bread, has lifted up his heel against me" (Psalm 41:9 NIV).	Luke 22:47–48
Betrayed for Thirty Pieces of Silver	"And I said to them, 'If you like, give me my wages, whatever I am worth; but only if you want to.' So they counted out for my wages thirty pieces of silver" (Zechariah 11:12).	Matthew 26:14–15
Thirty Pieces of Silver to the Potter	"And the LORD said to me, 'Throw it to the potter'—this magnificent sum at which they valued me! So I took the thirty coins and threw them to the potter in the Temple of the LORD" (Zechariah 11:13).	Matthew 27:5–7
Disciples Will Scatter	"'Awake, O sword, against my shepherd, the man who is my partner,' says the LORD of Heaven's Armies. 'Strike down the shepherd, and the sheep will be scattered, and I will turn against the lambs'" (Zechariah 13:7).	Mark 14:50
Did Not Respond to Accusers	"He was oppressed and treated harshly, yet he never said a word. He was led like a lamb to the slaughter. And as a sheep is silent before the shearers, he did not open his mouth" (Isaiah 53:7).	Matthew 27:12–19; Mark 15:4–5; Luke 23:9
Unjustly Condemned	"Unjustly condemned, he was led away. No one cared that he died without descendants, that his life was cut short in midstream. But he was struck down for the rebellion of my people. He had done no wrong and had never deceived anyone" (Isaiah 53:8–9).	Luke 23:22–25
Insulted	"Everyone who sees me mocks me. They sneer and shake their heads, saying, 'Is this the one who relies on the LORD? Then let the LORD save him! If the LORD loves him so much, let the LORD rescue him!'" (Psalm 22:7–8).	Matthew 27:27–31
Beaten and Whipped	"He was beaten so we could be whole. He was whipped so we could be healed. All of us, like sheep, have strayed away. We have left God's paths to follow our own. Yet the LORD laid on him the sins of us all" (Isaiah 53:5b–6).	Matthew 27:26
Pierced Hands and Feet	"My enemies surround me like a pack of dogs; an evil gang closes in on me. They have pierced my hands and feet" (Psalm 22:16).	Luke 23:33; John 20:27
Thirsty	"My strength has dried up like sunbaked clay. My tongue sticks to the roof of my mouth. You have laid me in the dust and left me for dead . . ." (Psalm 22:15).	John 19:28
Gambled for His Clothing	"They divide my garments among themselves and throw dice for my clothing" (Psalm 22:18).	John 19:23–24
Offered Sour Wine for Thirst	"They give me poison for food; they offer me sour wine for my thirst" (Psalm 69:21).	Matthew 27:34
Interceded for His Accusers	"I will give him the honors of a victorious soldier, because he exposed himself to death. He was counted among the rebels. He bore the sins of many and interceded for rebels" (Isaiah 53:12).	Luke 23:34
Abandoned on the Cross	"My God, my God, why have you abandoned me?" (Psalm 22:1).	Matthew 27:46

Cont'd . . .

Prophecy	Old Testament Scriptures	New Testament Fulfillment
Entrusted His Spirit	*"I entrust my spirit into your hand"* (Psalm 31:5).	Luke 23:46
Sacrificed for our Sins	*"But he was pierced for our rebellion, crushed for our sins"* (Isaiah 53:5).	Romans 5:6–8
Pierced in the Side	*"Then I will pour out a spirit of grace and prayer on the family of David and on the people of Jerusalem. They will look on me whom they have pierced and mourn for him as for an only son. They will grieve bitterly for him as for a firstborn son who has died"* (Zechariah 12:10).	John 19:34; 20:27
No Bones Broken	*"For the Lord protects the bones of the righteous; not one of them is broken!"* (Psalm 34:20).	John 19:33
Buried in a Rich Man's Grave	*"He had done no wrong and had never deceived anyone. But he was buried like a criminal; he was put in a rich man's grave"* (Isaiah 53:9).	Matthew 27:57–60
Will Not Remain in the Grave	*"For you will not leave my soul among the dead or allow your holy one to rot in the grave"* (Psalms 16:10; 49:15).	Mark 16:6
Swallow Up Death Forever	*"He will swallow up death forever! The Sovereign Lord will wipe away all tears. He will remove forever all insults and mockery against his land and people. The Lord has spoken!"* (Isaiah 25:8).	1 Corinthians 15:54–57

GOD'S PLAN OF REDEMPTION AND SALVATION

God's Plan of Redemption and Salvation is the series of events God so lovingly orchestrated to provide a way for mankind to live in fellowship with Him here on earth and throughout eternity. Mankind was originally created to live in fellowship with God. However, fellowship with our Creator was severed when the first man and woman rebelled against God and chose to follow their own selfish desires. As a result of their rebellion, every man and woman is born with this same rebellious attitude, doing things his or her own way apart from God, rather than allowing God to guide their lives. Rebellion against God is called sin. All of us are born spiritually separated or out of fellowship with God because of sin (Romans 3:10–12; 23).

God lovingly developed a plan to free mankind from sin (the spirit of rebellion) so that we can live in fellowship with Him. God's plan called for our redemption (deliverance by payment of a price) and salvation (freedom from the power of sin). God's plan required payment for our deliverance, but what would be the price and who would be willing and able to pay it? The Old Testament answers these questions for us. God promised to send a Messiah, who would die for our iniquities and cleanse us of our sins (Isaiah 53; Zechariah 3:8–9; 13:1). Throughout Scripture, it becomes clear Jesus Christ is the promised Messiah and that He paid the price of redemption with His "blood" (Hebrews 9:11–12).

God became a man, in the person of Jesus, and lived with mankind on earth. Jesus suffered death by crucifixion, paying the price for humanity's deliverance with the shedding of His blood. After three days in the grave, Jesus rose from the dead, conquering death and freeing humanity from the power of sin. Jesus' death and resurrection fulfilled God's Plan of Redemption and Salvation and provided a way for all mankind to live in fellowship with God now and throughout eternity (1 Corinthians 15:3–8; Romans 6:3–5).

ACCEPTING GOD'S FREE GIFT OF REDEMPTION AND SALVATION

God offers redemption and salvation to all mankind as a free gift. By offering His Plan of Redemption and Salvation, God is in effect saying, "I love you and want a close personal relationship with you. I knew you could neither redeem nor save yourself, so I sent My Son, Jesus Christ, to do it for you." Jesus paid the price for our redemption with His blood and provided for our salvation by conquering death and the power of sin.

Although God's Plan of Redemption and Salvation is a free gift, most people think it is something that must be achieved or earned. Many try to earn salvation by doing good deeds, such as giving to the poor, attending church, or giving up the things they know are morally wrong. However, our good deeds cannot save us. The only way we can be saved is by accepting God's gift of redemption and salvation. God's gift is a free gift and cannot be earned.

Accepting God's free gift of redemption and salvation is quite simple. Jesus has graciously done everything for us. All we have to do is have faith in (believe and trust in) Jesus Christ as our Lord and Savior, the One who has provided for our redemption and salvation (John 3:16; Romans 10:9–10). We are saved by God's grace (unmerited favor) when we believe in Jesus as our Lord and Savior (Romans 3:21–26; Ephesians 2:4–10). Jesus Christ invites you to believe and trust in Him. Jesus is saying *"Here I am! I stand at the door and knock. If anyone hears my voice and opens the door, I will come in and eat with him, and he with me"* (Revelation 3:20 NIV).

If you have already accepted Jesus Christ as your personal Savior, I pray that God strengthens your relationship with Him. If you are ready to accept God's free gift of redemption and salvation, all you have to do is believe in Jesus as your personal Savior and then begin a new life in Christ. You can confess your faith by praying the prayer below or one similar to it.

Dear God,

I thank You for extending Your mercy to me, a sinner in need of a Savior. Thank You for Your gracious plan of redemption and salvation. I believe Jesus Christ is the prophesied Messiah and that He sacrificed His life for me on the cross. I thank You for Your unconditional love, and humbly receive Your forgiveness and free gift of eternal life. I invite You to come into my heart and become the Master of every area of my life. My true desire is to follow You with all my heart all the days of my life. And I pray all of this in the powerful name of Jesus Christ.

Amen!

GLOSSARY

A.D.—Abbreviation for *Anno Domini*, meaning "In the year of our Lord." Dates after Jesus' birth are time stamped A.D.

Agape—Godly love. It is a love that is unconditional, sacrificial, and all-consuming.

Altar—A raised mound of earth or a platform used for sacrifices and praising God.

Anoint—To rub with oil in a ceremony of consecration. Anointing with perfumed oil was common in Jesus' days.

Apostle—A person sent on a mission. Jesus commissioned His twelve disciples as apostles and made an appearance after His death to commission Paul as an apostle.

Areopagus—Athens' high council of philosophers.

Ark of the Covenant—The chest containing the stone tablets inscribed with the Ten Commandments, kept in the holiest part of the Tabernacle. It was the symbol of God's presence with the people of Israel.

Armor of God—God is the faithful protector of His people and is often referred to as a shield for those who put their trust in Him. Putting on the armor of God is having faith He will protect you.

Atone, Atonement—To reconcile or make amends for sin.

B.C.—Abbreviation for "Before Christ." Events, which occurred before Jesus' birth, are time stamped B.C.

Baptism, Baptize—Immersion in water or the pouring or sprinkling of water over an individual, as a symbolic confession of one' faith in Jesus Christ.

Believers—(See Christians)

Bible—A compilation of writings, written by men inspired by God. God's Word; God's written message to mankind.

Bible Translations—The various renderings of Biblical manuscripts from their original language (Hebrew, Aramaic, or Greek) to English or some other language. (See the Introduction section titled, "Using this Study," for a list of Bible versions and translations used in this study.)

Blasphemy—Profane or contemptuous speech, writing, or action held to be irreverent or disrespectful to God. Any remark deliberately mocking or contemptuous of God.

Blessed—Holy; sacred; consecrated. Enjoying great happiness.

Blessings—Good wishes or approval. The gift of divine favor or blessings because of God's special favor.

Book of the Law—(See Mosaic Laws)

Calvary—Latin for "Skull Hill," *Golgotha* in Hebrew. It was the location of Jesus' crucifixion.

Canaan—Israel, also referred to as Palestine. The land God promised Abraham and his descendants.

Canaanites—A general term used to reference all the various non-Jewish peoples that lived in Canaan.

Canon—A word meaning "cane" or "measuring rod" and is the measure used to authenticate a book of the Bible.

Christians—Believers in the life, death, and resurrection of Jesus Christ. A follower of Jesus' teachings.

Church tradition—Ideas or beliefs within the church community of believers which have been passed down from generation to generation, especially by oral communication.

Circumcision—Removal of the male's genital foreskin. God initiated this rite as a sign of His covenant with Abraham.

Consecrate—To make sacred or holy.

Covenant (Testament)—Used to describe the various promises and agreements God entered into with mankind. When God enters into a covenant, He commits to bringing promised blessings to pass sometime in the future.

Crucifixion—To put to death by nailing or binding to a cross and leaving to die of exposure.

Crucifixion, The—Refers to Jesus' death by crucifixion.

Day of the Lord—Judgment Day. The Second Coming of Christ. The time when Christ returns to establish His New Jerusalem on the earth. The day Christ returns to judge the living and the dead. It is the Day of Judgment when the Lord renders eternal life and salvation to believers and eternal separation from God to non believers.

Demon-possessed—To be inhabited in one's body and soul by one or more demons, causing people to behave in ways or exhibit powers they ordinarily would not have.

Demons—Evil, supernatural beings. Demons are spiritual beings at enmity with God. They have certain powers over man, often relentlessly tormenting and torturing humans.

Devil—(See Satan)

Diaspora, The—The name used for the dispersion of Jews outside of Palestine (Israel) from the sixth century B.C. when the Jews were exiled to Babylonia. Also refers to present day Jews still dispersed outside of Israel.

Disciple—A student and devoted follower. One who embraces and assists in spreading the teachings of another; e.g., the twelve disciples of Jesus Christ.

Divine, Divinity—Coming directly from God; heavenly; God-like.

Dropsy—Edema. An abnormal accumulation of fluid in cells, tissues, or cavities of the body, resulting in swelling.

Dynasty—A succession of rulers from the same line of descent who are members of the same family. Also can be the period during which a certain family reigns.

Epistle—A letter. Apostle Paul wrote the majority of the epistles in the New Testament.

Eunuch—A castrated man in charge of a harem or employed as a high officer in an emperor's palace.

Excommunicate—To deprive an individual of church membership by overriding religious authority.

Exile—Self-imposed or enforced removal from one's native country. The Exile was the period in 6th century B.C. during which the Jews were held captive in Babylonia.

Faith—Believing in. Trusting in Jesus Christ as Lord and Savior. Under the Christian doctrine, salvation is not earned. Salvation is a gift from God to those who believe and have faith in Jesus Christ as Lord and Savior.

Fall, The (The Fall of Man)—Refers to the first man and woman's (Adam and Eve's) rejection of God's rules, which marked the beginning of sin in the world.

False Prophets (False Teachers)—People communicating messages contrary to the Truth of God. False prophets are those who have not received God's special call to communicate His message.

False teachings—Messages contrary to the Truth of God.

Flogging—A severe beating with a leather strap or metal spiked ball attached to an iron chain.

Foreshadow—To be a sign of something to come; to indicate or suggest beforehand.

Foreshadowing of Jesus Christ (Picture of Redemption)—A scriptural preview of how God would send Jesus Christ to save mankind and restore our relationship with Him. It is also any scripture that illustrates an aspect of Jesus' character or mission, or one that provides a symbolic representation of Jesus as Redeemer and Savior.

Gentiles (non-Jews)—Any person who is not a Jew. Historically among Jews, heathens (people regarded as uncivilized) and pagans (people with little or no religion) were considered to be Gentiles.

Gethsemane—A garden grove at the Mount of Olives where Judas betrayed Jesus.

God—The Creator of the universe and everything in it. He is not limited by time or space and has no beginning and no end. God is all-knowing, all-powerful, and in all places at all times.

Golgotha—(See Calvary)

Gospel—Good News. The Gospel is the New Testament teachings of Jesus Christ and His apostles.

Grace—Unmerited or undeserved favor. The unmerited love and favor of God toward mankind.

Great Commission—Jesus' commission to the apostles and all future disciples to share the Good News. Those who believe in the name of Jesus Christ as Lord are commanded to go and make disciples.

Hanukkah—Jewish Holiday also known as Festival of Lights or Festival of Dedication, celebrating the rededication of the Temple after Israel's revolt in 165 B.C.

Hebrew—Any member of a group of Semitic peoples tracing their descent from Noah's son Shem, Abraham, Isaac, and Jacob; an Israelite or Jew. The word also refers to the ancient Semitic language of the Israelites.

Holy—Dedicated to religious use; belonging to or coming from God; sacred; made spiritually pure by God.

Holy Spirit—The Spirit of God. The third being in the Trinity with God the Father and Jesus the Son. After Jesus' resurrection, the Holy Spirit came to indwell Christians and guide them toward God's righteousness.

Hosanna—A Hebrew word that means, "Save us now!"

Host—Those in God's heavenly army (angels).

House Arrest—Apprehending and detaining a person in their own home under guard instead of in a prison.

Hypocrisy, Hypocrite—Pretending to be what one is not, or to feel what one does not feel; especially a pretense of virtue or piety, etc. One who pretends to be better than one really is.

Idolatry—The worship of a physical object as a god. The blind or excessive adoration of someone or something.

Intercessory Prayer—A petitioning of God's special favor for someone other than oneself.

Israel—After God changed Jacob's name to Israel, his descendants became known as the nation of Israel, also called the Israelites or the twelve tribes of Israel. It is also the name of the land God gave to Jacob's descendants.

Jerusalem Council—The apostles and elders of the early church in Jerusalem who met in 50 A.D. to resolve the issue about requirements for salvation. The council wrote a resolution freeing Gentile believers from having to be circumcised and obey most Jewish laws as a requirement of salvation.

Jesus Christ—God made human. The second being in the Trinity with God the Father and the Holy Spirit. God became a man, in the person of Jesus, and lived among us to show us how to live a life that is righteous and pleasing to God.

Jews, Jewish—A person descended from the ancient Hebrews of Biblical times. A person whose religion is Judaism.

Judaism—The religion of the Jewish people. Believers in Judaism follow the Hebrew Bible (the Old Testament); and for the most part, do not recognize the New Testament.

Judaizers—Jewish believers who insisted Gentile believers must adhere to the law of Moses and be circumcised as a requirement for salvation.

Judge—The name Israel called the people God used to perform a special work for Him during the period after Joshua's death and before Saul became king. God used Judges to rescue Israel from their enemies.

Judgment Day—(See Day of the Lord)

Leavening—(See Yeast)

Leprosy—A term used for a variety of dreaded skin disorders. Symptoms included white patches on the skin, running sores, and loss of fingers and toes. The disease rendered its victims ceremonially unclean; i.e., unfit to worship God.

Levite—A member of the tribe of Levi, Jacob's third son. The name often applies only to those descendants of Levi who assisted the priests and handled more routine duties in support of the Tabernacle and the Temple.

Lord's Supper, The—Also called "The Last Supper," "Communion," and "Eucharist." The central Christian rite in which bread and wine are consecrated and distributed as the body and blood of Jesus or as symbols of them. It is a memorial service celebrated by the church to signify Jesus' sacrificial death for humanity's sins.

Maccabean Revolt—The Maccabees were a family of Jewish patriots of the 2nd and 1st centuries B.C. The Maccabean Revolt was a Jewish uprising led by the Maccabee (Hashmon) family against the Seleucids.

Manger—A trough or open box in which food for animals is placed.

Manna—A Hebrew word meaning "What is it?" The substance God provided the Jews for food as they traveled to Canaan.

Martyr, Martyrdom—One who chooses to suffer or die rather than give up their faith or principles. Martyrdom is when a person is tortured and/or killed because of his or her beliefs.

Mediate—To settle or bring about reconciliation.

Mediator—One who intervenes between two parties who are in conflict to reconcile them. Christ is the one and only mediator between God and man. He makes reconciliation between God and man by his all-perfect atoning sacrifice.

Mercy—Compassionate treatment, clemency. A disposition to be kind and forgiving.

Messiah—An expected savior or liberator of a people or country; a Hebrew word which is translated as "Christ" in Greek, and "Anointed One" in English.

Messianic Prophecy—Old Testament Scripture foretelling the coming of the Messiah, the Anointed One.

Mosaic Laws—The laws God gave Moses for the Israelites (Jews). The first five books of the Bible.

New Covenant—The covenant God entered into with mankind through the death and resurrection of Jesus Christ. Under the new covenant, a person is made right with God through faith in Jesus Christ as Lord and Savior.

New Testament—The second of two main divisions of the Christian Bible. It includes writings inspired by God from Jesus' birth to about seventy years after His death. It tells the Good News of the new covenant God entered into with humanity through Jesus' death and resurrection.

Old Covenant—The covenant God entered into with the nation of Israel under Moses' leadership. Under the old covenant, Israel was made right with God through obedience to His Old Testament laws.

Old Testament—The first of two main divisions of the Christian Bible. The Old Testament provides a record of God's relationship with mankind from the beginning of the world to about 400 years before Jesus' birth.

Pagan, Paganism—One who has little or no religion. One who worships nature or man-made objects.

Palestine—The Jew's homeland, called Canaan in the Old Testament and later called Israel.

Parable—A short story with an underlying spiritual meaning or lesson.

Passover—One of the most important Jewish holidays, commemorating the Jews' deliverance from Egyptian bondage. It is kept in remembrance of the Lord's angel of death *passing over* the houses of the Israelites when the firstborn of all the Egyptians died. The Israelites' firstborn were spared because of the lamb's blood smeared on their doorposts.

Patriarch—One of the scriptural fathers of the human race or of the Hebrew people (Abraham, Isaac, Jacob, and the twelve sons of Jacob (Israel)). A patriarch is a ruling ancestor or the founding father of a family, tribe, clan, or nation.

Pentecost—A Jewish festival occurring fifty days after Passover to thank God for harvested crops. As recorded in Acts, the Holy Spirit descended on 120 believers on the first Pentecost after the resurrection. Today, it is a Christian festival held on the seventh Sunday after Easter to celebrate the Holy Spirit's descent.

Persecute—To oppress or harass because of race, religion or beliefs. The apostles were persecuted because of their faith.

Pharisees—A religious party of Jesus' time committed to strict observance of the law of Moses and other Old Testament Scriptures.

Picture of Redemption—(See Foreshadowing of Jesus Christ)

Praise—An expression of approval, esteem, or commendation. For Christians, it is thanking God for what He has done. To praise God is to proclaim His merit or worth.

Priest—A representative before God, authorized to perform sacred rites and intercession. According to the law of Moses, only Aaron's descendants could serve as priests.

Prophet—A person divinely chosen by God to communicate His message to His people.

Ptolemies, The—The family who ruled Egypt and controlled the Jews' homeland from 321 to 198 B.C. The dynasty is named after Ptolemy, one of four generals, who received a division of Alexander the Great's empire after his death.

Purify, Purification—To cleanse from defilement or free from guilt, moral, or ceremonial blemishes.

Purim—A Jewish holiday, also called the Feast of Lots, commemorating the deliverance of the Jews by Queen Esther from a genocidal massacre of the Jews plotted by Haman.

Rabbi—A Hebrew word translated "master" or "lord" or more literally "great one." A person trained in Jewish law. It is the title given to Jewish religious teachers, including Jesus, and is still in use today.

Rebuke—To reprimand or express strong disapproval.

Redeem, Redeemer—To buy back. To save from captivity by paying a ransom. Biblically, to deliver from sin and its penalties. One who redeems or sets free. A reference to Jesus who redeemed us from sin by giving His life as a ransom.

Redemption—Deliverance by payment of a price. The buying back of something that has been lost by paying a ransom. Christ's blood was the "ransom" that bought back our freedom from sin's power.

Remission (of sins)—Cancellation of sins. When we repent, God forgives and forgets our sins.

Repent—To feel remorse, contrition, or self-reproach for what one has done or failed to do. To turn away from sin.

Resurrection—A rising from the dead or coming back to life. The state of having risen from the dead. The Resurrection in the Bible refers to Christ's resurrection on the third day after His Crucifixion.

Righteous—Acting in a just, upright manner; doing what is right; virtuous.

Righteousness—The actions and positive results of a sound relationship between God and a person or between God and His people. In the Bible, righteousness is the fulfillment of the terms of a covenant between God and humanity.

Right Standing—When used Biblically, refers to a restored relationship with God. In the New Testament, God declares us not guilty of sin and makes us righteous in His sight when we accept Jesus as Lord and Savior.

Sabbath—The seventh day of the week (Saturday) set aside for rest and worship and observed as such by Jews (from Friday sunset to Saturday sunset).

Sacrifice—Offering the life of a person or animal or giving up something precious. Christ was sacrificed to redeem us.

Sadducees—A wealthy, political-minded religious party of Jesus' time, which included high ranking priests.

Saints—A holy person. In Protestant religions, all who have accepted Jesus as Savior are saints. For Catholics, a saint is a person officially recognized as having lived an exceptionally holy life and able to intercede for sinners.

Salvation—Saved or rescued from danger, evil, difficulty, or destruction. Biblically, freedom from the power and penalties of sin, and the guarantee of eternal life with God.

Samaritans—The offspring of poor Jews who escaped the exile and Gentile migrants living in Samaria. Jews despised Samaritans because they were not racially, culturally, or religiously pure.

Sanctified—To purify. To set apart as holy, to consecrate. To be made free from sin.

Sanhedrin Council—A Jewish high court authorized by Rome to maintain limited civil order in Palestine.

Satan (Devil)—God's adversary; the accuser opposing God's people and tempting them to do evil. He fights against righteousness. Satan is also identified as *Lucifer,* leader of the fallen angels.

Savior or savior—One who saves: When written with a small letter "s" (savior), it means one who saves from danger or destruction. When the letter "s" is capitalized (Savior), the reference is to Jesus Christ.

Scribes—A special class of men responsible for interpreting, teaching, and making copies of the Scriptures. They were well-educated and influential leaders in their communities.

Scriptures—In Jesus' day, the term was used for the Hebrew Bible, which is our Old Testament; The Word of God.

Second Coming—(See Day of the Lord)

Sect—A group of people having a common leadership, philosophy, political or religious belief.

Seleucids, The—The family who ruled Syria and controlled the Jews' homeland from 198 to 143 B.C. The dynasty is named after Seleucus, one of four generals, who received a division of Alexander the Great's empire after his death.

Sin—Rebellion against God; rejection of God's Word; misdeeds or actions that are morally wrong.

Spirit-directed—Led by the Holy Spirit.

Spiritual separation—The barrier created between mankind and God after the first man and first woman (Adam and Eve) sinned. Their unrighteousness created a rift in the relationship man had once enjoyed with God.

Synagogue—A building or place used by Jews for worship, religious study, and community activity.

Tabernacle (Tent of Meetings)—A mobile tent used for religious worship after the exodus and before the Temple was built.

Temple—A building used for religious worship. In the Bible, God's house of worship for the Jews located in Jerusalem.

Testament—(See Covenant)

The Way—A first century name for Christianity.

Tithe—One tenth of one's earnings set aside as a gift to God.

Transliteration—The writing or spelling (of words, letters, etc.) in corresponding characters of another alphabet.

Trinity—The term used to express God's existence as three distinct beings: God the Father; Jesus the Son; and the Holy Spirit. All three are fully God, and yet these three beings are one God, and not three Gods.

Unclean—To be morally impure; unchaste, obscene, or defiled according to Moses' laws in Leviticus.

Unleavened bread—Bread baked without yeast so that it does not rise. A symbol of freedom from slavery or sin.

Unrighteous, Unrighteousness—Wicked; sinful.

Works—Good deeds. Strict adherence to the Old Testament law of Moses to achieve right standing with God.

Worship—To have intense admiration for; to show reverence or devotion; to glorify God for who He is.

Yahweh—Often rendered "Jehovah," it is the Hebrew name of God, which is translated "I AM" in English. It is the personal name of the One True God, the Self-Existent One.

Yeast—A fermenting agent that makes bread dough rise. Used as a leavening to bake bread.

Zealots—A political terrorist group of Jesus' time who openly resisted Roman occupation of the Jews' homeland.

BIBLIOGRAPHY

Anders, Max, *What You Need to Know About the Bible*, Nashville, Tennessee, Thomas Nelson, Inc., 1995

Benware, Paul N., *Survey of the Old Testament*, Chicago, Illinois, Moody Publishers, 1988, 1993

Benware, Paul N., *Survey of the New Testament*, Chicago, Illinois, Moody Publishers, 1990, 2003

Bromiley, Geoffrey W. (EDT), *International Standard Bible Encyclopedia*, Eerdmans Publishing Company, 1979

Halley, Henry Hampton, *Halley's Bible Handbook with the New International Version*, Grand Rapids, Michigan, Zondervan Publishing House, 2000

Harpur, James and Braybrooke, Marcus, *The Journeys of St. Paul*, Pleasantville, New York, Reader's Digest, Marshall Editions Developments Limited, 1997

Henry, Matthew, *Matthew Henry's Concise Commentary on the Whole Bible*, Nashville, Tennessee, Thomas Nelson Publishers, 1997

Hybels, Bill, *Too Busy Not to Pray*, Downers Grove, Illinois, InterVarsity Press, 1998

Lightfoot, Neil R., *How We Got the Bible*, Grand Rapids, Michigan, Baker Books, 1963, 1988, 2003

McDowell, Josh, *The New Evidence That Demands a Verdict*, Nashville, Tennessee, Thomas Nelson Publishers, 1999

Myers, Allen C., *The Eerdmans Bible Dictionary*, Grand Rapids, Michigan, William B. Eerdmans Publishing Company, 1987

Nave, Orville J., *The New Nave's Topical Bible*, Grand Rapids, Michigan, Zondervan Publishing House, 1969

Richards, Lawrence O., *The Illustrated Concise Bible Handbook*, Nashville, Tennessee, Thomas Nelson Publishers, 2000

Strong, James, LL.D, S.T.D., *The Strongest Strong's Exhaustive Concordance of the Bible*, Grand Rapids, Michigan, Zondervan, 2001

Telchin, Stan, *Betrayed*, Grand Rapids, Michigan, Chosen Books of Baker Book House Company, 1981

Tenney, Merrill C., *New Testament Times*, Grand Rapids, Michigan, Baker Books, 2004

The American Heritage Dictionary, Boston, Massachusetts, Houghton Mifflin Company, 1992

Unger, Merrill F., *Unger's Concise Bible Dictionary*, Grand Rapids, Michigan, Baker Book House, 2001

Wilkinson, Bruce and Boa, Kenneth, *Talk thru the Bible*, Nashville, Tennessee, Thomas Nelson Publishers, 1983

Study Bibles

Life Application Study Bible, New Living Translation, 1988, 1989, 1990, 1991, 1993, 1996 by Tyndale House Publishers, Inc., Wheaton, IL

The Open Bible, New King James Version, 1997, 1990, 1985, 1983 by Thomas Nelson, Inc., Nashville, Tennessee

Web sites

www.Jesuscentral.com, JesusCentral.com

www.crivoice.org, The Voice, CRI/Voice, Institute

ABOUT BIG PICTURE MINISTRIES

Equipping, Inspiring, and Promoting Spiritual Growth

John and Lorna Nichols are the co-founders of Big Picture Ministries, LLC, an organization devoted to encouraging spiritual growth through the study of God's Word. John and Lorna currently live in Chesterfield, Missouri, and are members of Grace Church-Saint Louis, a non-denominational church, where both serve as facilitators, leaders, and mentors.

Big Picture Ministries provides resources and services designed to help people better understand the message of the Bible. The goal of Big Picture Ministries is to encourage Bible reading and Bible study, and to promote spiritual growth. Our vision is to glorify God by providing tools designed to help people develop a deeper, more meaningful relationship with the Lord.

Big Picture Ministries' Bible studies are perfect for individual or group studies, Christian schools, and homeschooling. If you are interested in facilitating a Big Picture Ministries group study, please visit our Web site or call for information about bulk order discounts. If you would like to book Lorna Daniels Nichols for a speaking engagement or a tele-conferencing session, e-mail us or call to schedule.

Big Picture Ministries, LLC
P.O. Box 67
Chesterfield, MO 63006-0067

Web site: www.bigpictureofthebible.com
Phone: (636) 536-0197   Fax: (636) 536-0138

Please feel free to contact us with your comments or questions. Our e-mail address is:
info@bigpictureofthebible.com

Books Available from Big Picture Ministries:
Big Picture of the Bible—Old Testament

Big Picture of the Bible—New Testament

To order additional copies of this title call:
1-877-421-READ (7323)
or please visit our Web site at
www.winepressbooks.com

If you enjoyed this quality custom-published book,

drop by our Web site for more books and information.

www.winepressgroup.com

"Your partner in custom publishing."